Autism and the Social World of Childhood

D0141435

A key issue for researchers and practitioners is how to support the social engagement of children with autism in ordinary, everyday social processes that are transactional in nature and involve mixed groups of children, with and without autism, in rich and varied relationships.

Autism and the Social World of Childhood brings together current understandings about the social engagement of children with autism, gained from psychology-based research into autism, with well-established ideas about children's everyday social worlds, gained from sociocultural theories of childhood. It describes the experiences of interaction, friendship and play from children's own point of view as a way of giving insight into children's lives as they are lived and understood by them. Such an understanding serves to inform educational practice and aids the provision of more effective learning environments.

Autism and the Social World of Childhood includes sections on:

- the nature of play, social interaction and friendship in autism
- the nature of children's ordinary social worlds, including children's cultures of communication and variation in children's play
- research approaches to investigating the social engagement of children with and without autism in natural contexts
- educational approaches to supporting the integration of children with autism within a school setting
- the importance of reflective teaching in autism education
- the development of play in children with autism.

Autism and the Social World of Childhood includes real-life descriptions of children's social experiences taken from ethnographic research into the play and interaction of children with and without autism. Practical guidance is provided on educational approaches to supporting the inclusion of children with autism within the ordinary social worlds of childhood.

Carmel Conn is a teacher and researcher, and has a background in special educational needs and inclusive education. She has many years of experience in supporting children with autism, their friends, schools and families in included educational settings.

Autism and the Social World of Childhood

A sociocultural perspective on theory and practice

Carmel Conn

Routledge
Taylor & Francis Group

LONDON AND NEW YORK

KH

First published 2014
by Routledge
2 Park Square, Milton Park, Abingdon, Oxon OX14 4RN

and by Routledge
711 Third Avenue, New York, NY 10017

Routledge is an imprint of the Taylor & Francis Group, an informa business

British Library Cataloguing in Publication Data
A catalogue record for this book is available from the British
Library

Library of Congress Cataloging in Publication Data
Conn, Carmel.
Autism and the social world of childhood : a sociocultural
perspective on theory and practice / Carmel Conn.
pages cm
1. Autistic children–Social conditions. 2. Autistic children–Social
networks. 3. Autistic children–Research. 4. Socialization. 5.
Friendship in children. 6. Child psychology. I. Title.
HQ773.8.C66 2014
618.92'85882–dc23
2013039411

ISBN: 978-0-415-83833-7 (hbk)
ISBN: 978-0-415-83834-4 (pbk)
ISBN: 978-1-315-79545-4 (ebk)

Typeset in Bembo
by Saxon Graphics Ltd, Derby

10/17/15

For Phyllis and Douglas
with love and gratitude

Contents

Illustrations

Figures

Table

Acknowledgements

A book such as this is not possible without the interest, participation, support and opinion of the people who are described in it. I am deeply grateful to the children and adults who have given me permission to exemplify the discussion of social contexts with descriptions of their social experiences. I would especially like to thank the children who participated with such enthusiasm in the research that is used centrally here. Their willingness to share with me, to be observed and to answer my questions was invaluable to me in gaining a different perspective on their social worlds and achieving a much better understanding of what children do when they interact.

I would like to thank the two support workers who helped me gain permissions for the book, who gave so generously of their time and who have provided support and assistance throughout my research and writing. My thanks go to the parents and practitioners who have given me much encouragement over the last few years and who have provided feedback on drafts of the text. Thanks, too, to all the families who have given me permission to use the photographs that are provided in Chapter 3.

Warmest thanks go to Dr Anthony Feiler who supervised the research project that forms the basis of this book. This project was carried out whilst I was at the School of Education, University of Bristol and I would like to thank the staff and students there for their interest and support. Thanks, too, to the Economic and Social Research Council for providing the funding for the project, which is referenced ES/I901884/1. Special thanks go to Professor Chris Jarrold for his extremely supportive interest in the project.

I would like to thank Rich Chitty at Ctrl Alt Design for producing the diagrams that are used in the book, Gerald Conn for his help and advice with the photographs and other visuals, and my work colleague Sheila Haddock for reading drafts of the chapters on practice.

I want to acknowledge the personal support and the practical assistance that have been provided by my family and friends throughout my research and the preparation of this book. Much love and heartfelt thanks go to them.

Introduction

Richness and variation in children's lives

Sophie is running round the edges of the playground, running along the lines that are marked on the ground. A girl from her class, Abby, who school staff describe as a friend, runs towards her to say hello. Sophie veers quickly around Abby, not looking at her and leaving Abby looking puzzled by this lack of engagement. Abby goes to join a small group of girls who are picking dandelions. When Sophie has completed a circle of the playground, she joins Abby and looks at her flower. Abby blows the clocks of the dandelion into the air for Sophie to see, who smiles as she watches them fly away.

This is a book about children playing and being together, communicating and having friends. Its subject is children's ordinary social worlds and social experiences, but it is also a book about autism because some of the children who are described have been diagnosed with the condition. The aim of the book is to describe the experience of social interaction, friendship and play from children's own perspectives. The concern is less with what autism is and more with exploring how it manifests itself in children's lives as they are lived and experienced by them. Descriptive accounts similar to the one above, of Sophie, aged 6, who has autism and her friend Abby who does not, illustrate that we should not make hasty conclusions about children's experiences of each other in interaction. In the case of autism, patterns of difficulty may exist, but all individuals bring differing personal resources, interests and needs to relationships, and social contexts emerge, evolve and unfold over time. In this instance, Abby brings persistence in wanting to make contact with Sophie and an investment in the friendship, whilst Sophie shows motivation to be with Abby, despite being surprised by her sudden physical presence in the playground and unable to change her activity quickly. Descriptions such as this help us to gain a rich understanding of the quality of children's social experiences and the shared nature of social processes.

How we look at Sophie's experience of being with Abby in some ways depends upon our point of view. Autism is a gene-based condition that manifests as social difficulty and affects how people relate to one another, communicate and interact. The view that is most often taken in the academic literature on autism is one that focuses on the individual with autism, their impairment and the ways in which their abilities do not correspond with a preconceived 'norm'. It is a medicalized view that is not concerned with the dynamic and unfolding nature of the social contexts with which individuals with autism must engage. Indeed, the differing circumstances that influence social engagement are often factored out of this viewpoint as a way of getting at a 'core truth' that applies across large numbers of individuals with the same condition. The view taken here is that interaction is essentially a transaction between two or more people, where the personal resources and efforts of one are interpreted and creatively responded to by the other, using their own resources, efforts and interpretations. This is a social-based view that, of necessity, takes a wider perspective than individual behaviour alone and tries to account for how individuals participate together in social relations. A wider view is a more complex view, of course, with more factors coming into view, ones that cannot be factored out and must be taken into account. There is not one person's behaviour but the behaviours of two or more people, there is a richness of possibilities in terms of responses and a whole-group process, as well as influencing features within the social and physical environment.

A wide view of social processes is essentially a sociocultural one that locates the behaviour of the individual within the context in which it occurs. Socioculture refers to real-life social contexts where people are physically present and engaged with one another; for example, through their talk, gesture and gaze. However, importantly, socioculture also refers to contexts where people are not personally engaged but where culture exists anyway; for example, in the form of social structures, norms and practices. Socioculture takes many forms and is present in our customs, values and everyday routines, in cultural 'tools' such as language, texts, pictures, signs and other forms of media, and in our involvement with community practices and social institutions of all kinds. Sociocultural theory is thus less focused on individual behaviour and more on how the individual participates in group processes: how they engage with each other and the sociocultural environment using all the cultural resources that are available to them. Socioculture concerns how people make sense of each other's actions and communications and how they respond, using these interpretations. Crucially, unlike the classic view of autism which focuses on 'deficits', difficulties and what people with autism cannot do, a sociocultural view is interested in competencies, that is, what individuals understand, believe and do within a social context, whether socially effective or not.

Though aspects of sociocultural theory are used within explanations of autism, it has seldom been applied fully as a theory to autism. The defining feature of autism is reduced amounts of social engagement – reduced levels of social interaction and social communication, fewer friendships and less play – and this has been seen to preclude an approach to studying and supporting the condition that focuses on how individuals with autism participate in social contexts. It is the case too that autism has a difficult history in connection to viewing it in terms of social relations. An explanation for autism that was widely promoted in the 1960s and 1970s was that of the 'refrigerator mother', which saw the condition in children as the result of a lack of experience of maternal affection. The theory resulted in considerable suffering for parents of children with autism who were forced into treatment for what was perceived as their inadequate parenting and emotional frigidity. This theory has now been completely discredited. We know that autism has a biological basis and that parents do not cause autism through their care. The legacy that has been left, however, is one of looking outside social relations for theories of autism and of sidelining the importance of social processes to the development of theory and practice.

Yet, for those of us who live and work with children with autism, the idea that they cannot be viewed in terms of being socially engaged, of playing and of having friends can feel not quite right. Many children with autism do show social interest and seek out other people to be with. Recent research into the development of children with autism indicates that they do not stand outside social relations, with considerable variation in the autism population in how far individuals are engaged with others. Children with autism do interact, can play to some extent and tend to have at least one friend. There may be differential experience in this, with difference existing in preferences for types of play or cultural activity, and interaction and friendship taking particular forms. However, children with autism can experience feelings of loneliness and may want to be socially involved, but not know how to go about it.

Since the 1970s, theories of autism have developed apart from developments in general theories of childhood. There is some irony in the fact that, within the same time frame, theories of ordinary child development have *increasingly* focused on children's experiences of social processes and the innate sociability of the child. From the 1980s onwards, social theories have strongly influenced our understandings of the form and purpose of ordinary human communication, how children without autism participate in social contexts and the sociocultural nature of human development. Vygotsky (1978), whose ideas influenced this paradigm shift, argued that learning for the individual is essentially social learning, the ways in which the individual engages in social processes determining and driving their development. We know that children learn by engaging with the environment around them, including other people. They are not passive recipients of socialization influences but are themselves social players who participate in and contribute to social processes. The adults who know them support children in this, both children and adults engaging together in social experiences, making sense of them and each trying to create socially appropriate responses in increasingly sophisticated ways.

How children ordinarily interact and learn is critically important to our understanding of how to support children with autism to interact and learn. Children with autism do develop, but conceptualizations within the literature on autism of how this occurs are often curious. Children are conceptualized as learning to act according to fixed sets of social rules which are taught and through adults transferring their skills in socialization in one-way transmissions to children. There is little sense of the richness, creativity and transactional quality that we know characterize ordinary human relations and growth. We know too that ordinary human development involves cognitive, affective and social features that are intricately bound up together and reciprocally related in terms of growth, yet many approaches to autism continue to support development as if it occurs in separate domains.

This book seeks to contribute to a better alignment in the literature on autism of knowledge about children's ordinary social development with contemporary understandings about the social engagement of children with autism. There is much greater emphasis here on children's ordinary social experiences – of social interaction, social communication, friendship and play – than is usually the case in a book about autism. How children without autism ordinarily communicate and for what purposes is explored, as is how they try to make sense of things and what they look for in each other. This is not with the aim of identifying what causes autism, but rather more practically, of conceptualizing the nature of children's ordinary social activity *within a discussion about autism* as a way of achieving a better understanding of how groups of children with and without autism can be socially supported to interact more effectively and develop.

The focus of this book is on children being with other children, on how children with autism engage with other children and on what the experience of this is for both parties. Inevitably, many of the descriptions provided of children interacting, playing and being friends concern children within included educational settings where there are mixed groups of children, with and without autism. This is not a book, therefore, about all children with autism. It is not about children with autism who have little or no language and high sensory-processing needs, and who might be educated in more specialist settings. But neither is it about high-functioning children with autism only. It is about children engaging with other children and, though this usually requires some language, social knowledge and willingness to engage, many children with autism who communicate at a basic level nevertheless do seek out other children to play with, who might themselves not talk that much. What 'type' of child with autism is the focus of this book is in fact hard to pinpoint, since autism is a developmental disorder and children often achieve unexpected amounts in terms of their socialization. Part of the premise here is that we should not draw premature conclusions about what children can and cannot do and how their communication is received by others. The age range of children described within this book is within the primary school phase, that is, children aged between 5 and 11 years, though the social experiences of babies, young children and adolescents do constitute part of the discussion about children's social development.

This book is organized into two sections. Part I addresses theory and concerns the nature of social experience for children with and without autism. There is a discussion of the experience of social communication from the point of view of children with autism, but also from that of children who do not have autism. This is with the aim of theorizing more fully what it means to 'be social' and so understand what happens when a child with autism joins in with the activity of others. Findings from social-based research into the ordinary world of childhood are used to illustrate key features of ordinary social development. These are presented alongside descriptions of children's everyday understandings, values, concerns and practices, using children's own perspectives wherever possible. The focus is on the differing ways in which children conceive of issues such as 'what is play', 'what is a friend' and 'how do I enjoy myself' that are so central to our understanding of how to support the social inclusion of children with autism.

Part II focuses on practical matters in relation to supporting the social development of children with autism, focusing on education and learning contexts within ordinary school settings. The majority of children with autism are educated in mainstream settings and how we support children's social development and learning within these contexts is explored. The case is made for a reflective approach to teaching and learning within autism education where school practitioners take time to find out about and consider the nature of social relations within their particular setting and children's real-life learning experiences. It will be argued that effective support for learning is one that meets the needs of the actual social contexts in which the individual child with autism and his or her peers engage and takes into account all children's experiences of group processes.

Several themes about children's social experience run through both parts of the book. The first of these concerns point of view, which has already been mentioned in relation to how we view autism. What view is taken and what that subsequently allows us to see is critically important not only to our understanding of autism but also to our understanding of other related areas. The experience of disability, for example, can be seen as biologically determined and individually based, but it can also be viewed as partly determined by cultural factors and the social influences of family background and history. The individual and what they are capable of can be defined in terms of the context in which they find themselves since other people's knowledge, understanding, attitudes and values can crucially determine how disability is experienced or whether it even exists. However, the significance of viewpoint applies to our conceptualizations of ordinary social learning and development too. Developmental psychology and the idea of individual stages of cognitive development are most frequently used in the literature on autism to conceptualize the nature of human development, but advances in psychobiology and affective neuroscience are challenging this view as too narrow and providing an insufficient account of the social, affective and cognitive features involved (Panksepp, 1998). Indeed, so important is the issue of point of view in this book that it pervades most areas of discussion including, in addition, how we research the experience of autism in natural contexts and how we achieve quality in terms of practical support in schools for children's development and inclusion.

A second theme, one closely related to this issue of points of view, concerns the issue of complexity. Human behaviour is determined by multiple factors, including people's prior experiences, beliefs and interpretations about a situation, their feelings and perceptions, and their capacities, interests, values and ideas. People's participation in social contexts is also an ongoing process where factors are evaluated and re-evaluated in the light of events as they unfold. Thus, social phenomena should be thought of as complex; complexity existing not only in the multiple contexts of behaviour but also in the emergent nature of social experience as it happens.

In a discussion about autism, however, complexity should be seen as existing within the condition of autism too. Having the condition of autism implies difficulty with social interaction and an understanding of other people. But there is great variation amongst individuals with autism in this, with some people with autism experiencing mild or particular areas of difficulty and others great challenge in a number of areas. Autism is described as a spectrum disorder that is characterized by marked diversity across the population. Individuals with autism appear to experience different amounts of difficulty within different areas of cognitive, social, perceptual, affective and motor functioning, but should expect to develop their capacities in some, if not all, of these areas.

A central tenet in this book, therefore, is that the issue of complexity (that is, the complexity of autism and that of social phenomena per se) requires holding in mind a number of differing, diverse and even conflicting factors, some of which may be in tension and not easy to reconcile but all of which together make for a better understanding of human experience within a social context. Norwich's (2008) ideas about the tensions that inherently exist within special educational needs and disability are informative on this point. He argues that tensions — or 'dilemmas of difference' as he describes it — are always present within special needs education in the form of sameness and difference, integration and segregation, and similar versus special treatment debates. He puts forward the idea that keeping these tensions in mind is, in fact, part of the challenge of inclusive education, a proper engagement with these contributing to quality within practice. Autism involves many tensions, including the individual's disability versus their abilities, their social versus their non-social selves, and the degree to which they are the same as and different from people without autism. Tension exists too in seeing autism as belonging to the individual or to the group and as the result of local versus universal factors. The argument put forward here is that the existence of these tensions is not something that should be put to one side. Of necessity, a range of differing and diverse perspectives on autism is required, the combination of which provides *an appropriately complex view*. A sociocultural perspective is helpful since it provides additional information about social contexts that is complementary to the information provided by an individualized, psychology-based view and so contributes to a more complete account of social functioning of the individual with autism and the responses of others to them.

A sociocultural perspective views human behaviour in the context in which it occurs and tries to account for all the social factors that are in play at any one time. It is a holistic and ecological view that describes different social influences within the individual's immediate social environment as well as layers of influence from the wider world around. When people act or speak or respond, it is seldom a situation of single cause and effect and should be thought of more in terms of foreground plus background social influences. Children also participate with each other and the world around in this way, bringing whatever knowledge and understanding they have and trying to make sense of social situations. Their social worlds relate both to the dominant adult world around them and to what familiar adults say and do, as well as to their own interests, ideas, beliefs and perceptions, which they may negotiate with other children. Adults who seek to understand children's social worlds, therefore, should see them as characterized by richness and variation and requiring careful, close and detailed investigation.

Both these themes relate to how we look at autism and ordinary social engagement. The third and final theme concerns how we describe individual behaviour within social contexts. Within autism research, a preferred form of description has been a numerical one where children's social activity is quantified in terms of its amount and statistical relevance to normative measures. This is seen as a way of clearly defining what autism is and of providing evidence of children's progress following the implementation of support for their learning. Measurement, however, is not the method that is usually employed to describe ordinary social activity in children's social worlds, with qualitative descriptions, often in the form of narrative accounts, being much more likely. There is a long and respectable history of using narrative accounts within studies of children's learning which has influenced contemporary approaches to describing children's social experiences. Charles Darwin's observations and descriptive notes about the development of his eldest son, William, is an early example of the form. In the 1930s, the early years educator Susan Isaacs (1933) also famously produced narrative assessments of the children in her care, as did Vivian Gussin Paley (1992) in the 1980s and 1990s, who wrote up her action research explorations into children's learning as a series of books. Qualitative descriptions of children are good at capturing the details of the contexts in which they engage, including features within the environment and the nature of other people's responses. The narrative form, moreover, helps to convey the complexity of situated learning and integrates the social, cognitive and affective factors that together constitute human experience and development.

A conventional construct of the condition of autism is that it is 'atypical' and cannot be viewed or described in the same way as what is 'typical' in human behaviour. The behaviour of the individual with autism is seen to relate to their cognitive capacities rather than a more generalized experience of the world. People with autism do indeed describe a differential subjective experience and a different relationship to language and thought, often describing how they make sense of the world through individualistic and sensory-based interpretations that are not readily available to rich cultural sharing. However, research shows that people with autism are also partly engaged in social contexts, investing in and using some aspects of culture. It is argued here, therefore, that a case can be made for the use of descriptive accounts alongside other measures of social behaviour in children with autism. Children do not experience each other as a set of symptoms or skills, but they do make assessments of each other based on how they and others participate in real-life contexts. Understanding their points of view and the details of what happens is vitally important if we are to offer effective, reliable and socially relevant support for peer groups that include a child with autism.

Descriptive vignettes of children with and without autism playing and being together are provided throughout this book. This is by of way illustrating the quality of what happens within groups of children, but it also shows the uniqueness of detail such a method provides. Some of the vignettes are an amalgam of information about children's social experiences that has been gained from years of observing the real-life interactions of children with and without autism, though most are taken from participatory research into the social activity of peer groups that include a child with autism within mainstream school settings. What the vignettes show are the naturalistic ways in which children with autism engage with other children, including some of the difficulties in this but also some of the positive experiences and unexpected opportunities. Always of interest are descriptions of how children receive each other's communications, the uniqueness and variation with which they create their responses, and the differing social outcomes that can occur as a result.

Much more will be said in the chapters that follow about how we can describe children's social experiences and about the importance of complexity and point of view in relation to autism and the social world of childhood. One final point to make in this introductory section concerns the issue of terminology used in the book. Sociocultural theory is centrally placed as a construct within the text and draws heavily on Vygotskian ideas about the basis of human development being wholly within the experience of social contexts. Vygotsky argued that all learning is fundamentally social learning and that development is contingent upon the individual's participation in social processes. Vygotsky himself did not write about 'socioculture' but about 'culture' as the aspect of human activity that involves all social processes. Culture is the term that subsequent prominent scholars have used too, including Cole (1996) in writing about cultural psychology and Rogoff (2003) writing about the cultural nature of human development. The use of the term implies the understanding that there is no social activity that is not cultural and no aspect of culture that stands outside social processes. The view taken here is that the term 'socioculture' does not describe anything other than culture, but merely serves to emphasize the social basis of culture. It is particularly useful to use this term in relation to a discussion of autism – a social disability – since it highlights the social context of culture. However, the terms 'socioculture' and 'culture' are used interchangeably and do not refer to contexts or practices that are different in any way. Socioculture is sometimes used to emphasize the social nature of some aspect of children's activity, though the term 'culture' would do just as well.

Part I

Theorizing autism and children's social worlds

Part I addresses theoretical issues in relation to autism and children's ordinary social worlds, exploring in depth the experience of social communication for children with and without autism. Chapter 1 sets out current understandings about the social engagement of children with autism, looking at the experiences of play and interaction for children with autism and the nature of friendship. The issue of how we choose to view shared experiences of communication will be raised, making reference to the social model of disability taken from disability studies. Chapter 2 outlines the purpose of social activity in the lives of children without autism and its importance to learning and development. It makes the case for sociocultural theory as a perspective on social learning that is complementary to ideas within developmental psychology, the discipline most often used in autism theory and practice. Communication is a key area of difficulty in autism and Chapter 3 specifically explores the issue of children's communication in ordinary social contexts, looking in particular at how non-verbal and multimodal communication has greater significance for children than it does for adults.

Chapters 4 and 5 address the issue of how we can investigate and gain knowledge and understanding of children's social worlds. Chapter 4 presents case-study material about two children with autism and their friends to illustrate important features of social contexts where children with and without autism play and interact. Chapter 5 explores methodological approaches to researching the social experiences of children with autism and makes the case for participatory research with a mixed methods design as the form most suited to investigating the natural social contexts in which children with autism engage with others.

Chapter 1

The social experiences of children with autism

Since he was a young child, Richie, aged 8, has had a special interest in cars. His mother describes how, when he was young, he got deeply immersed in his play with toy cars in a way that was different from other children of his age. As he got older, Richie's interest in cars continued, but also developed with him becoming particularly interested in fast cars. His mother describes how he often likes to imagine that he is a car. She thinks that in doing this, his imagination has a particular quality that differs from children without autism. She believes that he is not concerned with imagining that he is a driver of a car and is instead imagining the much more sensory experience of being the car itself, of wheels going round and road markings passing underneath.

She thinks that this imaginative experience is no less rich for Richie than it is for other children, and believes that it has a peculiar intensity for him. She says, 'Sometimes when we're walking along the pavement, he will try and go off. He doesn't make the noises but he is pretending to be a car. I do let him because that's something he needs. It's his passion, but I do try to keep it under control. He just loves doing it, pretending that he is a car. He just goes with the racing, the lines on the road, the fences going past, whatever is in his head.

This description of how a mother of a boy with autism imagines his experience of imagining raises the question of difference for an individual on the spectrum. Richie's mother expresses a belief that her son has a fundamentally different experience of imagining, one that is intensely experienced and is focused on sensory detail. It is a belief that reflects the many first-hand descriptions of conscious experience produced by writers with autism. These emphasize the sensory, perceptual, motor and affective experience of the condition rather than its social-cognitive impact, and give the impression of a consciousness that is perceptually overwhelming, sensorily compelling and prohibitive to a small or large degree of social sharing (see, for example, Williams, 1996). What is being described is an essential difference to individuals without autism, a subjective experience that does not automatically 'convert experience into abstractions and words', as Temple Grandin (Grandin and Johnson, 2005) describes it, but processes the world in primarily sensory ways.

The essential difference of autism probably accounts for the fact that children with autism are often viewed and treated in ways that are different from children without autism. However, everyday knowledge and experience of being with children with autism indicates that, in many ways, 'difference' does not describe all that they are. We may see, for example, that children with autism are socially engaged – sometimes or for most of the time – in their families, schools and communities. We may see them communicating, playing and sometimes having friends. We may know that they are interested in people and want to be with other children. Close attention to the activity of a child with autism sometimes reveals a logic that is not easily apprehended or understood, but that does make social sense when considered from the child's point of view. What is at question in this book is the nature of that engagement given the essential difference of autism and given too that social experience is importantly a dyadic situation experienced by more than one party. What happens when a child with autism engages with other children and what is their experience too? How do children together, and left to themselves, make sense of and engage with each other's communication? What are the misunderstandings that arise and the nature of any conflict? In order to address these questions, there needs to be an acknowledgement that children with autism are *both different and the same* as children without autism and that to think about what autism means in any situation involves, above all, engaging with more than one way of looking at things.

A recurring theme of this book, which is introduced here, is that any discussion of the social engagement of children with autism necessitates consideration of how we 'see' autism. Our knowledge of any complex phenomena, such as social engagement, children's play, friendship and so on, depends to some extent on how we choose to view it. How we look at autism – whether we focus on sameness or difference, the individual or the group, strengths or weaknesses – affects our understanding of what autism is and our ideas about how to support it. The typical view of autism that is used in theory and practice is a medical one, sometimes known as the medical model of disability. This uses a normative discourse and positions autism as a situation of 'deficit' compared to the 'norm' of 'typical development'. The view is reductionist where 'what is autism' is simplified to single variables that can be studied, measured and supported. Part of the premise of this book is that social processes are not straightforward but are inherently complex and that it is not helpful or indeed possible to separate out social functioning into discrete areas of capacity. The argument being put forward is that an understanding of children with autism within ordinary social contexts must come from engagement with complexity, not only with the complexity of autism but also with that of social phenomena per se.

The idea of a sociocultural perspective on autism will be introduced in this chapter as an important framework for thinking about autism which provides a complementary view to that provided by the medical model of disability. The view is a wider and augmentative one that looks beyond the individual and takes in layers of cultural influence. Sociocultural theory is concerned less with the individual and more with the group, looking at the details of cultural practices within a setting and how people individually participate in these. It focuses on *contexts* and is concerned with competencies, that is, what people actually do in relation to the social context rather than their 'difficulty' and what they do not do. A sociocultural perspective supports the social model of disability which views disability as the result of a confluence of factors in impairment as well as cultural and social relations and seeks to describe positive social identities for individuals with a disability.

A discussion of the medical versus social models of disability will be provided at the end of this chapter. Before this, the chapter will outline what we currently know about the social engagement of children with autism. Since this has been gained predominantly from investigations of discrete areas of social functioning, these will be used as a starting point here. The chapter will outline current understandings of the play, social interaction and friendships of children with autism, taking each in turn. It will be noted that research evidence shows children and adolescents with autism are at least partly socially engaged, though with some differences in the nature of their engagement compared to children who do not have autism and with considerable individual variation across the autism population. Specific issues have been highlighted by research in relation to the possible differential experience of social engagement and the difficulties inherent in researching this area of study, and these issues will also be outlined.

The play of children with autism

Although we know that autism is a developmental disorder that has a strong genetic basis (Abrahams and Geschwind, 2008), social factors are used as the criteria for singling out children with autism from other children (American Psychiatric Association, 2013). Play is key amongst these; children with autism are characterized by their lack of variety in play and unusual play behaviours. However, what we know about how children with autism participate in play contexts presents a mixed and complex picture, of some play participation as well as some areas of difficulty. We know that children with autism can play but tend to produce less play that would be described as spontaneous, that is, produced without any support or ideas provided by an adult (Rutherford *et al.*, 2007). They also spend more time looking away from play situations (Libby *et al.*, 1998), and are less likely to share or engage the interest of others when they are playing (Mundy *et al.*, 1986; Williams *et al.*, 2001). Though children with autism do express positive feelings when they are interacting with an adult, these expressions tend not to be evident in shared playful situations that involve joint attention on an object of interest (Kasari *et al.*, 1990).

Children with autism have noted difficulties with the development of pretend play and this was thought to reflect what is the core difficulty in autism. Leslie (1987) made a strong distinction between the capacities needed for pretend play compared to those needed for other forms of play and argued that the child's capacity for pretence depends on their capacity in terms of theory of mind. The link was made to autism and the child with autism's difficulties with pretend play, but subsequent research has shown that pretence does not necessarily involve metarepresentation and that children with autism can produce pretend play (Jarrold *et al.*, 1994; Jarrold, 2003). Children with autism tend to underuse pretence in natural play situations, but can be encouraged to increase the amount of pretence they carry out when structure is provided by an adult (Lewis and Boucher, 1995). In a large intervention study designed to develop joint attention and pretend play skills in children with autism, Kasari *et al.* (2006) showed that both these areas of functioning can be developed in children with autism and can be generalized to everyday play and interaction with their caregivers. There is evidence that young children with autism respond to a range of structured and naturalistic interventions and that progress is better if the approach used is child-centred as opposed to adult-led (Bernard-Opitz *et al.*, 2004; Kasari *et al.*, 2006).

It is possible that the distinction made between the competency of children with autism in pretend play situations and other forms of play has been overstated. In actuality, children with autism display difficulties in other areas of play too; for example, in simple functional play with objects where they show less varied play with fewer play ideas compared to other children (Williams *et al.*, 2001). They also demonstrate different preferences in play, showing a clear preference for sensorimotor play beyond the usual cut-off age, for physical play that involves rough and tumble, and for play that has clear interactive turns (Boucher, 1999; El-Ghoroury and Romanczyk, 1999; Libby *et al.*, 1998). Anecdotal reports by individuals with autism about their play experiences as a child describe preferred categories of play that stand apart from recognized notions of relational, functional and pretend play. Such things as collecting items, playing with words and sounds, making lists, dropping and spilling objects are not often thought of as developmentally significant types of play (Donnelly and Bovee, 2003; Williams, 2008). However, the categories of play that are used in the literature on autism are narrow and tend not to recognize the many different ways that children without autism play at different ages (Anderson *et al.*, 2004).

Play is a particularly complex phenomenon that involves biological, sociocultural and ecological contexts and research into autism and the development of play increasingly recognizes the need to take a more integrative approach, investigating different types of play, focusing on naturalistic settings and incorporating a range of measures of play behaviour (Barton and Wolery, 2008; Boucher and Wolfberg, 2003; Jarrold and Conn, 2011; Luckett et al., 2007). Some studies have tried to combine measures in play behaviour – for example, in motor, manipulative, functional and symbolic capacities – with measures of mental state understanding and qualitative assessments of social orientation and social behaviour in play (Brown and Whiten, 2000; Thorp et al., 1995; Wolfberg and Schuler, 1999; Yang et al., 2003). Wolfberg has been particularly prominent in considering the cultural context of children's play, using natural settings and other children as play partners in her Integrated Play Groups (IPGs) to assess and develop levels of children's play (Wolfberg, 2004). She uses mixed groups of 'expert players' (children without autism) and 'novice players' (children with autism) who are both supported in situ by the teacher as they play, the teacher providing prompts in terms of play and social communication. Across studies that have used an IPG-type approach, success in terms of play development has been consistently reported, but the difficulty of identifying which aspects of the approach are critical to that success is regularly noted (Ingersoll and Schreibman, 2006; Yang et al., 2003; Zercher et al., 2001).

A key issue within the literature on autism and play is whether the development of play, if and when it does occur, takes the same form as it does for children without autism. Some play interventions assume a kind of 'kick-start' to development. Wolfberg's IPGs are conceptualized in terms of Vygotsky's 'zone of proximal development', specifically that play with objects and play with people is a primary driving force behind the development of other capacities in symbolic thinking, interpersonal skill and social knowledge. Wolfberg reasons that play serves a quite similar function in the development of children with autism as it does for other children and that development in play will lead to development in other areas (Wolfberg, 2008). Others conceptualize development in autism as qualitatively different from neurotypical development. Hobson et al. (2009) have made the case that children with autism lack the fundamental biological background in social–emotional relatedness that underpins ordinary psychological development. They emphasize difference in terms of autistic and neurotypical experience and development. Research into the progression of early development of children with autism shows that difference does exist. Carpenter et al. (2002) looked at this in their study into the development of social-cognitive skills in young children with autism. They found that the ordinary developmental pattern of shared attention – so critical to the later development of social cognition and language – emerges first in ordinary early infant joint engagement with an adult, the child alternating their gaze between an object of interest and the adult, but that this pattern is reversed for young children with autism. The children with autism in their study differed from other children in that they used imitation and referential language before any joint engagement with an adult. Findings such as this have given rise to the idea that children with autism do not follow a typical developmental pathway, but learn to compensate cognitively for social-emotional barriers to learning. The social-cognitive skills that are demonstrated by some older individuals with autism, particularly those with higher cognitive ability, may be acquired through 'artificially' learned strategies and understandings (Kasari *et al.*, 2001).

However, as Carpenter *et al.* (2002) point out, there is no consistency across the autism population in terms of the early acquisition of social-cognitive skills, with the input from parents and teachers being a possibly important factor in the development of a child with autism, as it is for all other children. There are also clear differences between the development of play in low-functioning and high-functioning children with autism (see, for example, Kok *et al.*, 2002), and within these two groups differences are also evident, with most studies showing differential responses by individual participants within one of these groups to situations of play (Libby *et al.*, 1998). A study of the play interactions of children with autism and their siblings compared to that with their parents, found that within-child difference also exists, children with autism making more effort to initiate interactions with their siblings (El-Ghoroury and Romanczyk, 1999).

We will return to the issue of play and the nature of development in autism in the chapters that follow, particularly Chapter 4, in which descriptions of children with and without autism playing in natural contexts are provided, and Chapter 8, which focuses on the development of play. This chapter will now look at what we know currently about the social interactions and friendships of children with autism and provide an overview.

Children with autism and social interaction

As with the play of children with autism, little is known about how children with autism interact with others in real-life situations or about the quality and nature of those interactions (Kasari *et al.*, 2011). It is apparent that children with autism are socially active but are more often socially peripheral, though not completely isolated (Chamberlain *et al.*, 2007; Locke *et al.*, 2010). Compared to other children, children with autism spend less time in proximity to other children and are less likely to look at or talk to them (McGee *et al.*, 1997). The social behaviours used by children with autism appear to be less complex than those used by children without autism, with fewer combinations of behaviour, such as smiling whilst looking at something (Lord and Magill-Evans, 1995).

In Sigman and Ruskin's (1999) comprehensive study comparing high-functioning children with autism with typically developing children, children with Down's syndrome and children with developmental delay, children with autism spent more time in solitary play or in play that was not well coordinated with the activity of their peers. They were less likely to begin an interaction with a peer or respond to a peer's social invitation. More recent findings have shown that, in classroom settings, children with autism are more likely to interact with others where groups are small or in one-to-one situations and where the engagement is child-directed as opposed to teacher-led (Boyd *et al.*, 2008).

Although findings point to the fact that children with autism as a group are engaged socially to some extent, as with play, the nature and frequency of those engagements presents a complicated picture across the population. Sigman and Ruskin (1999) note a marked difference in the naturally occurring social behaviour of high-functioning and low-functioning children with autism, the former making a greater number of attempts at social engagement, possibly reflecting a greater desire to be socially engaged. However, again as with play, within-group and within-child variation is evident. Studies show that some high-functioning children with autism participate in the same amounts of social engagement (Sigman and Ruskin, 1999) and with identical proportions of social behaviour as children without autism (Bauminger *et al.*, 2003). High-functioning children with autism also show differential interaction patterns depending on whom they are interacting with, using more complex interaction with non-autistic peers compared to interactions with children with autism (Bauminger *et al.*, 2003).

It is likely that social development will occur in children with autism, though this may be more dependent on the mediation of others than is the case for other children (Bauminger and Shulman, 2003). Children with autism are responsive to a wide range of interventions designed to increase the amount and quality of their social engagement. Intervention methods include strategies such as adult mediation of a child's social interactions with their peers (Kohler *et al.*, 2001), peer mediation of social engagement (Roeyers, 1995), social training for high-functioning children with autism (Bock, 2007) and parent-assisted social skills training (Laugeson *et al.*, 2009). In recent years, the trend has been towards the use of naturalistic techniques, peer mediation and social-skills training for children with autism and away from adult mediation as the way of providing socially relevant structure for a child (White *et al.*, 2007). Peer-mediation techniques, where the children engaged with the child with autism are taught more effective ways of making and responding to social interaction, often use children who are socially competent, in a similar vein to Wolfberg's 'expert players'. Roeyers (1996) purposefully selected children who were known to be 'excellent players' in a proximity alone approach, Whitaker (2004) selected older children to facilitate the inclusion of two children with autism, and Owen-DeSchryver *et al.* (2008) chose peers who showed good cooperative skills and who were able to make up class work missed through participation in peer-training sessions. The important concepts behind peer-mediation interventions are the idea of 'transmission' of social behaviour, from competent peer to less competent child with autism, and the facilitation by an individual peer of entry into the general peer group.

Though most studies on social interaction interventions report success, no single intervention can be pinpointed as especially important (Parsons *et al.*, 2009). The demand is for robust empirical research using large samples that can be replicated, but the increasing focus on natural settings, real–life situations and the support of other children throws up difficulties in terms of the complexity of the research field (Wang *et al.*, 2011). The need is to identify variables that support social development, but in rich and constantly changing natural contexts, it is difficult to single out one or two aspects of the environment that might be critical to success. As Prizant and Rubin (1999) point out, it is seldom the case that studies take account of other interventions that go on outside the study, but which are probably present. Given the marked diversity within the autism population, it is likely that different needs exist for different individuals requiring different kinds of interventions (Parsons *et al.*, 2009). Since social development covers such a wide range of functioning, including language, cognition, communication, social understanding, self/other awareness and play, it is likely too that no one intervention is sufficient for one individual (Prizant and Rubin, 1999).

The focus in autism research on social interaction has been on amounts of engagement, but there is a perceived need to consider the quality of interaction as well (Bauminger *et al.*, 2003; McConnell, 2002). A high number of social initiations may indicate sociability but may also point to a lack of social effectiveness and necessity for repeated attempts. Lists of social activity give little away. Bauminger and Shulman (2003) carried out a survey with children with autism and their friends on the types of social activities they enjoyed together. 'Watching TV with a friend' was the highest rated social activity of children with autism and their non-autistic friend, but this gives no indication of whether this meant watching television sociably, that is, talking about the programme and using its content in subsequent play activity, or simply sitting side by side.

There is an identified need too for greater use of our understanding about what goes on socially for children without autism. Bauminger *et al.* (2003) conclude from their study of peer interaction and loneliness in high-functioning children with autism that the issues involved are highly complex and they call for more qualitative documentation of 'chains of ongoing interaction' as a way of providing some clarity. Similarly, Rogers (2000) argues that social inclusion methods must be strongly grounded in actual peer behaviour, not in the assumptions of practitioners and researchers. As Frankel and Myatt (2003) point out, the social skill technique of coaching in scripts and social routines, so often advocated for children with autism, may completely miss the point of everyday interactions. For example, the polite use of the script 'Can I play with you?' may well result in a resounding 'No you can't!' from two children trying to protect their precious play space and friendship in a shared play environment (Corsaro, 2011).

The friendships of children with autism

Children with autism usually have at least one friend, though that friend might also have some sort of social difficulty or learning need. Studies of children's social networks have found that children with autism are peripheral in terms of social groupings, but not isolated (Chamberlain *et al.*, 2007; Rotheram-Fuller *et al.*, 2010). Several studies report a pattern for naturally occurring friendships between children with autism and another child with special educational needs (Bauminger and Kasari, 2000; Bauminger and Shulman, 2003; Ochs *et al.*, 2001). The friendships of children with autism present a mixed picture, however, with some children with autism being nominated as having a central status within their peer groups.

Similar to the social interactions of children with autism, there is a paucity of information about the details of children's friendships and a call for more qualitative descriptions of how friendships are formed and the pattern of dyadic two-way activity within a friendship (Chamberlain *et al.*, 2007). Bauminger *et al.* (2008) is one of the few studies that tries to address this issue by looking at different social factors in friendships between high-functioning children with autism and typically developing children, compared to those between high-functioning children with autism and other children with autism or another disability. This study used a large range of measures to assess the quality of 'mixed' and 'non-mixed' friendships and found that mixed friendships, that is, those between children with and without autism, were more mutually responsive, exhibited higher levels of social cohesion and orientation, and achieved more complex levels of play. However, findings from the study suggest a complicated picture. Mixed friendships provided the children with autism with fewer opportunities for leadership and the authors concluded that non-mixed friendships may have benefits in terms of self-esteem and the practice of social skills.

As for children without autism, there is an indication that the experience of friendship has an impact on how children with autism view themselves. For high-functioning pupils with autism, the knowledge that they are someone who has friends supports good self-esteem, resilience to negative experiences and acceptance of their diagnosis (Humphrey and Lewis, 2008). In Bauminger and Kasari's (2000) study into the experience of loneliness of high-functioning children with autism, greater feelings of loneliness were reported, indicating a desire for greater involvement in relationships with others. The authors conclude that children with autism do not seek out aloneness, but are outside social relationships because they lack the social knowledge and skill to be included. They point out that it might also be the case that the nature of friendship means something different for children with autism than it does in the ordinary case. In defining friendship, Bauminger and Kasari found that children with autism had a less complex concept of friendship, rating 'closeness' higher than qualities such as companionship, affection and intimacy that they looked for in a friend. It is possible that friendship for an individual with autism is more about actual physical presence and less about mental forms of relationship.

There is some evidence that friendship with a child with autism has an impact on the non-autistic friend. Studies into peer-tutoring programmes report that, though lasting friendship did not always result, the non-autistic participants often experienced enjoyment, increased self-confidence, enhanced self-esteem and disappointment when the programme came to an end (Jones, 2007; Whitaker et al., 1998). It is possible that the experience of friendship and interaction between a child with autism and a peer addresses needs of the non-autistic child, such as shyness or their own social exclusion (Jones, 2007; Laushey and Heflin, 2000).

Studies into the friendships of children with autism and into their experiences of play and interaction indicate that social engagement for children with autism presents a highly complicated picture. The complexity of autism, that is, the complexity of what children with autism can and cannot do, needs in itself to be taken into account within autism theory and practice and is something that is explored more fully below.

Complexity as a key issue for autism theory and practice

Whilst it is apparent that children with autism are socially engaged, do play and can have a friend, difficulties in all these areas of functioning exist when children with autism are compared to other populations of children, including those with developmental delay. However, autism is a spectrum disorder and though the same criteria are relevant for all individuals along the spectrum (Leekam et al., 2000), there is clear diversity within the population. It is evident that different individuals experience differing degrees of social and cognitive difficulty, which probably helps to explain the marked differences in levels of social functioning (Prior et al., 1998). In some cases of high-functioning people with autism, the difference between their level of functioning and that of the typical population is really quite small. Further complication exists when one considers that autism is a developmental disorder and that individual change and development is to be expected. All children with autism are responsive to a wide range of interventions designed to develop social inclusion and play, though which aspects of an intervention are critical to success is unclear. Autism is associated with multiple difficulties in different domains – cognitive, social, motor, sensory, perceptual – and it is not clear how these separately contribute to difficulties experienced by the individual.

Part of the complexity of autism rests in the fact that the associated difficulties of the disorder are in turn highly complex in nature. For the purposes of study, autism research has tended to separate out the different aspects of children's social behaviour. Social interaction, emotional responsiveness, play and friendship have largely been treated as discrete areas of operation, but any consideration of children's activity in ordinary circumstances shows that this is far from the case. Play is not just about playing with objects but also crucially concerns playing interactively with play partners and playing out stories and ideas about social experiences. Even solitary pretend play is closely linked to children's social play with others in the ordinary case (Howes *et al.*, 1989), and for young children without autism, pretending is an inherently social activity (Lillard, 2006; Rakoczy *et al.*, 2005). Friendship has more aspects to it than simply proximity to another child or willingness to take turns and share. It is brought about by the sharing of a similarity in terms of social interactive skills and is partly distinguished by the complexity of play and communication achieved together (Howes *et al.*, 1994). Friends feel that they are friends because they achieve a satisfying coordination of behaviour, the enjoyment of friendship promoting social skills in conflict resolution, negotiation of play interests and dealing with distress in others (Howes, 1998). The influential work done by Dunn (2004, 2005) on children's friendships shows that children's social behaviour is best studied in situations that have real emotional significance for them and that involve experiences of affection as well as conflict, when playing and joking, shifting blame or getting what they want. Friendship for all children is marked out from 'being playmates' by the degree of affection and intimacy present and quality of emotion in the interaction, none of which are easily quantifiable. Attention to everyday social encounters shows a discrepancy between children's capacity in classic research situations and much greater capacity in real–life family or peer group situations (Dunn, 1991).

The complex nature of the social phenomena involved in play, interaction, friendship and the emotion involved probably accounts for the often-noted 'fuzziness' of these concepts in the literature on autism (Jordan, 2003) and, indeed, in the literature on child development and childhood generally (James *et al.*, 1998). A review of articles on the social engagement of children with autism will throw up any number of terms for what is being described, including 'social involvement', 'social networks', 'social play', 'peer interaction', 'socialization', 'social skills' and 'circle of friends'. In separating out areas of 'skill', the idea is that it is then possible to investigate, measure and support the individual factors that underlie autism, but this overlooks the fact that children's social and emotional worlds are incredibly rich, multilayered, interactive and constantly changing. They are not easily described in terms of individual factors or as single cause and effect.

Naturalistic study is increasingly seen as a priority in autism research to help clarify what is unclear about the social engagement of children with autism (White *et al.*, 2007), but this presents a challenge in terms of conceptualizing a more complicated ontological frame. Of necessity in naturalistic study, the behaviour and functioning of the individual child must be seen against a wider ecological background that includes groups of children as well as children and adults in social situations and play encounters. The focus of research is no longer the individual only, but a much richer social, emotional and interactive context in which the individual with autism is situated.

Taken together, the complexity of autism and the complex nature of social phenomena per se necessitate a rethink of approach to the social engagement of children with autism. We have a great deal of knowledge about individual behaviours that are evident in children with autism, but not how they play out in real life. A sociocultural perspective is needed that seeks to understand social contexts in all their complexity and without intruding on what occurs naturally between people. This is concerned with describing the network of interactions within any one community and how individuals make sense of and respond to each other using the mental and material resources that are available to them in that setting. It focuses on specific contexts and preferentially seeks contextualized accounts of behaviour, not in order to make premature generalizations but to uncover patterns of behaviour across different communities.

What a sociocultural approach can contribute to the study of and support for autism will be explored further in the chapters that follow. In the final section of this chapter, more will be said about the issue of complexity, particularly in relation to how we choose to view autism. How we construct our idea of 'what is...' – whether it is what is autism, what is play, what is social interaction or what is friendship – is heavily dependent on our point of view. This is a recurring theme of the book that is a particular focus in Chapter 5 on research into autism. The next section will look at how debates on autism research and practice are largely medically rather than socially driven, with a focus on the individual and their biology rather than on social systems, their structures and processes.

Medical versus social models of disability

Of relevance to a discussion of the nature of the social experiences of children with autism is the concept of the medical model of disability. This is a model of how people with a disability are 'seen' and described which focuses on the individual and their impairment. Its roots are in the positivist traditions of the nineteenth century which sought to objectively study the social world and compile universal laws for individual development (Barnes, 2004). The model as it stands today is most informed by research into child paediatrics that took place in the second half of the twentieth century. This used a large number of different measures for children's physical, behavioural and emotional development to build a framework for 'normal development'. According to the medical model of disability, these normative measures are useful in identifying the 'abnormal child' too and in indicating what areas of development require special 'remediation' in order for the child to progress along the same developmental pathway. Within the model there is little idea of cultural differences between groups of people. The influence of social factors on development also plays a minor role, with the idea of a fixed and biologically determined developmental trajectory of childhood being a much more dominant discourse.

The medical model of disability dominates autism research and practice and underpins the strong focus on the individual child with autism and on interventions to address 'deficits' that are measured against the 'norm' of typically developing children. The 'typically developing child' is constructed within the literature on autism as part of a homogenous group who follows a set pattern of development; for example, in their play, moving inexorably from sensorimotor to relational to symbolic capacities. There is little sense of diversity within different childhoods or that different cultural expectations around children's activity exist in different societies. The continuing influence of behaviourism in autism education also reflects the dominance of a biomedical discourse. An approach to autism that persists is one where the 'behaviours' involved in social communication are identified and promoted with the view taken that these are fixed across different groups of people. The separation of social functioning into the 'skill' areas of play, social interaction and friendship that are somehow stand alone, as has been noted here in the discussion above, is a reflection of this kind of thinking too.

In the last three decades, the social model of disability has been put forward as a counter-argument to the medical model of disability. This is a model that views disability as at least partly socially derived, barriers to 'being and doing' created within and by society. The idea of impairment is downplayed and viewed as not necessarily leading to disability. The argument is that any perceived difficulty in the individual person with a disability is actually constructed in social relations; in other words, in people's ability or failure to accept and accommodate individual differences (Connors and Stalker, 2007). Individuals with autism and their parents have adopted the social model of disability as a way of challenging medicalized views of the condition, using ideas such as 'We are not broken and do not need to be fixed' (Sainsbury, 2000: 30) in response to the idea of autism as a deficit. They argue that development in autism takes a different course to neurotypical development and constitutes a form of naturally occurring neurodiversity (Brownlow and O'Dell, 2009; Langan, 2011).

Some writers, indeed, have constructed autism as a type of culture and the difficulties that exist between people as instances of cultural difference (Mesibov and Shea, 1998). This is an interesting idea playing on the notion that, though autism is a developmental disorder and not a culture, it can be seen to operate as one. Culture refers to shared patterns of human behaviour and cultural norms that affect the ways people think, behave and communicate. Autism too affects the ways that individuals think, behave and communicate and it could be said that autism functions *as* a culture, yielding characteristic and predictable patterns of behaviour in people who have the condition. It is often suggested that understanding the behaviour of someone with autism involves thinking like a cross-cultural interpreter and making sense of cultural difference: autistic and neurotypical. Cumine et al. (2000) suggest that those working with children with autism must use an 'autism lens' to 'see' the behaviour of a child with autism. Part of their role is to 'translate' these behaviours for those who know the child but do not fully understand him.

A cultural perspective centrally places questions about how autism is viewed and who perceives it as different or problematic. In settings such as a school, for example, within-child capacity might be of less significance than environmental factors, including other people and their understandings and behaviour (Clough and Corbett, 2000; Sinclair, 1993). The social difficulty that exists in autism has a transactional basis, where meaning or failure to make meaning involves at least two people. Where difficulties in communication arise, it could be said that it is the result of a shared impairment (Gray, 2009). Thinking about cultural difference, different kinds of questions arise that do not concern within-child issues only but relate to the whole group, what they bring and the nature of their responses. For example, how do mixed groups of children, with and without autism, share meanings and learn from each other? By whom is difference noticed and how is it made consequential? What misunderstandings occur and how are they resolved? Thinking in terms of culture means that the focus shifts from what a child with autism cannot do in comparison with his or her peers, to what he or she *is* doing with them and what peers are doing too.

In some forms, the social model of disability posits that all difference is socially based. Recent thinking about disability has criticized this stance, taking the view that impairment makes for essential difference beyond the socially constructed (Scott-Hill, 2004). There is criticism too of a model that sets up universal concepts of the 'disabled child' without any recognition of diversity and the nature of individual experience within that. What has been put in place of this is the idea of disability as a confluence of factors – in impairment, social structures and culture – that relate to each other in different ways depending on individual circumstances (Watson et al., 2000). The key principles for effectively supporting people with disability are seen to be flexibility and a holistic approach instead of the use of fixed categories. Prevention rather than remediation is seen as important, as is a focus on strengths not deficits and providing support that is transactional rather than hierarchical (Dolan et al., 2006).

In line with Watson et al. (2000), it is argued here that an approach to autism must manage this fine line between competing factors and take a nuanced view. The disposition of the individual with autism is not overwhelmingly social and the experience of the disability must be viewed as relating partly to a core impairment. In educational research, autism has been singled out from other special educational needs as the one area that does need different consideration and a recognition of essential difference (Jordan, 2005). Unlike other areas of learning need, children with autism do not require 'more of the same' curriculum that is taught to all children, though this might be a feature of their education. Teachers of children with autism are also required to have special skills in viewing and translating behaviour, similar to that described above in relation to an 'autism lens'.

Yet, children with autism are *also* socially engaged – to quite a large degree in some cases and particularly in the mainstream settings that are the focus of this book. This makes social structures and culture absolutely critical factors to consider too, in addition to impairment. Thus, getting to grips with autism involves acknowledging factors that are not easy to reconcile but that must be brought together to gain a proper understanding of a child's functioning within their social world. Only in this way can a clear picture be gained of what autism means in the individual case and how we can support it.

To summarize, the following are the key points about autism as a disability to keep in mind:

- Autism involves an experience of the world that is essentially different from that experienced by people without autism and that is prohibitive to some extent of social understanding and engagement.
- Nevertheless, individuals with autism are socially engaged, though there is considerable individual variation in this.
- The difficulties experienced by individuals with autism are partly socially derived, social relations having an extremely important part to play in how the disability is individually experienced.
- Autism has a genetic and biological basis and the challenges of the condition are also physically derived.

A model of being that is most suited to thinking about the social engagement of children with autism is perhaps the 'affirmative model' as proposed by Swain and French (2000). This takes a middle way between acknowledging the core difficulties of an impairment and the key role social attitudes and barriers play in the way disability is experienced by the individual. The affirmative model of disability is predominantly concerned with describing positive social identities where individuals with disability are viewed as having a contribution to make that is of value to others. Such an approach is highly relevant to the case material that is presented in Chapter 4, which describes mixed groups of children, with and without autism, playing and being friends. Some difficulties for the child with autism in each case is described, but it is also evident that they are socially engaged in ways that are appreciated, enjoyed and perceived as socially competent by other children and adults. Before this, the focus of the book will turn to the social experiences of children who do not have autism, setting out children's experiences of everyday interactions, friendships and play. This is done as a way of gaining a fuller understanding of the nature of social experience for mixed groups of children, with and without autism.

Summary

This chapter has noted that research into the social experiences of children with autism presents a complex picture in which they are partly socially engaged, do play and can have a friend, though difficulties in all these areas of functioning exist. There is a marked difference in the level to which children with autism are socially engaged across the autism population and a recognized need within research to know more about the actual social experiences of children with autism, the quality of their participation in social contexts and the nature of other people's responses. The chapter has highlighted the fact that ordinary social processes are also complex. Aspects of children's social behaviour, such as play, friendship and social interaction, are not separate but highly interactive social phenomena that are intricately networked together. The issue of how we view autism has been raised and a sociocultural perspective on autism and social model of disability has been introduced. This provides a complementary view to the medical model of disability by focusing on social contexts and group processes rather than within-child deficits only.

Chapter 2

The social world of childhood

Rachel is a 12-month-old baby, the first-born child of her mother and father. Her mother, who is her main carer, has grown into her role as a first-time parent. She has gradually become 'attuned' to Rachel's actions and interactions, more lively and coordinated in her reciprocity and more resourceful in her care.

On this day, Rachel is sitting on the floor of the living room at home, playing with some toys that have been placed there. Her mother puts new items on the floor: a wooden pot with a lid and, inside, a brown comb. She says that in recent weeks Rachel has become very interested in containers with lids and that she has been looking out for such items. Rachel immediately crawls towards the wooden pot on the floor. She removes the lid and looks inside. Keeping her head down and with great focus, she repeatedly removes the comb from the pot and then replaces it, carefully closing the lid. As she does so, she watches the gap closing between the lid and the pot. Rachel's mother watches intently as she does this, leaning towards her but not saying anything. After a time, the mother puts a wooden cube inside the pot and replaces the lid. Rachel immediately looks inside and her mother smiles. In playing with the pot, Rachel's hand movements at all times are skilful and she concentrates on gripping and grasping things.

Mother goes to fetch her cup of tea and, whilst she is out of the room, there is the sound of an aeroplane flying overhead. Rachel stops what she is doing with the wooden pot and looks up. She looks out of the window and appears to freeze, staying very still for a time. Rachel's mother returns with the tea and looks out of the window herself, noticing a cat that is lying outside in the garden. She picks up Rachel and draws her attention to the cat, but Rachel does not focus on this. Then there is the sound of another plane flying over the house and Rachel's mother makes an exclamation, pointing at the ceiling and saying with interest, 'Plane!' Rachel and her mother look up at the ceiling together, both staying very still and paying close attention.

The intensity of this kind of micro-focus on the detail of actions and interactions allows one to see how much happens in a child's experience, even within a few minutes. Close attention to the detail of social interaction for a child who does not have autism shows the strong emotionality that exists in the baby's contact with her environment and the richness of the communication between her and her carer. It is apparent that for a young child such as Rachel, the environment crucially includes other people and that learning within it is fundamentally social. For an infant, experience of the world is heavily contingent on the actions, responsiveness, attitudes, values, concerns and personal resources of her mother and father. Yet an important detail within Rachel's experience is that she also brings innovation to her environment – her attention, attitude and responsiveness also determining the course her experience will take.

Social-emotional learning of this kind, which is typical of a young child's early experiences of the world, is different from traditional notions of school learning, although ideas in educational practice are increasingly influenced by this understanding of children as learners. It is a type of learning that does not depend on verbal language alone, but does heavily involve emotionally regulated situations that are strongly relationship based. A key feature of social learning is attunement within relationships and a degree of mutuality in identifying objects of shared attention. Rachel and her mother do not always share their focus of attention, but the nature of their relationship partly concerns finding ways of orienting the self to the other, particularly on the part of the parent. This is a barely conscious process, but one that crucially describes all social relationships.

This chapter will focus on the social worlds of children who do not have autism, looking at social experience from the inside, that is, from the child's own point of view. It will note that the construction of ordinary human development in the literature on autism presents a slightly skewed picture, one where the typically developing child is seen as a passive recipient of external socializing forces and the process of development as one that conforms to universal and unvaried laws. An alternative view of child development will be presented which is based on well-established ideas about the sociocultural nature of learning found in the work of Lev Vygotsky, Urie Bronfenbrenner and later social theorists. This posits that human cognition is not individualistic but social in nature, guided and constrained by understandings gained through interpersonal relationships and transactional experiences. It will be argued that this is equally the case for adults and for children, the latter also engaged in appropriating cultural resources in order to interpret and participate in social processes. Key theoretical constructs within children's social learning will be outlined as a way of providing insight into what it means to 'be social' and what it therefore means to be partly or mostly non-social and so to have autism.

The construction of ordinary social development in the literature on autism

Anyone who tries to facilitate social engagement in children with autism, or research key factors in this, will have to have a notion of what constitutes social engagement in the typical case. Whether we are teaching skills for joining in with a conversation or developing a child's capacity to play with others, we need an idea of what it is that we are aiming towards, that is, the form a conversation or play encounter typically takes for children without autism.

Ideas about what children typically do come up again and again in the literature on autism. There is the idea that children follow social rules and that children with autism need to first learn then apply these rules in order to engage with others more effectively. There is the idea too that norms exist in children's social worlds, so that children usually have a 'best friend' and usually develop to the point where they engage in imaginative play with others. Research into social engagement is often predicated on the belief that children 'initiate' play with others, possibly saying a phrase such as 'Can I play with you?', the more initiations taking place the better and seen as an indication of social inclusion.

For those of us working with children with autism in typical contexts, such ideas often seem curious. Are there really social rules which other children, those without autism, know and consistently use? Do most children have a best friend? Do all children engage in imaginative play? And is it really the case that the more times a child goes up to others and asks to play the better? Those of us working with children will know that the answer to these questions is a 'yes' and a 'no': there is variation in all of these things and children's social contexts are much more complex than only one idea of it.

The idea of what constitutes social engagement in the typical case is a construct that is taken largely from psychological theories of development. These put forward the notion that the dominant issue of childhood is the achievement of age-related competencies, with children passing naturally through stages of increasing sophistication in social organization. Development is seen as biologically based, an individual and linear process, which takes place according to universal laws of change in psychological functioning. Children are viewed as moving towards the endpoint of becoming a fully developed adult, with any 'failure' in this an indication of 'deficit', 'deviance' or incompetency (Hogan, 2005).

Consistent with this view of childhood is the idea that children are the passive recipients of socializing forces. They are seen as 'a project in the making', moving towards adulthood, but incomplete, dependent and not fully formed (Woodhead and Faulkner, 2008). They are unskilled and acquire skills gradually through the internalization of external socializing influences and norms, which are mostly adult directed. An important concept here – one that is often alluded to in the literature on autism – is that of 'transmission', where social learning is transferred from a more competent, older or developmentally advanced individual to a less competent one.

Consistent too with this notion of the 'socially developing child' is that processes of change in childhood can be objectively studied and that development in the individual child can be measured against a standard of age-related capacities. Science-based methodologies are seen as most suited to studying child development, with predominance given to quantifiable data gained from experimental research designs and sociometric surveys.

Piaget, whose work dominates this field, was a constructivist and believed that human development was the result of both nativistic capacities and social influences. He described the child as active and engaged with his environment, a 'little scientist' who strives continually to engage with the world around him. However, he used a discourse that constructed the child as undeveloped and development as a natural process of increasing stages of competency. The child's development is essentially decontextualized and viewed as one-way, the child absorbing learning from an environment that remains unchanged and autonomous.

These ideas in psychology-based theories of development, which dominate thinking in autism research and intervention, are focused on cognitive growth but are not especially good at taking account of the quality of children's lives as they are lived by them. The positivist methodologies used are unable to describe subjective experience and the quality of social engagement or the nature of individual differences. Social theorists, using naturalistic 'bottom-up' ethnographic methods to investigate individual social experiences and real-life interactions, have argued that cognitive developmental theories have not taken sufficient account of more recent understandings about how children actively take part in their social worlds and contribute to their learning (James et al., 1998; Woodhead and Faulkner, 2008). These understandings are gained from social-based theories of what children do, sometimes described as the 'new sociology of childhood'. James et al. (1998) have put forward the concept of the 'sociological child' as a counterpoint to the construct of the 'socially developing child'. This accepts the developmental stage theories of child development, but with much more emphasis on the unfolding, contextualized nature of human development, the child conceived of not only as the product of biology, but also as one of history, society and culture.

The sociology of childhood

Arguments against the dominance of developmental psychology, and its emphasis on stages of development and the accomplishment of adulthood, were first put forward in the 1990s and could therefore no longer accurately be described as 'new'. However, since that time they have became well established in contemporary thinking about children and childhood in Western society. A central tenet of the sociology of childhood is that children are competent social players who steer their way through complex social worlds and deal with competing concerns and perspectives. According to this view, children should be seen as active participants in culture with a role to play in constructing and creating social relationships. The value of what children do should not be read simply in terms of their future capacities, but also in what it says in the present about how they are interpreting and shaping social relationships (Christensen and Prout, 2005).

Children should not be viewed as incomplete or asocial, the passive recipients of socializing influences provided by parents and teachers. They are 'social actors' whose activity contributes to social processes and children's own learning. Children's culture is not a private world – a mysterious and separate world of childhood – but is heavily influenced by their association with their families, other adults and the wider world around them. What is important to understand in children's worlds is how they are making sense of things and using these understandings in their interactions with the environment, including other people.

Working within this new paradigm, Corsaro (1992) has devised an interpretive model of development that is reproductive rather than linear. His longitudinal ethnographic studies of children showed that their reproduction of culture was neither imitation nor a result of direct transmission, but more a *creative* appropriation of the adult world. Children creatively participate in a collective process of socialization. Their contribution is always embedded in social context and language and cannot be extracted as something that is only 'individual'. Of his ethnographic studies of young children, Corsaro wrote:

> Little by little I began to see that I was not simply verifying young children's impressive social skills and the positive effects of peer interaction on their individual development. I found myself studying collective, communal and cultural processes. I was documenting the children's creative production of and participation in a shared childhood culture. My full grasp of this revelation was gradual because I clung strongly to the typical adult tendency to try to interpret and evaluate almost everything children do as some of sort of learning experience that prepared them for the future.
>
> (Corsaro, 2003: 5)

According to Corsaro – whose important ideas about children's social activity will be described more fully in the following chapter – children's peer cultures are characterized by persistent attempts to understand and gain a footing in social activity. They may not always understand things fully, but will continue to interpret and interact anyway. Children do not carry round culture in their heads, but reproduce it publicly. This makes close attention to children's responses, in their play, to each other and to adults, absolutely essential to the study of childhood socialization (Corsaro, 2011). Corsaro draws a parallel between children's attempts to gain social entry and adult access rituals when joining in with conversation. He points out that a direct request to join in would be deemed inappropriate by children and adults alike, but that an indirect approach, using non-verbal behaviour and appropriate cultural knowledge, will have much more success.

Such an interpretation of children's actions does not distinguish between different types of social activity. Play, interaction and friendship can all be described as 'temporal sites of cultural reproduction', where children learn about culture and reproduce it (James et al., 1998). All exist as responses to socialization processes, where knowledge of the social world is appropriated and exchanged. Children's peer groups are vitally important in facilitating cultural reproduction, but all interaction and cultural activity involves this same process of interpretation and reproduction. The emphasis is on what children are doing and on their competencies, rather than on what they cannot do. By focusing on competencies, an insight is gained into how children make sense of things and use their understandings to navigate and negotiate social interactions. Children's cultural routines – the activities that they repeat together again and again – must be studied since it is these that are their 'cultural arenas' where understandings, concerns and values are explored.

Different aspects of children's play are not more cognitively relevant than others. Typically, the value of some aspects of children's play, including rough and tumble play and silly or 'dizzy' play, has been treated with ambivalence by adults, with pretend play viewed as more central to children's development (Pellegrini and Smith, 1998). However, all aspects of children's activity are culturally relevant, even those viewed as educationally irrelevant, such as gibberish, jokes, teasing, silly noises and ideas taken from junk media (Kalliala, 2006). Corsaro (2011) points out that market research and commercial interests often pay more attention to children's actual toy preferences and processes of play. Superhero play, absurd and grotesque humour, fantasy and group identities are often key aspects of children's play experience that are overlooked by educators and academics. Children's play experiences and cultural activity should be viewed as part of the much wider culture and the process by which they appropriate and interpret varying cultural identities, roles, events and ways of interacting.

It is important to remember that children's culture is understanding and knowledge in the making and therefore only emergent and partial. It is difficult to measure in test settings since, for children themselves, it is something that is still developing (James, 2001). Ideas about interaction, play and friendship have a strong public and performative element at this stage, rather than a secure cognitive one. Friendship, for example, may be less of a fixed and stable phenomena and more a working out of what it means to be a friend whilst locating oneself in discourse as someone who 'has friends'. It is also the case that children who are more skilful socially, who know good games and make interesting play transformations, will be fun to be with and desirable as a friend, though this should not be confused with actual friendship (Howes, 1998).

Ideas about how children participate in and contribute to their own learning are based in the conceptualization of human development as an essentially cultural process. Using theoretical constructs taken from Vygotsky, Bronfenbrenner and other social theorists, these understandings are well established in contemporary ideas about child development, though much less understood in the literature on autism. The dominance of positivist methodologies in autism research and of directive interventions in autism education probably accounts for this, but the degree to which an understanding of sociocultural processes is absent in the autism literature must constitute a major gap and a concern. Children with autism are partly socially engaged and understanding what form that engagement takes and how it evolves within ordinary social contexts can only come about through more theoretical engagement with what we know about the sociocultural nature of human development and learning.

What is socioculture?

Socioculture refers to the behaviour of individuals as it relates to the context of their social setting. The relationship between the individual and their environment is viewed as encompassing 'transactional arrangements' rather than straightforward single interactions and one-way influences (Bruner, 1986). Socioculture is better thought of as 'processes' in which communities of people participate in ways that are ongoing, two-way and multilayered (Rogoff, 2003). People's participation in culture can be observed, but being rich, continual and ever-changing, it is impossible to record in its entirety (Stern, 2004). The sociocultural context refers to people's everyday social routines which are often ordinary, taken for granted and mostly unnoticed, but which are actually strongly rooted in historical and ongoing cultural practices and understandings. Different sociocultural contexts exist with their own distinctive features, but all individuals are embedded in culture, unable to stand outside it and take an objective position.

A sociocultural perspective differs in its view of the individual from the classic cognitivist model of being. The cognitivist model is derived from Descartes and conceives of a private 'self' that is located somewhere in the body, probably in the head, and is essentially separate from the outside world. The connection between inner self and outer world is not a direct one and involves a process of 'mentalization' where the world – which in this model is seen as being fixed and pre-given – is taken in and reflected upon through a higher-order process of thought (Gallagher, 2004). Access to other people's minds is problematic since they are hidden away, closed in inside the body.

More recent developments in theory have questioned this Cartesian notion of the individual; the idea of an internal self that exists before or outside culture is seen as a strong cultural bias of Western philosophical thought. A paradigm shift occurred in the 1960s with the emergence of social constructionism which dissolved the whole idea of a subject that exists separately from social relations. Since the 1980s, sociocultural theory has contributed to this the idea that the individual actively participates in cultural processes, creatively producing shared understandings of the world (Prout and James, 1997). It is the individual who constitutes their experience by directing their attention towards something, doing this by virtue of the object's meaning for them. The relation between the perceptual experience of the individual and its object is not a passive one. Consciousness is not free-floating, but is guided or constrained by understandings gained through interpersonal relationships and experiences. Thus, for a child playing in a playground, the world may consist of the movement of a ball, the lines of a football pitch and their own performance measured against the actions of other children playing. For an adult in the same playground who is directing a group of children away from a fence, it is probably none of these and much more an attention to boundaries, expectations and issues of control. The world is made sense of in terms of the elements of a scene that are in operation for the individual at any one time together with their understanding of how those elements play out culturally.

Ideas about socioculture as they have developed in the last few decades have been strongly influenced by the work of Vygotsky in the 1920s and of Bronfenbrenner in the latter half of the twentieth century. The ideas of Bronfenbrenner, Vygotsky and more recent sociocultural theorists have underpinned our current understandings of how human beings develop and learn. We know that the human brain in the typical case is essentially a social brain and that all learning and development is socially based. Though autism has a strong genetic basis and does not have a primary cause in social factors, the social basis of development in individuals without autism means that it is nevertheless important to fully grasp this. The view taken here is that, only by focusing on our understanding of the sociocultural nature of human development, can we get closer to an understanding of how to support the activity of individuals with autism and their engagement with others.

What is of paramount importance is that knowledge of sociocultural contexts is essentially knowledge about what actually goes on between the individual and the environment, which includes other people. It is knowledge about how individuals engage in social processes and how social contexts unfold. Essentially, it is practical knowledge about experience as it is lived by the individual. For practitioners who seek to find ways to support the individual with autism, this kind of knowledge and understanding is fundamental to their work and of much greater value than more generalized ideas about 'what is autism'. The practical knowledge that is available in a sociocultural approach will be discussed in the chapters that follow. Before this, the next two sections will discuss in more detail Vygotsky's sociocultural-historical theory and Bronfenbrenner's ecological systems model.

Sociocultural-historical theory

In the case of the typically developing human being, individual perception and participation is always constituted in wider cultural understandings, culture providing templates for the individual to 'see' and act in situations, with language used to overcome ambiguities and agree meanings. The writings of Russian psychologist and founder of sociocultural-historical theory, Lev Vygotsky, have provided the theoretical framework here. Vygotsky's ideas were based in psychology, but added an important and radically new sociocultural dimension. According to him, individual effort can never be viewed as separate from social contexts, the capacity for thought coming about in the way individuals participate in these.

Vygotsky put forward the idea that children's activity must always be located within society, specifically within cultural and collective actions with other people. He described how human development is not the result either of biology or of the influence of culture, but occurs through the constant interaction of each, biological behaviour and social conditions. Interpersonal exchange leads to the internalization and appropriation of culture, developmental capacity always appearing twice: first on the social level and then intrapersonally, within the individual (Vygotsky, 1978). He believed that humans are active in 'making themselves from the outside' as they participate in, produce and modify cultural practices. He argued that the goal is not to find out how many 'units of heredity' combined with which aspects of the environment, but to retrace the historical development of behaviour or, as he described it, to discover 'the historical child' (Vygotsky, 1987).

The idea of psychological 'tools' that enable people's participation in culture is central to Vygotsky's ideas, with language seen as key amongst these (Vygotsky, 1978). Language is a cultural tool that is used by the individual to mediate thought and behaviour, the act of speaking – whether externally or as inner speech – helping us to do our thinking. By studying language, it is possible to see the development of mental concepts within the individual and the nature of their cognitive awareness. Other cultural tools exist such as counting, texts, maps, pictures and conventional sign systems, but Vygotsky emphasized verbal language as the main cultural tool available to human beings. Recent theorists have argued that non-verbal communication, particularly in young children, would also constitute a key cultural tool (Rogoff, 2003). Infants use their limbs to reach and move, but also as mental tools for communication in episodes of joint engagement with their caregivers; for example, raising their arms to indicate that they want to be lifted up. In the chapter that follows, on children's cultures of communication, some of the many non-verbal ways in which children communicate will be described more fully.

Vygotsky pointed out that cultural communities are constantly changing and cannot be said to exist separately from the individuals who participate in them. People continually produce and reproduce culture, using and enhancing cultural practices in continually ongoing transactions with each other and with the environment. Cultural practice, which includes tool use, is socially and historically constituted, passed on, recontextualized and refined across the generations. Vygotsky argued that culture and biology should not be viewed as two separate entities but should be seen as historically intertwined and mutually shaping. He described how cultural learning occurs within four time frames: the biological inheritance of evolutionary time that leads to species change; the accumulation of cultural artefacts and traditions that occurs within historical time and that is passed on generationally; the learning that occurs across an individual's lifespan; and individual learning in micro-moments of time (Scribner, 1985). Within all four time frames, biological, cultural and individual aspects of human functioning are interlinked and together contribute to the overall process of human learning. In contemporary thought, reductionist views of humanity, such as are found in the nature versus nurture debate, have been abandoned in favour of a more complex view. As Prout (2005) argues, biology, culture and, indeed, technology should not be viewed as existing as separate phenomena. Each contributes to the other, in some cases over millennia, and none can be described as purely 'natural' or purely 'social'. Even technology involves components that are natural and will include many features that are derived from the social.

Bronfenbrenner's ecological systems model

Urie Bronfenbrenner's ecological systems model of development has also served to highlight the importance of a sociocultural perspective. His ideas shifted the focus of research away from studying within-person capacities alone towards an interest in the combination of intrapersonal, interpersonal and historical-communal processes involved in individual experience. Bronfenbrenner (1979) put forward the idea that individuals and environments are interdependent systems and said that it is possible to look at the individual and their environment separately, but it is better to take in both. He argued that the more we understand the multiple contexts of any piece of behaviour, the better we understand the behaviour and advocated a wide perspective that brings together, rather than separates out, the cultural variables involved. He believed that theories of psychological development that focused on intrapersonal processes were only partial descriptions of behaviour and offered a wider and more complete account of human behaviour.

Bronfenbrenner tried to move away from linear ideas of cultural transmission and proposed a system of concentric circles to depict the individual's relationship to their environment. He proposed that the individual and their environment consist of a number of systems that work together and so help to create one another. He identified four systems altogether, each one becoming larger and wider in terms of influence. The smallest systems, the microsystems, concern the individual's immediate experiences and closest relationships, but this is in operation with ever-widening social systems involving the settings of home, school and local neighbourhood (mesosystems), the local community, social institutions and the wider social society (exosystems), its values, traditions and norms (macrosystems). In Figure 2.1, it is possible to see that the child is not in direct contact with these wider systems, but all are in continual interaction and help to shape each other. Bronfenbrenner described individuals and environments as mutually constituting, each changing and reacting to change in each other. In his ecological model of development, the individual and their unique personal resources, history and expectations interacts with the distinctive patterns of activities, roles and interpersonal relations in their immediate environment and, indirectly, with those in the wider society around.

Central to Bronfenbrenner's model is the idea of the system which is conceived of as an integrated whole consisting of a number of interdependent elements that are dynamic and in constant interaction. The system as a concept refers to arrangements that are found in nature as well as within society and is concerned with connectivity, feedback loops and networks. Systems are self-regulating and made up of interrelating groups of elements which feed backward and feed forward, changing shape and reacting to change in each other. A system may be closed, and so follow fixed principles of cause and effect, or it may be open and described as complex, with varied possible outcomes. Closed and open systems can be found in nature and society. Prout (2005) gives the example of the laws of thermodynamics as a closed system in nature, where change in one of the variables of pressure, volume and temperature always has a predictable effect. In contrast to this, he gives the weather as an example of a system that is open, where constantly shifting variables interact with each other to produce outcomes which are hard to predict. The literature on autism often depicts social systems as fairly closed – people's actions giving rise to certain predictable reactions and behaviours – but social systems would more accurately be described as open. People's interactions with each other and the environment involve a whole range of factors in personality, knowledge, understanding, experience, culture and affect, and should be thought of as complex. Links within complex systems are not straightforwardly linear in terms of cause and effect so that small differences in variables in two systems that are similar will produce quite different outcomes over time. Thus it is hard to predict how social systems will develop, the system itself not being produced by outside forces but emerging from internal features that are interactive, fluid and constantly in play.

The final section of this chapter will explore in more depth the sociocultural nature of human development, discussing some key theoretical constructs in relation to this that are particularly relevant to a consideration of autism.

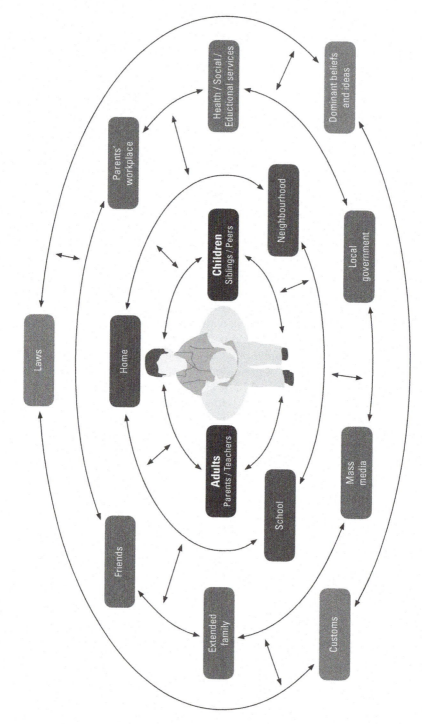

Figure 2.1 Bronfenbrenner's ecological systems model showing the multiple contexts of behaviour (adapted from Cole et al., 2005)

The sociocultural nature of human development

Vygotsky argued that the development of thought and all 'higher mental functions' are socially formed in transactions with other people. Culture is not simply a trigger to early development, though this is what it has been reduced to in interpretations of Vygotsky's ideas (Corsaro, 1992). In the literature on autism, for example, sociocultural theory underpins ideas about executive function deficit but is used in a way that is cognitively focused. The capacity for inhibiting external information in favour of internal thought – what Vygotsky saw as the basis of the child's capacity for pretence – is seen as a single and separate capacity that is either present or not present in the individual with autism. Within executive function explanations of autism, there is little sense of interpersonal experience as an ongoing feature of human development and that all learning should be viewed as involving cognitive, affective and social features, as Vygotsky argued.

For Vygotsky, the development of conceptual understanding goes from spontaneous, everyday concepts, which are concretely and practically formed by the individual in their everyday actions, to more abstract and general concepts that are supported by formal systems of thought. He described conceptual understanding as a progression from natural, spontaneous and everyday knowledge, that is based on the here and now and what we can see, to what he described as constructed 'scientific knowledge' (Vygotsky, 1987). He argued that these scientific concepts are not simply transmitted in a pre-packaged pedagogical form, however, but develop in ways that are intertwined with the individual's experiences of culture. Systematic and organized thinking – what Vygotsky associated with scientific knowledge – becomes gradually embedded in the individual's everyday use of language and thereby achieves greater contextualized richness and real meaning. Vygotsky wrote:

> Pedagogical experience demonstrates that direct instruction in concepts is impossible. It is pedagogically fruitless. The teacher who attempts to use this approach achieves nothing but a mindless learning of words, an empty verbalism that stimulates or imitates the presence of concepts in the child. Under these conditions, the child learns not the concept but the word, and this word is taken over by the child through memory rather than thought. Such knowledge turns out to be inadequate in any meaningful application. This mode of instruction is the basic defect of the purely scholastic verbal modes of teaching which have been universally condemned. It substitutes the learning of dead and empty verbal schemes for the mastery of living knowledge.
>
> (Vygotsky, 1987: 170)

By focusing on questions about the nature of social learning as outlined in sociocultural theory, we are more able to understand what it means to be social. This in turn allows us to understand more fully both the core difficulties of autism and what we can hope to achieve when we support the development of individuals with autism. Some questions about social learning – ones that are key to our understanding of and support for autism – are addressed below.

What is the zone of proximal development?

Vygotsky's conceptualization of the process by which learning occurs in early development is the 'zone of proximal development' (ZPD), the site where learning is imparted from a more knowledgeable adult to a less knowledgeable child. There has been much theoretical focus on the importance of the ZPD to the process of learning, though it is not clear from Vygotsky's writings how far he envisaged it as a space where an actual social other is present with the young learner. It is possible that he allowed for the existence of different forms of participant structure, not all of which involve the actual presence of an adult partner and which include texts and other media, number systems, community practices and social institutions (Daniels, 2005). However, ZPD activity should not be seen as a one-way transmission of learning, with children on the receiving end of adult creativity (Daniels, 2008). Vygotsky envisaged the ZPD as a creative space for both participants, where children can develop ideas as much as adults, where participation is collective and where learning can occur on both sides.

ZPD activity is sometimes used to describe the interaction that goes on between teachers and students in schools (Pollard, 2008). In some areas of education, children's learning is envisaged as a process of extending the child's capacity to make sense of a topic and so move themselves forward in their understanding. The teacher's role is one of 'scaffolding' the child's learning and this involves finding out what they bring in terms of knowledge and understanding to the learning context, and then supporting further learning by asking questions or introducing new cultural material. The emphasis is on engaging with the child within meaningful and constructive relationships, noticing and responding to how a child participates in learning contexts. ZPD activity is particularly evident in early years education, but is increasingly being used to theorize what goes on in classroom activity in the later years too, all children seen as continuing to engage with learning in this way. Chapter 7, which focuses on the educational assessment of children with autism in schools, goes into much more detail on this point, looking more closely at children's activity as learners and the purpose of teaching.

How does children's participation in learning contexts contribute to their development?

Participation is a central idea in our understanding of children as learners and the social nature of development. Children participate in, contribute to and help to shape their learning experiences. Thought comes about through a process of internalizing social experience and an important aspect of this is the way in which children engage with, appropriate and use cultural tools and make them their own. Appropriation has occurred when the individual has adapted sociocultural resources in a way that is meaningful to them, that fits in with their pre-existing schema and that they can use as their own.

Building on the work of Vygotsky, Rogoff (1990) introduced the concept of 'guided participation' to describe the process by which learning takes place. This involves situations of cooperative activity that have a strong emotional and relational basis and differ from traditional notions of didactic school learning. Participation in learning situations involves an individual's past experiences as well as their own efforts and understandings of socially constituted practices, making the process by which development unfolds a transactional, dynamic and creative one. People – children and adults – bring what they know and understand to cooperative situations of learning, using and adjusting these according to events and understandings as they unfold.

Development comes about as the result of changes in the way in which an individual participates in culture. Perceptions, motivations, feelings and understandings are socially constituted so that cognition, emotion and action could all be said to be aspects of sociocultural activity. Rogoff (2003) describes development as 'transformation' of cultural practice, that is, in the way an individual notices, remembers, classifies, feels, understands and problem-solves. Development can be studied by attending to changes in the way the individual participates in and contributes to sociocultural processes.

However, in viewing human activity within a setting, the focus should not be individual actions, but people's participation in events. For sociocultural theorists, 'context' is a more important concept than 'agent', and 'action' is more indicative of human mental processes than 'skill' or 'ability'. Rogoff (1990) argues that mental processes should not be thought of as objects – language, thought, memory, perception and so on – which are internal and the fixed property of the individual. It is much better to think of them as actions that are related to goals – expressing, thinking, remembering, perceiving – so that we can see more clearly the mental process involved. For example, the child in a classroom who shouts 'Yes!', making a celebratory fist pump gesture when he gets a right answer, is not simply using his language, but *expressing himself* in a way that is appropriate to being a 'winner amongst peers'.

What is the significance of intersubjective engagement to the development of cognition?

It is thought that the protracted length of infancy in human development, compared to other primates, is actually for the purpose of prolonged social engagement. For a considerable period of time, the human infant's interactions with the world are almost always socially mediated – social engagement, affect and infant cognition tied together in continuous action patterns between parent and baby. The infant acts and its actions are given a gloss of social meaning through the emotional response of the parent; for example, the baby's vocalization of 'da!' translated into delight and a greeting by the mother. Young children are not egocentric in the Piagetian sense, incapable early on of taking a perspective that is social and needing to be brought to sociality, but should be viewed as socially focused from the outset (Bruner, 1968). Analysis of infant–carer interaction has shown a clear pattern to this social behaviour, one that is characterized by 'cycles of communication' with the constant gaining and withdrawal of attention between parent and baby rhythmically repeated over time. Interaction is described as a two-way process, where both participants are mutually and bodily engaged, and where expressions of face, voice and hands act out affective and narratorial 'protoconversations' that have an overture, escalation, resolution and ending (Trevarthen, 1979).

The interactions of baby and caregiver from nine months onwards mark a turning point in the nature of social engagement. From nine months of age, babies demonstrate a new understanding of actions that are directed towards hidden objects and goals that are separate from immediate behavioural means. The baby is able to see the intentions of their communicative partner behind their actions, focusing on and coordinating themselves to the intentionality present in the situation rather than any immediately perceived meaning. This understanding and way of operating is markedly different from the perception and memory-based cognition of other primates (Tomasello, 1999). The baby experiences the caregiver, not as an object, but *intersubjectively*, taking in something of that person's orientation towards the world and seeing the mind of the other in their action. By focusing on intentions, the baby is able to recognize that one action can have several meanings and that meaning itself is separate from the action. The baby sees, for example, not just that the plate is removed but that it is tidied away or snatched away angrily or playfully hidden. Play situations often concern the playful negotiation of meanings, where a system of checking looks is used that go back and forth between an action or object and the other person (Lillard, 2006). In early social infant interaction, it is the adult who creates these kinds of symbolic acts, with the baby at first watching and copying and only later inventing their own (Striano *et al.*, 2001).

The case for intersubjectivity as the basis for learning and development is strong and found not only in the sociability of parental care, but also in the innate capacities of infants. Recent developments in neurophysiology, which focus on how the mind works with the body, indicate that infants show responses at the neural level to the actions and intentions of others. In particular, neural schema in the infant do not react to any action by others but specifically to those that have a social meaning (Petit, 1999).

How do children develop a capacity for symbol formation?

It is not clear how higher-order thinking comes about from this kind of primary social-emotional engagement. Cognitive explanations, such as Tomasello's (1999), put forward the idea that experience cannot be directly accessed and must be intellectually constructed by the individual, with human relations perceived mentally from the 'outside' even whilst the individual is engaged in interaction. By contrast, relational approaches to human development emphasize the direct connection that exists between people within intersubjective engagement, an understanding of other persons coming about through an intense perceptual and affective relatedness towards their body and behaviour (Hobson, 1993a). The development of mind, including an understanding of other people's mental states, is not a separate process involving the 'switching on' of cognitive abilities at particular ages, but a slow accumulation of learning based in intersubjectivity. The repeated, rhythmic, richly and emotionally experienced nature of early social engagement gives rise to 'metaphors of experience' that begin to exist separately from their original actions. The elaboration of movement that goes on between an infant and its carer together with the communicative intent within it becomes part of an 'out there' expression available for cultural and symbolic use.

Espanõl (2007) provides a case study of a 19-month-old child, Habib, that provides a good illustration of how early experiences of movement in repeated encounters of interaction, together with access to culture give rise to the creation of symbols for use in communication:

> Habib has seen a video in which a flamenco dancer, Joaquin Cortéz, dances accompanied by other dancers. He has frequently imitated the movements of the legs and arms, varying the speeds, passing one hand through the opposite arm, turning his head, going round in circles, and tapping his feet in different directions. On one occasion when he saw the video-player was off, Habib looked at me and moved his arms and hands over his head in a waving manner, imitating the movements of flamenco dancing. My immediate response was: 'Do you want to see Joaquin Cortéz's video?' The arm movement performed by Habib is not a 'natural' movement. It forms part of the repertoire of resources that culture offers him for symbolic formation. In the same way as the word 'papa', the patterns of movement 'are out there' prepared to be appropriated by the child.
>
> (Espanõl, 2007: 249)

Hobson and Hobson (2007) have been prominent in proposing a relational approach to development that involves a 'two-person psychology' where the infant mentally incorporates the psychological stance of another person alongside their own stance. Thought comes about through a process of increasing awareness of and differentiation between what belongs to the self and what belongs to the other. Different intentions towards the object are recognized, giving rise to different possible meanings of the object so that symbols become distinguishable from their original object as 'thoughts from things' (Hobson, 2006). Hobson (1990) posits the idea that intersubjectivity underpins the early construction of the 'psychological architecture' of mind, including the development of a theory of mind, though some writers within cognitive science argue that intersubjectivity is not something that 'switches off' with age and operates throughout life (Gallagher, 2011).

More will be said in Chapter 9 about how young children develop a capacity to symbolize from participating in social experiences with their carers. The next chapter continues to explore children's ordinary social worlds, focusing on their experiences of social communication.

Summary

This chapter has outlined the social basis of ordinary human development and the nature of social activity for children without autism. It has been argued that the reliance on psychology-based theories of development in the literature on autism and the emphasis on an individual model of deficit overlook important features in children's social worlds. These include the fact that children are social actors, active in creating group processes and contributing to the development of their cognition. The rich, continuous and encompassing nature of people's participation in sociocultural processes has been described and it has been noted that social contexts must always be considered in terms of their complexity and emergent dynamic. A relational and embodied approach to development has been outlined. This views interpersonal engagement that is experienced intersubjectively as the basis for growth in human cognition, including the capacity to create and use symbols.

Chapter 3

Children's cultures of communication

Taylor, aged 9, is a high-profile member of his class group and attracts a good deal of staff attention and management, both for his learning needs as well as refusals to comply with teacher direction. A regular occurrence is that Taylor walks out of the classroom or leaves the group in some way, raising considerable management issues for the teacher. Children in the class help Taylor with his work and the everyday skills he finds difficult. They are also observed on several occasions taking on a management-type role with him in the playground, where he regularly infringes the rules and gets into disagreements with other children.

One day in the playground, Taylor is using a large branch to retrieve his jumper, which he has thrown up in a tree. The branch swings back and forth making it difficult for him to get his jumper. After a while and instead of trying to retrieve his jumper, he starts to use the branch to swipe at some of the children who are standing near to him. Three girls from his class, who are part of this group, tell him to calm down, staying very calm themselves and talking to him in an adult-type way. Suddenly, however, they jump on him and pin him to the ground. One of them, Molly, tells him they will only let him go once he is calm. He does become calm and the girls release him, but then Taylor gets the branch and starts to swing it again and the girls pin him to the ground once more. This keeps happening, the girls releasing Taylor, Taylor getting hold of the branch and then being pinned down by the three girls. There is something playful about the whole engagement and it is not clear whether Taylor is really not calm or only pretending to be badly behaved.

A central theme of this book is that the interaction between individuals and their environment, which includes other people, is not a straightforward one. Participation in culture involves an individual's past experiences and their personal resources, efforts and concerns as well as their understandings of social situations in the here and now. This makes people's engagement with others a process that is dynamic and unfolding. The above description of children's play provides a good example of this. In the playground, three girls are 'managing' the behaviour of another child, a boy in their class. The manner in which they do this is reminiscent of the way in which they regularly see their teacher managing the boy's behaviour in class. The attitude and gestures they adopt have the quality of an adult-type role of 'care and control', telling him authoritatively to give them the stick and making slow 'calm down' gestures with their hands. However, the manner in which they do this is not fully 'adult' since they also jump on him and pin him to the ground. As an adult watching these children interact, it is difficult to be sure whether they are playing or being serious. Both Taylor and the three girls appear to be enjoying the engagement to some extent, with Taylor repeatedly getting upset and the girls repeatedly remonstrating with him and pinning him down.

Corsaro (1992) has conceptualized this type of behaviour in children as 'interpretive reproduction', where children do not merely learn about the social world, but also actively interpret it and reproduce it in creative ways in their interactions with each other. The concept of interpretive reproduction extends the idea that children simply act on their environment, highlighting the fact that they *creatively* appropriate sociocultural information within the process of socialization as well as using it to meet their own individual and peer culture concerns. The play these children carry out has a flavour of this, the children partially understanding what goes on between adults and children, playing with roles and trying to make sense of the meaning of adult care and control of children, whilst also concerned with their own issues, perhaps in this instance issues of gender and sexuality.

This perspective on children's actions and childhood culture highlights the fact that children are not simply socialized by adult influences, but also respond innovatively to socialization processes. Their social activity is not simply mimicry of what they see adults do, but has more in the way of agency on the part of children. This chapter will employ the ideas of Corsaro and other theorists who use social-based accounts of children's cultural worlds to provide an alternative description of children's social communication to that typically found in the literature on autism. Communication is a key area of difficulty in autism and it is worth exploring the issue of children's communication in ordinary social contexts as a way of understanding what happens when children with and without autism interact.

The chapter will outline children's varying forms of communication – what Christensen (2004) has described as their 'cultures of communication' – and note that for children, unlike adults, non-verbal communication is a particularly important communicative feature. It will describe some of the concerns that children typically communicate about, including those to do with personal identity and social competence. Finally, it will look at children's use of media culture, which is also a strong feature of their communication. It is surprising that, given the extensive use made by children with autism of media resources

– a typical behaviour being to repeat lines, phrases and songs from films and television programmes – there has not been more focus on this in discussions of autism. This chapter will describe the extensive use children without autism make of media resources in their communication and so help us to understand how the communication of children with autism may be experienced and made sense of by other children.

The hundred languages of children

In discussions about how to develop the social communication of children with autism, the idea of communication is often put forward as one of 'transmission of a message' (see, for example, Paul, 2009). This involves a person, autonomously knowing what they want to say, relaying that message verbally or non-verbally to another person or group, who then receives it and processes whether they understand it or not. The system described is a fairly mechanistic and unilateral one where communication is 'sent out' and 'taken in'. Such an idea is consistent with the view of the individual that dominates thinking about autism: that of a private, internalized self which is essentially separate from the world around and must intellectually create links with it.

In fact, studies of human communication in both children and adults find that it is less about the verbal transmission of single items of information and more to do with orientation, states of mind and a whole range of verbal and non-verbal communicative processes (Schore, 1994). Communication is much more than turn-taking, involving, as it does, layers of interaction and the continuous creation of meaning between communicative partners. During communication, individuals often overlap in their contributions and simultaneously communicate through their body movement, facial expression, gaze, sound and posture. Communication is a co-construction of meaning that happens in the here and now, where people continually check out and negotiate with each other what is being communicated (Finnigan, 2002). It is an ongoing process that does not always have a clear beginning or end, but does involve several levels of awareness of self and other.

In children's communication, Vygotsky put a heavy emphasis on verbal communication, but more recent theory has emphasized playful, non-verbal expression as the primary currency of children's social worlds. Rogoff (1990) points out that Vygotsky was influenced by the Soviet agenda on widespread literacy and the importance of speaking and listening. She argues that children's communication should in fact be viewed much more widely than this and should centrally include non-verbal aspects of language and communication. In contemporary theories of early childhood education, children's communication has been conceptualized as the 'hundred languages of children' where communication takes a great number of different forms and importantly includes behaviour, gesture, sound, art, movement and what children choose not to say (Malaguzzi, 1993). Children communicate with each other in diverse ways, not many of which use the spoken word. To give a flavour of what this means, Box 3.1 describes some of the many forms of communication that might be observed in children aged 5 to 11 years old within one minute of playground activity.

Box 3.1 Children's communication in the playground

Two girls sit on a wall and watch their legs swing in rhythm. The rhythm changes slightly every so often and the children smile, not looking at each other and all the time looking at their legs.

One child stands in front of another, looking intently at him and talking to him in an angry manner. The child being spoken to does not say anything and looks unperturbed, but a third child who stands beside him answers for him, speaking seriously and looking worried.

Two children talk gibberish, facing each other, talking fast and at the same time.

A group of children collect fallen leaves during the autumn. When a gust of wind blows, many of the children simultaneously raise their arms, wave them in the air and shout 'Hoorah!'

Groups of boys do fighting moves that involve running, dodging, crouching, jumping out on each other and making 'karate chop' noises.

In a small group of boys and girls, one boy dramatically folds his arms and walks away from a group. He goes to sit on a nearby wall, looking fed up. No one in the group looks to see where he has gone.

Two boys make bleeping sounds as they run around the playground.

Two girls stand side by side, looking up at the sky and screaming at the top of their voices.

One girl talks to another who does not say anything, but only shrugs her shoulders.

Several small groups of girls perform singing and clapping games, whilst some children look on.

Two boys, on a large climbing frame that is full of other children, climb quickly to the top, taking different routes but always keeping each other in sight.

Four children, each with a medium-sized ball, stand near each other and throw the balls in the air. The children do not look at each other or say anything, but nevertheless move around the playground space together, managing to keep roughly together as a group.

One girl shows another a feather, not saying anything as they look at it.

Four girls do synchronized dance routines along crossed lines that are painted on the playground. Each girl starts at the most distant point on the lines. They dance along the lines, meet each other at the centre of the cross and smile.

Two boys sit on a bench, facing away from but leaning against each other's back.

Research into children's cultural worlds is increasingly framing communication as something that is more than language. Children's communication is viewed as being 'multimodal', that is, involving a number of different communicative modes in image, sound, gesture, body posture and use of space, as well as in spoken language (Bishop, 2011). There is, of course, a clear understanding within autism research and practice that communication involves important non-verbal features. Autism implies difficulty in social communication and necessitates a view of language that takes in all aspects of communication. However, it is often the case that social communication training programmes for children with autism base ideas about appropriate forms for children's communication on adult-type models. Ideas about non-verbal features of communication are usually viewed as fixed and universal and sometimes have little to do with how children really communicate with each other. Such programmes may include the development of 'correct' body language and social distance, that is, at what distance to stand in communication, where to look, for how long and so on. But such ideas mistakenly conflate what goes on socially between adults with what goes on socially amongst children. There is no understanding that children communicate in slightly different ways to adults – that are playful and not necessarily fixed – and often for different purposes too.

Multimodality is a concept that gets closer to what children actually do in their communication. It is an innovative approach to describing how children select and combine different communicative modes depending on what they want to say and how they want to be seen by others. It emphasizes the many creative ways – non-verbal, verbal, sound, movement and so on – in which children do communicate. It tries to capture children's use of language and communication as it is 'performed' in the here and now and embedded in the 'social semiotics' of the present situation and the wider world around (Jewitt, 2006). Children together make meanings, employing all the cultural resources that they have, reorganizing material in the present moment to contribute as best they can and in whatever form to what is being said or done. In the new media age, where children consume and make use of a wider range of media resources than at any other point in history, children's use of multiple modes of communication must be seen as prevalent in their worlds (Marsh, 2010).

Examples of the communicative modes that mixed groups of children use, children with and without autism, are provided in the next chapter. The discussion here will look more closely at what it is that children want to communicate about, exploring how children use their communication in displays of social competence, social control and as a challenge to adult dominance of their social worlds.

Children's communication as interpretive reproduction

It has been noted in Chapter 2 that childhood is a social structural form which is useful to study in its own right. Children should not be viewed simply as 'adults in the making' and recipients of adult culture, but as social actors who participate in and help to create social contexts. William Corsaro (2011) is an American sociologist who has carried out extensive ethnographic investigations of children's social worlds across age groups and within different countries. He has used the paradigm of childhood as a structural form to produce rich descriptions of children's cultural activity that shift the focus away from interaction as interpersonal exchange only. He argues that little attention has been given to how children make sense of the world around them and to the interpretive basis of children's social engagement. Children do not always have full knowledge of social situations, but continually seek to gain a footing in social engagement by making interpretations about what is going on and acting on these. In his view of social development, Corsaro uses a reproductive model rather than a linear one. Children do not simply copy what adults do but *reproduce* it, manipulating and transforming material to suit their own interests, ideas and concerns.

The conceptualization of children's activity as 'interpretive reproduction' puts much more emphasis on social engagement as an active, public and shared phenomenon. It moves away from individualistic theories of social action towards a cultural basis for human interaction. Children do not individually and internally receive culture, but *actively* reflect on social processes by engaging in them. They try to act in ways that they think are appropriate to social contexts and negotiate this with others as they go along. Thus, Corsaro describes children's social activity as pre-eminently creative as well as collectively produced. He notes that children may not be able to put into words what it is they are doing or what they know. Theirs is more of an emergent 'practical consciousness' where the interpretation and creation of children's culture are one and the same thing.

Corsaro argues that children's persistent attempts to understand and engage in what is going on around them come from a desire to gain control over their lives. He describes children's cultures has having the key rationale of generating shared meaning, coordinating social activity with other children and challenging adult control. Figure 3.1 illustrates the different processes that operate with and within children's cultures, showing the interactive relationships that exist between them. Cultural routines are an important feature of both adult–child

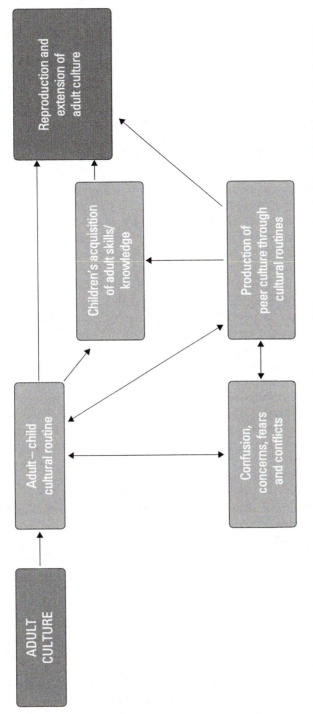

Figure 3.1 Corsaro's interpretive model of socialization processes showing the different processes involved in children's social development

relations as well as child–child or peer relations. These are the stable set of routines, artefacts, values and concerns that people produce and share in their interactions with each other. It is important here to note that these are stable and can be recognized, but given the ever-changing nature and diversity of culture, are not fixed over time nor necessarily exist in the same way in different cultural contexts.

Cultural routines have a general framework that is recognizable, predictable and recurrent, but what emerges out of them is not, being a refinement and extension of existing cultural skills and knowledge. Corsaro (1992) gives the example of approach-avoidance play as a distinctive and commonly found routine in children's cultures. In this type of play, where one child plays being a threat from which other children run, there is a primary frame or 'working hypothesis' with features that are immediately recognizable to children in a group, in this instance, the manner in which the child-as-threat walks, the expression on their face and their possible verbal declaration of intent. This process activates relevant social scripts which guide *but do not dictate* individual behaviour. Again, scripts should be thought of in terms of words, phrases and actions that are recognizable within a smaller and perhaps wider group, but not as something unvarying over time and universal. Individuals use their working knowledge of the recognized cultural routine to 'embellish' on it, creating a customized version of the routine that is in some way novel, may be collectively understood and produced and does not necessarily refer to aspects of adult culture. Figure 3.1 shows the existence of peer culture, depicting it as a 'subculture' that consists of special knowledge and competency different from dominant adult culture. Children creatively appropriate sociocultural information, transforming it according to their own understandings and to meet the concerns of their peer world. Aspects of peer culture will be unknown by adults, but peer culture is not something that is separate from dominant adult culture, an 'unknowable world of childhood'. It is related to it and can be understood by adults if explained by children.

In participating in these kinds of cultural practices, children explore and express concerns that differ depending on their age. Pre-school and younger school-age children find it challenging to coordinate their play to that of other children and spend more time creating and gaining access to peer play. In the busy shared play environments of early childhood settings, where increasing numbers of children in Western societies are spending their time, children must find ways of protecting their play and the space in which it occurs from unwanted peer intrusions (Corsaro, 2011). By contrast, children from around 7 to 13 years of age are more able to sustain peer activity and generate play. Their principal concerns are with peer acceptance, popularity and group solidarity and with finding ways of expressing these. A dominant feature of pre-adolescent peer culture is an increasing differentiation in peer relations and the production of stratified sets of peer groups. Children of this age are concerned with constructing identities that ally them with some peers whilst separating them from others, as well as finding ways of asserting their own individuality and creativity (Corsaro, 1999).

When observing children's social activity, it is possible to see many examples of interpretive reproduction. Boys playing football in a playground, expressing their camaraderie through high-five gestures and team hugs, and their aggression using pointing fingers and accusatory verbal mutterings, has the feel of children constructing for themselves an experience of being part of a group in a male world. Boys carrying out superhero play, doing fighting moves and blasting pretend guns, can be interpreted as playing with an overblown notion of masculinity. In such play, children try to resist taking on the role of 'baddie' if they can, preferring to leave it to be imagined only (Holland, 2003). Figure 3.2 shows a group of girls singing and performing coordinated dance moves from a popular song. This could be read as a way for them to 'perform' and re-confirm their friendship in the here and now, which their teacher says is sometimes affected by conflict and fallings out.

Social theories of childhood also point to other concerns which children communicate about and these are discussed below.

Children's communication is increasingly concerned with constructing acceptable social identities

Children and adolescents exist in worlds that are populated by other children and adolescents and an important part of what children communicate about is how they fit into these worlds. Children's communication partly concerns the construction of a social identity to present how children see themselves and would like to be seen by others. Given that children operate in different worlds – at home, in school, in clubs, in the local community – it might be more

Figure 3.2 Four girls perform singing and dance moves. The girls perform the music single 'All the Single Ladies' to support their friendship in the here and now

accurate to use the plural term 'identities' since children can present themselves differently in different situations. An increasingly key issue for children and adolescents as they get older is that of carving out identities that are acceptable to others in a group. This is not always the same thing as identities that are acceptable to adults. Children may express a dislike of someone for different reasons from adults – children judging others much more on the basis of whether they get them into trouble, for example, or if they are 'too bossy'.

Very often, children's social identities are supported verbally or performed in actions with other peers, children verbally and physically marking the fact that they are associated with a peer or peers within a group. James (1993) has noted that children's bodies and what they can do take on an important communicative significance here. Children find visible ways that show they are the same as or different from each other, often comparing themselves physically in terms of their height, hand size, hair colour, skin colour, age or speed in doing something. However, comparisons can also be drawn in terms of other information that is equally tangible, such as birthday dates, family structure, food preferences, drawing ability and knowledge of media culture.

As they develop, children and adolescents increasingly make assessments of each other based on the practical achievements that they can see their peers perform. Within public 'arenas of action', children engage in social actions and bring together play material and other cultural resources in an effort to construct for themselves acceptable social identities that can be appreciated by others (Hutchby, 2005). Again, this is in contrast to adults who will make assessments of children partly based on other kinds of knowledge; for example, on educational attainment, attendance at school and family background. Children do not necessarily have this kind of knowledge, but are aware of their own and others' competency in relation to arenas of action. Figure 3.3 shows a skilful drawing made by a boy with autism, aged 8. A routine within his group of

Figure 3.3 One of many skilful drawings of a fast car made by a boy with autism, aged 8

peers – consisting of boys who themselves have an interest in cars – is for the boy to make a drawing of a fast car whilst his peers sit and watch, admiring his drawing skill. When a drawing is finished, one peer in the group often asks if he can show it off to other members of the class.

Socially successful children, perceived as such by their peers, are those who are able to demonstrate social competence, though their ability to do so involves some complexity. For example, children who have shortcomings but who are able to make light of them are perceived as competent by other children (James, 1993). Children who are able to switch easily between different identities are also seen as competent; for example, children who can adopt peer-valued roles such as being tough or being funny, but who are also able to recognize the requirements of different social situations and know when to drop inappropriate roles and conform to adult rules and expectations.

Many children do not have this level of social sophistication and the flip side of children's activity as displays of social competency is that children also act to cover up their incompetencies. As children develop in terms of their awareness, an important communicative behaviour can be trying not to reveal what they struggle with in everyday tasks and ordinary social situations, that is, their lack of competency and knowledge. This can be particularly the case for children with a disability and special educational needs (though not necessarily children with autism) who may be hesitant in asking checking out questions, show uncertainty when carrying out tasks, be wary when they are being watched and try to cover up whatever it is they are trying to do. Such children may be aware of their difference from others and not want to be seen identifying with it.

Participation in discourse is key to children's construction of social identities and perceptions of social competence in each other. Discourse refers to how communication is used within a social setting, particularly the ways in which it relates to the patterns of meaning that exist for individuals within that context. Children's discourse would include verbal elements, but also, of course, important multimodal features, children recognizing each other's use of gesture, posture and so on. A good illustration of this is children's discourse around friendships, how children construct themselves socially as 'a friend' in their conversations and their actions with others. In talking to children about their friendships, what often comes across most strongly is the sensitivity of the subject and how closely it is tied up with issues of personal identity. Questions about whether a child is someone who has friends, how many friends they have and for how long, often feel too sensitive or potentially hurtful to be asked. Children often become wary when asked about friendship, or quickly fire off answers to be sure there are no misunderstandings on this point. What comes across in children's talk about their friends is how important it is to make verbal declarations about friendship. The discourse around being friends and having friends seems as important in some ways as friendship itself (Dunn, 2004). Children declare themselves someone's friend and hope that that declaration is reciprocated. The idea of a 'best friend' often exists as an ideal that is keenly appreciated, but one that has not been personally known. In some settings, the number of 'best friend' dyads can actually be quite small.

Barnes (2003) argues that friendship for children differs from friendship for adults, having not only a cognitive-affective aspect but also a strong performative one too, one that clearly defines the child's identity within the larger peer group. He points out that children's friendships do not endure in the same way as adults and can be more affected by momentary factors, such as the trading of favours, but that being seen to be someone who has friends is of great importance. Children often have a 'language of friendship' that takes verbal and non-verbal forms and recognizably signals to themselves and others 'we are friends' and 'I am someone who has friends'. Examples would include choosing to sit next to each other and inviting each other to a birthday party. Figure 3.4 shows children posing for a photograph and choosing to pose as friends, even though some of these children say they are actually not. The children depicted here show an easy facility in engaging in the discourse around friendship that exists in their setting, of putting an arm around someone or standing close to them in some way and, in some instances, of including a token of friendship, such as the object which you enjoy sharing. It is notable that in these photographs the child with autism also demonstrates his ability to participate fluently in this postural discourse of friendship.

Friendship and other concerns and values that children communicate about must be seen in the light of influences that exist within all cultural contexts. Constructing acceptable identities and demonstrating social competency will take different forms depending on the general cultural features of gender, race and class. Taking gender for example, it is well documented that difference exists in how boys and girls communicate in play. In North American and European cultures, boys play more ball games and imaginative action-adventure play in larger, looser groups whilst girls engage more in conversation, sedentary play, singing, jumping and verbal games in smaller and tighter groups (Blatchford et al., 2002).

Children's play preferences can be further influences on the form that communication takes within a group. Equipment play, using items such as balls, hoops, ropes and construction blocks, gives rise to a high level of parallel play where children play alongside each other, engaging separately in activity and communicating in minimal ways only. Parallel play should not be seen simply as what happens for children at a certain stage of development. All children can revert to parallel play given the nature of what it is they are doing (Kalliala, 2006). The same group of children who engage in parallel play when playing with building blocks, for example, can carry out more collective actions and dyadic and group behaviours when playing competitive team games. Similarly, there is evidence that children engaged in imaginative role play will organise themselves into a situation of leaders and followers: one player assuming a dominant communicative role in the play, giving instructions, assigning make-believe identities and narrating the story of the game, with

Figure 3.4 Children with and without autism are asked to pose and choose to pose as 'friends', though only some of them say they actually are

others following and only offering suggestions (Harris, 2000). An important fact about children's cultural worlds, one that needs always to be kept in mind, is that different children have different play preferences. Not all children like to carry out physical play and only some children choose to play imaginative games and it is possible that the communicative modes present in one form of play determine to some extent individual children's play preferences.

The influence of media culture

In the last decade, there has been increased interest in the subject of children's consumption of media culture, particularly in relation to new digital technologies. The term 'the new media age' has been coined to describe the fact that children's lives have been transformed by new technologies, changing the nature of their relations with others, the world around and their own sense of self (Buckingham and Willett, 2006). Computer games, the Internet and other forms of media and popular culture are an increasingly diverse and rich resource for children to draw on, providing a counterpoint to competing influences in their lives. This reframes the tension that has always existed in children's peer cultures between adult-directed structures within the family, school and community, and the norms, expectations and constraints of other peers (Pollard and Filer, 1996). Children must manage two sets of relationships – adult–child and peer–peer – and the new media and other popular culture resources outside the home and school play an increasingly important role in this, children using these to counteract what their parents, teachers and other adults say is meaningful or educationally relevant.

Products from popular media can be described as 'symbolic resources' and serve as markers of interest and identity that are easily shared within a group of children (Willett, 2009). Examples of media products would include characters, actions, sound effects, narratives, dialogue and branding. They are often the primary source of symbols drawn on by children in their play, recontextualized and transformed for children's purposes in the way they are included, adapted and re-arranged (Götz et al., 2005). Part of the pleasure in play is derived from players' ability to exert control over these kinds of representations and to use them in exploring and challenging rules, roles and identities. However, this part of children's cultures is often dismissed by adults as one that is on the fringes of what children legitimately do, crudely dictated by television and film with repetitive material of unchallenging content and limited value.

Recent studies of children's play and interaction show that media products form the basis of commonly used communicative modes in children's cultural worlds. Children routinely use 'intertextuality' – the referencing of 'texts' from the media and other sources – in their communications with each other. In a study of the play and interactions of typically developing 7-year-old boys, Taylor (2006) found that their communication took both a verbal and an important non-verbal form. 'Postural intertextuality', comprising children's communication through gesture, posture, body distance, facial expression and gaze, took up a considerable portion of the boys' communication, but the study also identified 'auditory intertextuality' as present in the children's communication, where reference was made to certain sounds and popular tunes. Ways of referencing were commonly recognizable within the group with similar postures and sounds used by different individuals. This kind of multimodal intertextuality constitutes forms of communication that children can be seen using in any playground. Peers within a setting recognize in each other certain positions, hand gestures, ways of looking, noises, sound effects and phrases and use these as a kind of language mode of play and communication. Figure 3.5 shows children in one setting of a mainstream school playing different games on different days but referencing shared postural 'texts' that are borrowed from the films they watch and computer games they play. These children belong to different peer groups, one group including a boy with autism, and these photographs are taken on different days, but the same postural language is used. Their postural language is shared by many children in the playground and expressed in the way they position their head, arms and legs, and how they fire their pretend guns. This 'language' is what children say they enjoy the most when they play, though supervising adults express some disapproval of this type of play.

Children often describe the use of symbolic resources taken from the media as the thing they particularly enjoy in their play and admire in their peers. However, it is an aspect of peer culture that tends to be outside adult knowledge, adults not having consumed the original media source and generally not having access to the play *in situ*. Children are sensitive to the presence of an adult and will usually stop what they are playing when approached (Corsaro, 1985; Tudge and Hogan, 2005). An ever-present issue for children is the degree to which their activity is acceptable to adults and whether it will draw criticism or sanction by them. This means that adults have limited access to children's play, although in situations of trust they can ask questions and children will be forthcoming. It is also the case that adult experience of cultural resources might be different from that of children. Corsaro (2011) gives the example of the Tooth Fairy which, for parents, may mark an attempt to keep their child young and innocently unaware of the nature of reality, whilst for children, the losing of a tooth may be experienced as a mark of their maturity.

It may feel as if we have moved a long way from the experiences of a child with autism. However, as some of the illustrations used in this chapter show, children with autism are able to participate to some extent in forms of communication that are socially appropriate, perceived as such by their non-autistic peers and by adults who know them. The next chapter will provide more in the way of illustration here, providing narrative descriptions of how a child with autism participates socially in ways that are the same as and ways that are different from other children.

Figure 3.5 Children with and without autism in one playground share a common postural language when playing action-adventure games

Summary

This chapter has noted that human communication involves processes in the co-creation of meaning between communicative partners in the here and now. This is much more than simply the transmission of a message and has important performative and creative features. Children's communication differs from that of adult's in that it uses a large number of non-verbal communicative modes. Children use the cultural resources that are available to them in their families, schools and in the wider society for their interactions with each other, interpreting and recontextualizing cultural material for the purpose of expressing their own thoughts and concerns. This process produces peer culture that is linked to, but differs from, dominant adult culture and may exist outside adult knowledge, understanding and value systems. Children's communication differs depending on age. Younger children use their communication to gain access to situations of play whilst pre-adolescents and adolescents use it to demonstrate social competency and construct positive social identities that are acceptable to the group.

Chapter 4

Finding ways to play and make meaning

Social engagement is an ongoing process of negotiation of meaning between the individual, other people and the cultural sources available to them in their environment. It involves any number of communicative modes and is much more than simply turn-taking. The construction of meaning – or making of meaning – is a critical element within social engagement that involves a recognition and appreciation of the cultural material, understandings and concerns being produced. Social engagement is a process that unfolds so that those involved do not always fully understand what is being said, done or created, but will continue to engage in an effort to achieve meaning. They can be successful in this and so have a satisfactory experience of engagement, but they can also be unsuccessful, with continuing such experiences leading to feelings of confusion, frustration or even anger about engagement with a person, group or cultural platform.

Chapter 1 highlighted the fact that children with autism are at least partly socially engaged but that research indicates we know little about the details of this. We have little detail, for example, about the quality of engagement and the experiences of all the people involved. This chapter presents research designed to gain detailed information about children's social experiences where children with autism engage with other children. The question asked was: what conditions naturally support children with and without autism to find ways to play and make meaning? Two case studies, each of one child with autism and his group of peers, are presented as 'cognitive ethnographies' (Daniels, 2008) into what goes on when a child with autism engages with other children in the natural setting of a school.

Instances of actual interaction are described in narrative accounts as a way of illustrating some features of children's ordinary experiences of social contexts in which a child with autism engages with others. What will be described are the many contexts in which a child with autism participates appropriately in peer culture, and also some of the ways in which his participation is perceived as 'different', 'odd' or 'wrong'. However, what is provided is not a conclusive or finite list of contexts. It is a basic tenet of a sociocultural approach that social experience is infinitely rich and impossible to capture in its entirety. This would hold for the social engagement of people with autism too. There are many contexts in which an individual with autism engages in socially appropriate ways and many in which their behaviour is perceived as different.

The material presented in this chapter is based on information gathered from observations and conversations with children, practitioners and parents in two mainstream school settings. The process of research involved gaining details over a period of time about the social activity of the child with autism with his peers and compared to that of his peers, exploring issues of sameness and difference in his participation and the ways in which others experienced it as appropriate and of interest, or as different and inappropriate. The fact that most children with autism in a school setting have at least one or two children with whom they associate more regularly was used to design research that looked at social engagement within three social contexts: the wider class group as a background point of comparison, the smaller peer group of which the child with autism was part, and finally, the individual participation of the child with autism compared to this small peer group. The idea was to investigate all the cultural activity within one community of children, taking a wide view at first but then progressively focusing on the child with autism and his small group. In this way, the activity of a few, or even of the individual child, could be viewed against the wider sociocultural background and their experience of interaction made sense of within a particular setting.

In gathering information about children's social activity, an important consideration was Corsaro's (1992) idea of 'cultural routines'. These are the fairly stable patterns of cultural activity with which a group of children are engaged over a period of time and include play themes as well as cultural values, concerns and resources appropriated by children for use in their social engagement. Each case study will be used to describe features of children's social activity and cultural routines, and a child with autism's engagement with these. The discussion of the nature of these experiences for the child with autism and his peers is informed mostly by social theories of childhood. These seek to identify a range of factors that are present structurally and culturally within children's social worlds and do not concentrate solely on factors associated with intellectual functioning, individual characteristics or single features of the environment.

Case study 1: Richie and his group

The first case study concerns Richie, aged 8. Richie had been attending his local mainstream school since reception age, 4 years old, and was well known to staff and other children. He had been given a diagnosis of autism within the 'mild to moderate' range at the age of 4, but was described as having developed considerably within the time he had been at the school and was seen as fully included in his group. His educational placement was described as a successful one with no major concerns associated with his experience of school, though difficulties at home were reported. We have already met Richie in Chapter 1, where his intense imaginary experience of speeding cars was used to illustrate the possible nature of difference in someone with autism. At the time of the research, a key experience for Richie was that his functioning at home contrasted markedly to that in school. He lived with his mother, father and younger sister in a house near the school, but seldom went outside on his own because he had certain extreme fears about the sun falling out of the sky and dinosaurs coming back to life, and a fear too of being on his own. These fears were the source of considerable concern for his parents and something they felt they had been unable to address, but were not evident at school.

Richie's class group was a stable one, having remained roughly the same for three years. His peer group was identified as a group of mostly boys, though there was also one girl. These children played regularly together and shared similar interests and a similar attitude to learning. The group was said to be 'lively', their chatting and giggling requiring fairly constant low-level adult management in the classroom. However, the children themselves were well liked and described in positive terms by practitioners. The majority of children in Richie's group had additional learning and language needs, many of them receiving extra teaching and support.

Case study material about Richie and his group is being used to illustrate the following key features of children's social contexts:

- social contexts are multilayered and evolve;
- time is a feature of social engagement;
- aspects of children's culture are hidden from adults;
- experience is socially constructed and individuals play an active role in their cognition.

Social contexts are multilayered and evolve

The first narrative account concerns Richie's special interest of cars and how it was experienced within this setting. This was a strong interest within the group, not just for Richie but also for all other members of his peer group.

> Richie's special interest had been in cars and speed for some years. His mother said that his conversation was always 'cars and motorbikes', talking especially about racing cars and the details of different makes of cars. She said that the interest was not as overwhelming as it once had been and that he had developed other interests too, such as building with Lego, watching films and playing computer games, though these often involved cars or vehicles of some kind. When friends came round to the house and when playing with his little sister, Richie tried to get them to play with cars, which they were sometimes happy to do.

The play interests of Richie's group were also dominated by the theme of cars, especially fast cars, racing and speed. The children regularly carried out physical play where they ran races and competed against each other, imaginative games where they pretended they were riding motorbikes, did construction and toy play using small cars and building racing tracks, and made drawings of cars and motorbikes in their free time in class. When asked to name their favourite play activity, most children in the group said running races and 'running around'. Children also frequently mentioned popular culture in the form of brand names, computer games and cars. The attention of children in this group was drawn to pictures and logos related to these things and they regularly traded tag lines for products in their conversations, particularly in relation to fast cars. Richie was given status within the group as someone who could make sophisticated drawings of racing cars. He regularly did this whilst members of the group watched and then showed off his drawing to other children in the class group.

Competing against each other and with boys from older year groups was a routine that was present in this group; for example, in play fighting encounters or to see who was the fastest. One lunchtime play, Richie and some of the boys in his group were running races. Some of the boys had taken off their shoes and were taking turns to challenge the fastest boys. Calum was fast and a very good runner, and so was Evan. Joey eventually beat Calum, who had beaten everyone else. Richie stood with the faster boys to race them, standing to one side each time. He did not win, but he was not far behind. Older boys from other year groups challenged these younger boys. There was a general feeling of camaraderie as well as of appreciation of the fastest runners. A few of the children gave each other high fives. After a number of races, some of the boys sat on the grass and became spectators, chatting together and watching the others.

The following day it was wet play and the children were in their classroom. Richie's group had fetched the toy box from under the teacher's desk and was playing with Lego on the carpet. Kirsty was busy making a racing track for cars using some large green baseboards. Evan and Emir were with her. When asked what they were playing, Kirsty proudly indicated the track with cars lined up on it. 'Races', she said whilst the others nodded and smiled. Richie and Tyler looked in the box of car toys, Richie looking for a certain car, 'Number Uno' he said. They joined the others on the carpet. All the children were individually busy, building things from Lego or playing with a car. Morgan was racing a bright orange car down a Scalextric track that he had propped on a chair, Emir was sitting cross-legged, clutching a small red car. Evan was making a garage out of Lego, which tightly enclosed a car inside. Richie was busy building and had a flat Lego plate upended to which he was attaching Lego bricks. When asked what he was making, he said that it was a garage. Kirsty was adding more detail to the track layout she had made. When Emir was asked why he was holding the small red car he replied that it was special because of the detail on it, specifically the front end and the bumper.

For this peer group, the topic of cars and speed spanned many of the children's different activities: outside play, inside play, drawing, hobbies and their conversation. It had been a stable feature of the group for some time, though school staff who knew the children throughout their school career said it had grown as an interest over the years. What is not clear about this strong group play theme is the origins of this aspect of peer culture. Cars and speed were the special interest of Richie, the child with autism – his 'passion' as his mother described it. It is possible that the intensity of his interest had somehow influenced peers in the group. However, there are indications that other features of the environment were also present. The previous class teacher described how she had provided the only toys that were available in the classroom for wet play. These were cars and Lego because they were the toys with which her son had played and the only free resources available to her. A further factor is that running races was a feature of playground activity with which older boys joined in. Richie's peer group was interested in being seen to be grown up and regularly opted out of whole-class activities which they deemed 'too babyish'. The children running races in the playground with older boys – challenging them and expressing their solidarity – has the feel of children constructing for themselves an idea of what it means to be an adult in a male world. Richie's peers were interested too in appropriating the popular culture of fast cars and Formula One racing that existed outside the school and which they talked about in referential terms as something sophisticated and exciting.

In effect, it does not seem possible to identify a single cause for the cultural interest of this group in cars and speed and it seems likely that there are multiple causes. It is conceivable that many, if not all, of the variables described have contributed to each other in a dynamic way over time. Bronfenbrenner (1979) points out that it is more helpful to think in terms of contexts that contain multiple features and exist over time, and of processes that are in constant interaction with each other. Variables in social processes constitute each other, not as simple cause and effect, but in a dynamic, ongoing, two-way process.

With this in mind, it seems that Richie's special interest in cars and speed takes on a social meaning in this context that could not be assumed in advance. There is an intensity and a longevity about his interest, in the way that individuals with autism often experience their special interests, but by focusing on wider group processes rather than on the individual child, it is possible to see that this intensity is not viewed by other children and adults in this context as too intense, inappropriate or odd. A sociocultural approach seeks to identify the aspects of cultural knowledge available to a community and describe the ways in which individuals within it are interpreting that culture. Individual personality and behaviour traits are of less significance than *comparative facility* in producing culture within a group. The fact of this probably accounts for the high level of social inclusion that existed for Richie within this particular group of children.

Time is a feature of social engagement

A key feature of social contexts is that they evolve. Social contexts unfold, develop and change shape over time, change being dependent on what occurs within the context. People's continuing engagement in social processes, with each other and the environment, is greatly determined by the level of understanding, enjoyment and satisfaction they experience in the generation of meaning. This is the case for situations of play too and the following description of Richie's game of motorbikes with another peer shows how the unfolding nature of social engagement over time is an important feature of play experience.

Richie's support worker recalled a time when Joey and Richie had played and really enjoyed a game of motorbikes. This had occurred over several weeks in the summer term of the previous year. She described how the two children had played the game intensely, running round the playground for long periods of time and sometimes coming in to the school building covered in mud 'as if they really were motorbikes'. She said they played the game over and over again, mostly really enjoying it, though sometimes the game leading to conflict between the two boys and a falling out for a short period of time.

Richie's mother recalled the same time. 'For ages he told me that they played motorbikes in the playground, that is pretending to be motorbikes and running around the playground. They played that every single day because Richie encouraged them to play that. There is this boy, I think Joey, and he loves playing that with Richie. He will play with him, but some days he gets fed up and Richie says, "Oh, I'm not very happy because Joey didn't want to play motorbikes with me today." And I say, "Well, sometimes you've got to play what they want to play." That's what friendship is about, sharing ideas and games and everything else. I mean it's a two-way thing, it's not only "you, you, you." But he couldn't understand that. He said, "Well, I don't have fun with their games."'

Probably of relevance here is the fact that this situation of play involved Joey, a child within Richie's group of peers who particularly liked to play imaginative games. Joey liked to lead imaginative games and, when asked, described his play mostly in terms of imaginative role play, saying that this is the aspect of playing with others he especially enjoyed. There are individual differences between children in terms of what they play and the amount of play in which they engage. Some children are especially playful and some are especially imaginative, carrying out more imaginative play (Sutton-Smith, 1997). Joey appeared to be a child who was imaginative and interested in imaginative play and this was something he and Richie shared. The intensity with which they played motorbikes was perhaps something only they could experience within this group of children.

But what was the experience of imaginative role play for these two children, one with and one without autism? Recent research into the creation of pretend situations helps us to understand the nature of their experience. This indicates that pretence is a process of co-construction between players who do not perform individual pretend acts, but who try to act jointly (Rakoczy, 2008). The social realization of pretend play is envisaged as an ongoing process of sharing, where players continually verify a 'fit' in terms of a common pretence perspective, using a system of checking looks (Lillard, 2006). The process of pretending means that fit is not always fully realized, children engaging in pretend actions and recognizing actions in each other, without always or completely sharing joint aims in play (Lillard, 1993). Play fighting provides a good example of this since it can become real fighting, children not always reading each other's play signals correctly and interpreting them as aggressive when they are not (Dunn and Hughes, 2001).

With Richie and Joey's imaginative role playing of motorbikes, the play was made possible given their enjoyment of and commitment to the shared fictional 'reality' of going at speed, which they were able to create through shared acts with recognizable features. The boys played the game by pretending to hold the handles of a motorbike, by making engine noises and by trying to run around as if riding in a synchronized way. However, repeated playing of the game eventually led to conflict. Children naturally play the same games over and over again, sometimes for years, but they must have a continuing sense of enjoyment without too much conflict for a game to continue successfully. An important factor in this is that a game needs to change slightly over time. The experience of ordinary, effective participation for the individual should be one of recognizing familiar features within the environment as well as and alongside new and innovative ideas happening over time. Rogoff and Angelillo (2002) point out that the distinguishing nature of culture is that it is always changing, but that change exists within recognizable templates that are ongoing. Similarly, Corsaro (1992), writing about children's play, describes their creative participation in cultural routines as having both predictable features and newly produced elements. This is what children take pleasure in and gain satisfaction from, enjoying the experience of familiar routines in play presented alongside new and unfamiliar ones. For Richie and Joey, the ongoing nature of communication in creating pretend acts was probably the basis of the conflict they experienced. Participation in culture exists temporally. It is probably the case that Richie's communication in the play did not change in a socially appropriate way over time – with new pretend elements not shared or insufficiently shared alongside familiar ones – and that this was the cause of difficulty that existed intermittently between the two children.

Aspects of children's cultures are hidden from adults

In thinking about children's social worlds, it is important to remember that adults do not know everything about what goes on amongst children. Children have their own understandings and concerns, which may be meaningful to other children in their group but not necessarily to familiar adults. It is also the case that children actively exclude adults from their social activity. This next description concerns an aspect of culture in Richie's peer group and in the wider class that was very familiar to the children themselves, including Richie, but was unknown to adults in this setting and to Richie's parents.

Richie had fears and anxieties that were out of the ordinary. In particular, he was afraid that the sun might fall out of the sky, that dinosaur bones might reconstitute themselves and come alive, and he was afraid of being on his own. His support worker said that she had seen no evidence of fears in school, except for some reluctance to flush the toilet because of the gurgling sound of the drains. By contrast, Richie's mother reported that at home Richie was reluctant to go outside the house or be on his own in a room because of these fears. This caused great concern for his parents. Richie's mother said it had been impossible to persuade Richie that these were irrational beliefs. She described how his fear of dinosaurs coming back to life originated in a family trip to a museum where they saw a dinosaur display. She described how his fear of the sun, in particular the heat of the sun and the possibility of it burning up the earth, had originated from a documentary he watched at school which showed close up images of solar flares. She said that, though Richie enjoyed watching films, she had to ensure he did not watch anything that would unduly upset him and that many films, even apparently harmless ones, could have this effect.

There were indications from conversations with other children in Richie's class that fear and talking about frightening things was part of the culture of this wider group of children. Other children in Richie's class group when asked directly mentioned the fact that children frightened themselves and each other in school by talking about scary topics and describing imaginary things as if they were real. The toilets in the school were mentioned several times as a place that was particularly associated with frightening things, where children were on their own and could be frightened by others. One girl said, 'Sometimes my cousin says there's a ghost clown in the toilet', whilst another girl, Lindsay, commented, 'Children try to scare people in the toilets by moving the door.'

When this was mentioned to Richie, he admitted that other children had been telling him frightening things too. He said that one boy had told him a ghost had killed his brother. When asked if he thought this was really true, he said, 'Well, he only walks home with his mum and his sister.'

This description concerns the 'subculture' that existed within this group of children. The subculture of peer groups is often dismissed by adults as 'silly', containing crude ideas that are not fully thought through and hold dubious educational value. Children hide aspects of their subculture from adults too, knowing that certain ideas, values, concerns and actions will be criticized by adults or subjected to disciplinary control. Those of us working with children will be aware that it is sometimes hard to know what actually goes on within a group of children, children typically stopping what they are playing or talking about when approached by an adult and reluctant to discuss it when asked. It is only when they are sure that there will be no adverse consequences or control by the adult that they will usually be forthcoming.

In this instance, there is evidence that Richie had a socially appropriate awareness of the underground nature of peer subculture around frightening ideas, evidenced by the fact that he had not shared this aspect of culture with adults. Like other children in his group, he only did so after direct questioning and where no possibility of sanction for the behaviour was raised. On questioning, it was apparent that Richie was party to the routine of children talking to each other about unreal things in an exciting and frightening way. The more extreme nature of his fear, which was really only apparent at home, indicates that he was perhaps less able to cope with this aspect of children's culture in his group and this is something that is explored more fully in the description below.

Experience is socially constructed and individuals play an active role in their cognition

Vygotsky put forward the idea that people play an active role in their own cognition, with emotion closely tied up in this (Bruner, 1997). The way in which we turn our attention to stimuli, the emotion we experience in relation to this and our capacity to think are all heavily contingent on our social experience. The following description concerns a group interview in which Richie and his peers were asked to explore what 'imagination' meant for them. They were asked about this because the issue of what is real and what is imagined had emerged as a key feature of their peer culture, as described above. The children's responses to this question and the way in which their experience of participating in this group exchange unfolds, illustrates how human beings shift in the way they experience and subsequently think about something and how it is participation in a social process – and the emotion involved – that brings this about.

> Sitting in a large circle, Richie and his group of friends were asked to say what 'imagination' meant to them. Going round the circle, each child took a turn to give their definition of the word 'imagination'. Individuals said things such as, 'Something you think about', and 'When you want something but you can't have it, like Playstation 3', and 'Like Spiderman'.
>
> When it came to Richie's turn, he said, 'You really feel like something's behind you and you look but it's not there.' Richie's comment immediately set off a reaction amongst the other children in the group. Some made ghostly 'Oooo' noises and one girl commented, 'Like when we went to Wexley Manor', referring to a recent class visit to a stately home that is thought to be haunted. After that, a new tone of 'spookiness' was introduced to the group and there was much more mention of ghosts in relation to the imagination. One child gave his definition as, 'When you dream and you think it's really happening', and another, 'It's like seeing a ghost or something.' The discussion was brought quickly to a close since the group had started to become unsettled.

This description of participation within a group illustrates the fact that all children can shift in terms of their relation to the apparent reality of something and the degree to which they fear it. When Richie gave his definition of imagination as similar to seeing a ghost, the mood of the group became notably more 'nervy', some children making ghostly noises or mentioning frightening experiences of their own. In writing about the imagination, Harris (2000) points out that all children – and adults – exert control over whether they believe an event is real or imagined by thinking about it and considering whether something could be real. Consideration of how something has been produced, for example, reduces its apparent reality as well as its emotional impact. However, experience is influenced by environment and Harris gives the example of being in a dark house late at night as an instance where emotion is likely to overwhelm the capacity for thought about the perceived reality of an experience. The shift in the mood of the group interview has this feel, the children as a group shifting from a fairly relaxed attitude to the subject matter of the imagination, to one that is influenced by Richie's contribution and becomes much more anxious.

This raises the possibility that Richie's experience of having fears and anxiety is out of the ordinary, but is not wholly different from that of other children. What is being described here is the way in which experience is partly constructed by people participating in social events and how people adapt themselves in their understandings, attitudes, emotions and concerns according to how those events unfold. The information gathered from the wider class group about fears and the imagination indicate that they were not straightforward issues for them and other children in the school. From conversations with the wider group of children, it was evident that irrational fears existed here too, fears that particularly centred on areas of the school where adult presence was minimal; for example, the children's toilets. Other children in the group had the experience of finding themselves anxiously fearful at times. From the descriptions provided by Richie and his peers of how children frightened each other when adults were not around, which has been discussed above, this was part of the culture of the general group in this setting. It is perhaps the case that Richie's peers, by virtue of not having autism, were more able to seek and benefit from adult reassurance and social explanation about what they found fearful and that this made it less of an issue for them.

Professionals working with Richie and his parents had tried to address Richie's fears and the fact that he did not want to go outside his house. They had explained to him how things that appeared to be real are actually created – for example, special effects in films – but to no effect. When the multiagency team and Richie's parents saw the findings from this research, they began to think much more in terms of 'normalizing' Richie's response as something that was on a continuum with other children's experience. Richie's parents were encouraged in this by the professional team and were able to feel less anxious about the situation. In follow-up visits to the family that occurred several months later, the existence of irrational fears were no longer described as a significant issue for Richie or his parents.

Case study 2: Kyle and his group

The second case study concerns Kyle, aged 9 years, who had attended his local mainstream school since reception age, 4 years old. At this age, he had been given a diagnosis of autism, having been assessed as being within the 'severe' range of the spectrum. Kyle was seen as having developed in the time that he had been at school, though a number of concerns did exist at home and at school. He was viewed as a highly imaginative child who stood out as someone who talked to himself and existed in an imaginary world for much of the time. Concerns at school centred on his ability to stay on task in class and contribute ideas relevant to the topic. At home, there were concerns about whether he was perceived negatively by others as being different. However, Kyle was said by his teachers and parent to 'love school' mainly because of the imaginary play he carried out with other children at playtimes.

Within the classes of the middle school – of which Kyle's class was one – there was a generic specialist resource base for children with special educational needs. Kyle's classroom was adjacent to this and his peer group was identified as consisting of several boys in his class as well as some of the children from the resource base. Children with a physical or learning disability had a high profile within the school generally. This was partly due to the presence of the specialist resource base, but there were many children with a disability or special educational needs, such as Kyle, educated within the mainstream of the school. One member of Kyle's peer group and of his class, Joshua, was described by children and staff as Kyle's best friend, the friendship having lasted for several years and described as one of the few 'best friendships' that existed in that class.

Observations and conversations with practitioners and children indicated that Kyle's peer group engaged largely in imaginative superhero play involving elements of pretence as well as very active physical play. This was a dominant play theme in the playground at the school, played regularly by a number of groups of older children, mostly boys. Kyle's group constituted one of these groups, with some members of Kyle's core group joining other groups in this play on occasion.

This case study is being used to illustrate the following features of social contexts that concern children's play and friendships:

- children's play is varied and children have different play preferences;
- children have their own understandings of what is socially appropriate;
- children take on different social roles in play;
- children's games can begin away from the playground;
- discourse is a key feature of children's social experience;
- imagining has a cost for some children with autism.

Children's play is varied and they have different play preferences

Children's play is a complex phenomenon that has been notably hard to define. Different perspectives on play are possible and it can be variously conceptualized as involved in cognition, affect, communication, individual development, power relations and cultural activity (Göncü and Gaskins, 2006). Play occurs in multiple contexts, has multiple purposes and is determined by individual capacities, but it is also heavily influenced by children's experiences within their cultural communities (Howes, 2011). It has already been noted that children's reproduction of culture has itself an element of playfulness and it is evident that it is play that sustains many aspects of children's social activity. Children's play exists across cultures and different social structures, in forms that are recognisable as well as different, and is characterized by both continuity and variation.

Different play forms exist which include differing proportions of elements in social, physical, non-verbal and sensory experience. Pretend play has a strong social component and develops out of social relations, but there are natural forms of children's play that are strongly body-based or strongly sensory. Different play preferences exist: not all children, for example, play imaginative games and some children play in particularly imaginative ways. Individual children often have distinctive play interests which are stable over time. One play interest – for example, superhero play – can span a number of different activities, not just social play but also solitary play and non-play activities such as reading, drawing, taking part in lessons, walking around the school and talking to peers. Children think a good deal about what they play, even when they are not playing, recalling play experiences with pleasure and anticipating forthcoming play with keenness and excitement. This narrative account of the play carried out by Kyle and his group describes a form of play – superhero play – that is typically carried out by boys.

Kyle and his friends were one of several groups of mostly boys who played action-adventure games in the playground. These games had both a pretend element, involving fighting between goodies and baddies, capture, escape and battling monsters, as well as physical elements of running, chasing, creeping, hiding, jumping over obstacles, doing kung fu and other fighting moves. Children and adults alike described the play as 'run around, run around, run around' and this was something that children were always observed doing when playing. Like other groups of children playing the same games, Kyle's peer group acted out stories from the action-adventure films and television programmes they watched. The names they gave their games were inspired by these and included 'Transformers', 'Star Wars', 'X-Men', 'Police', 'Mummies' and 'Army'. They played these games every breaktime and clearly gained great enjoyment from them. When they were asked to describe their games, many children mentioned the name of a game with a smile and made a comment such as, 'I really love that game' or 'I really enjoy playing that game.' Playground supervisors agreed that these children regularly engaged in and really enjoyed playing these games. One midday supervisor said, 'They play with guns, but we stopped that because they're not allowed guns. They play space games. They're always running. They don't keep still. They've always played those sorts of games.'

The children's interest in the theme of superheroes and action-adventure was evident at other times of the school day. In the dining hall, they had conversations about their favourite media characters, always hero action figures such as Luke Skywalker or Ben 10. The children were especially interested in the poses and special movements of these characters and could be seen walking around the playground and the school in a way that mimicked a superhero character. Much of the children's conversations on and off the playground consisted of phrases taken from films and TV programmes and, in particular, the sound effects of the imaginary equipment they used in their play. Kyle's support worker commented that children's conversations were largely about their superhero play. She said, 'I don't think they would have a conversation as such, no. You know, where did you go on the weekend, or what are you doing after school. No. I think it would be "Ahhh", "Boom!", "Wham!", that type of thing.'

The superhero play carried out by Kyle's peer group included a strong element of play described as 'physical activity play' (Pellegrini, 2011). This is play with a strong physical component, such as running and chasing, but which can be multidimensional with the possible inclusion of symbolic activity and play fighting. Pellegrini makes the distinction between physical activity play, the distinguishing feature of which is a raised metabolic rate, and rough-and-tumble and play fighting which are primarily social. He argues that physical activity play is a type of play that many children engage in, but that is typically overlooked or viewed with ambivalence by adults. Physical activity play is seen as having less developmental value compared to other play forms, such as functional and pretend play, though, as Pellegrini and Smith (1998) point out, it does have the purpose of developing strength, endurance and economy of movement. In this instance, school staff were uncertain about what to think about the superhero play carried out by Kyle and his peer group, and by other groups of boys in the same playground. They described it as 'mucky play' and disliked elements that included firing pretend guns, or even actual weapons in the form of sticks and small stones. However, they saw that the children enjoyed the play and had not stopped these games from being played, though they had discussed this as a possibility.

Children have their own understandings of what is socially appropriate

Writing about the social world of the primary school, Pollard and Filer (1996) note that children's culture looks in two directions: externally to adult-directed structures within the family, school and community, and internally to the norms, expectations and constraints of other peers. They argue that a tension often exists between these two sets of relationships – adult–child and peer–peer – and that individuals must find a way of managing both. From his extensive research into children's cultural worlds, Corsaro (2011) has argued that playing with this tension and challenging adult authority is a large part of what children do; the media and other popular culture resources outside the school and home playing an important role in this. Within Kyle's group, this element of a subculture of challenge appeared to exist in their keen enthusiasm for their superhero play, which regularly merged with rough play and play fighting. However, it was also apparent that these children had worked out a shared understanding of what was socially appropriate within the group, behaviour that successfully managed the tensions between dominant adult culture and peer subculture being viewed optimally.

Several aspects of the superhero play carried out by Kyle's peer group were on the fringes of what was thought by adults to be acceptable behaviour in children. A fine line existed between the children playing their imaginative games and getting into trouble with midday supervisors and teachers on duty. The play was often carried out on the edges of the playground so that children moved easily into areas where they were not allowed. An area down the side of the school building, for example, which was out of sight of staff on playground duty, was often used in the children's games. This was where they hid from each other or played out an 'escape' element in the story. On some occasions, particularly when real conflict emerged, a supervisor was asked to intervene and would clear the children from the area, saying that they should not have been there in the first place.

More important than this, however, was that the superhero play was very physical, with the pretend fighting slipping easily into real hitting on regular occasions. Though many members of Kyle's group did engage in play fighting – and real fighting when it occurred – they frequently complained about this in others, saying they were too rough in the play.

Play fighting is a distinct form of play identified by its truncated actions and slightly exaggerated movements (Bateson, 1972). Again, it is an aspect of boys' play that is looked upon adversely by adults, though in children's activity generally the incidence of play fighting becoming real fighting has been found to be quite low (Holland, 2003). Both able and less able children engage in play fighting, but it is only really the latter for whom it escalates into real aggression, perhaps because they are more likely to misinterpret the signals used in the play (Dunn and Hughes, 2001; Pellegrini, 1988). What is notable about the play fighting in Kyle's group of peers is that, though it fitted peer-play interests and did present some challenge to adult authority, it did not accurately reflect the dynamic within the group itself. Children acted out being tough, but most said they did not like peers whose play was 'too rough'. Though some children in this group did engage in actual fighting and did get into trouble, peers criticized them for not knowing how to play properly with others.

Managing the tension between having fun and getting into trouble is the most important way in which children judge each other's competence or difference. Some of the children in this group who were identified by adults as standing out from the group because of learning or behaviour needs, also stood out in the perception of their peers as someone who was 'the baddie' or 'gets into trouble'. This was the case for children who had a high visibility in the playground because of outbursts of anger and management of their challenging behaviour by staff. However, it was not the case for all the children, some of whom were identified by adults as different from the group – usually because of learning needs – but who were not singled out by their peers. Conversely, other children who were not particularly seen as 'different' by adults were perceived warily by their peers as 'someone who gets into trouble' and who might get them into trouble.

Kyle showed that he was able to manage the tensions between peer culture and adult expectations and norms. Unlike some of the children in the group who also had special educational needs, Kyle was aware of the difference between having fun, messing about and pushing boundaries in play, and getting into trouble with staff and other children. One striking feature of people's perception of Kyle was that he was someone who disliked getting into trouble with adults and would take steps to avoid it. He was well liked and his ability to maintain a sensibility experienced by both children and adults as 'moral' was an important part of this. Kyle's likeability was described in terms of him being funny and imaginative, but also caring of others, kind to younger children, incapable of lying and wanting to do the right thing.

Children take on different social roles in play

From their research into playground games in the UK and the US, Blatchford et al. (2002) have identified five roles in children's play which they describe as 'key', 'central', 'team', 'hoverer' and 'solitary'. They found that the adoption of a role remained stable for individual children over the course of a school year and is associated with children's differing abilities and levels of development. The taking on of key and central roles within play correlate with such things as popularity, friendship, leadership and playground independence and features particularly in pre-adolescent imaginative role play, where one child's ideas about the play narrative prevail and their play instructions to others are tolerated. The following is a description of the imaginative play that was carried out by Kyle and his group in which Kyle always took a leadership role and routinely instructed the others in the game.

Kyle regularly led the action in the children's play, with others following behind him in a line. He was observed controlling the play by gesturing to where people should run, telling others what actions to perform and going to get a player who had wandered off, bringing them back to the game. Sometimes he told the story of the play which the other children acted out. School practitioners said that Kyle was 'the boss' in his group of peers. Kyle's class teacher said that it was his imagination that 'draws others in quite powerfully'. Kyle's support worker also commented that Kyle was 'a leader'. She said that he was not bossy as such, but just more enthusiastic about his play ideas than other children.

One day whilst playing a superhero game, Kyle, Conor and two girls from another class confronted Sam, who was the baddie in the game. The children stood facing each other and Kyle said in an American accent, 'Guys, why is he attacking everyone?' Kyle said something to Sam who pinned up Kyle's hands, his arms outstretched in a crucified position. Kyle said something quietly and Sam touched him on the temples. Kyle started to shake his whole body as if he was being electrocuted, then flopped forward. His head dropped onto his shoulder and his arms went limp. He whispered something to one of the girls who put Kyle's arm around her shoulders and helped him down. Kyle pretended to be hurt or dead and did not say anything for a while. Then he came alive and told the others to run.

Kyle had a number of skills in relation to his leadership or 'key' role. He had a great interest in media culture, particularly action–adventure films, and was described as having a 'perfect recall of events'. This aspect of his experience was used to advantage in the superhero play of his peer group where the recall of detail from film and television programmes was a central aspect of the play. Kyle's use of details and dialogue taken from media culture stood out in people's perception of his social participation, as richer, faster and more entertaining than that of other children. Kyle participated confidently in the imaginative play, giving instructions to other children, taking the role of play narrator, answering others' questions about the play and assigning roles.

Willett (2009) notes that access to media and the confident use of symbolic resources is important in play leadership since this is where play ideas mostly come from. Kyle was at his most confident in playing these games and full of certainty in a way that many of his peers were not. He competently negotiated the allocation of roles – with little evidence of conflict on this matter emerging – and was always able to secure a heroic role for himself, never taking on that of the baddie. In this, his participation was in marked contrast to many of his peers who were much less confident about what they were playing and accepted lesser roles, and some of whom were not able to resist the role of baddie.

The fact that his peers mostly accepted Kyle's leadership role is perhaps partly explained by the personal resources they brought to the play. Many of the children in the group had learning needs of their own: in language, memory, attention and the generation of ideas. Those children who did not, such as Kyle's best friend Joshua, were described as quiet and happy to go along with others, and so suited to Kyle's confident and enthusiastic leadership style. Others still, who were marginalized within the general group as children with challenging behaviour, possibly fitted in well with a group that played in marginalized ways. It is likely that Kyle's difficulty in sharing his imaginary experience at an interpersonal level, which was the result of his autism, meant that he always took a leadership role in peer play, but his peers' relatively weaker imagination and poorer play resources are probably the reason why they were happy for him to be the leader.

Children's games can begin away from the playground

Ethnographic studies of children's playground games show that children discuss what games they are going to play long before they start playing them (Burn *et al.*, 2011). Children's playground games tend to be ongoing, children using the same game themes again and again, some themes lasting for several years (Corsaro and Johannesen, 2007). With time short at breaktimes and children keen to resume their ongoing games, they tend to negotiate what they are going to play long before they arrive in the playground (Willett, 2011). Kyle's discussions with his peers over their lunch conformed to this pattern of behaviour, the children – including Kyle in a leadership role – routinely working out what they were about to play before they started playing.

> In the dining hall, children talked about what they were going to play at playtime whilst they were eating their sandwiches. They discussed whether they were going to carry on with a game they had been playing, what the story was and how it should start that day, who would take which role, and what actions would be performed. Kyle took part in these discussions too. The children sometimes referred to him when they planned what they were going to play. During one lunchtime, a group of children discussed what they wanted to play. One girl asked Kyle if he would chase her when they got outside. Kyle told another boy that he would meet him by the door to the playground when he had finished eating his sandwich so that Kyle could help him locate the game in the playground.

Discourse is a key feature of children's social experience

Friendship is a particularly important and sensitive component of children's construction of social identities. It can exist in many different forms for children, in small, tight friendship groups, for example, or larger and less exclusive circles of friends, but it is always important to assert oneself in discourse as 'someone who has friends'. It is important too to be able to participate appropriately in the form of discourse around friendship that exists within a setting. The following is a description of the way in which friendship was talked about within Kyle's group of friends.

From conversations with children it was apparent that they viewed some peers in the group straightforwardly as a 'friend'. Kyle described Joshua and Sam as friends, as did Joshua of Kyle and another boy, Finley, with whom he played football but who was not a regular member of Kyle's peer group. Sam described Liam in this way, as did Lewis about his friend in another class, Marty. Their descriptions of each other were almost wholly positive with the friend described mainly in terms of how they felt about playing with them. Descriptions of friends included, 'someone you play with all the time', 'someone who goes along with the play' and 'someone whose games you like'.

Other patterns of friendship existed in the group which were less straightforward. Children were described equivocally, for example, as 'plays along with different people, but talks too much', or 'is funny – a bit', or 'makes up kind of good games'. Several children insisted that some peers within the group were not a friend and even that they did not know them, a few continuing to maintain this after it had been pointed out that they had been observed playing together. A number of individuals made a distinction between 'my friend' and 'my friend's friend' to describe the other children engaged in the play. Several children used the term 'team' to describe how they played, small groups of friends 'teaming up' with others to play their superhero games. Joshua described his play with Kyle in this way, saying that they played against other children 'as teams and we split up'. Kyle described Liam in this way too, saying that he was not his friend but 'Sam's friend and sometimes teams up with me'. Kyle also said of Lewis that he was not really a friend, 'we just play as the same teams'. Sam described Joshua as someone with whom he had never played and, when it was pointed out that he had just been observed playing Scooby Doo and the Mummy's Curse with Joshua, remarked 'he was playing with Kyle'.

The peers in this group showed sensitivity to the subject of friends and were keen to point out that they were someone who had friends. Friendship appeared to depend on experiences of enjoyment, mutual support, reliability and willingness to sort out conflict, just as it is described in the literature on children's friendships (Asher *et al.*, 1998; Dunn, 2004). It is also apparent that friendship was partly maintained through play, with game playing used to support and enrich social relationships (Blatchford *et al.*, 2002).

What is interesting about Kyle's group is that they shared an understanding of what friendship meant, evident in the way they used the same terms and definitions even when questioned individually. The children had developed a clear system of thought around friendship that was not evident in the discourse on friendship in the wider class group. Adults who knew the children well did not share this discourse on friendship and did not seem to know about it. They did not use the language of 'teams' or 'friends of friends' and simply described the children as friends or friends who sometimes fell out. The understanding about friendship that was shared within Kyle's group – about what was a friend, a friend's friend and a team – conformed to the content of the children's play. It is an understanding that involved some nuance, making the distinction between someone you felt close to and others who you played with regularly but who were not so close. Kyle also participated in this aspect of group culture, using the terminology of friend's friend and team without prompting when he was interviewed. He had other skills too in relation to friendship. He was one of the few peers within the group who had achieved the status of having a best friend, Joshua, the two boys equally willing to declare each other as this. Like other children in the group, Kyle too based his idea of friendship on the experience of play, describing his friend Joshua as someone he had fun with and who 'I play with all the time'.

Imagining has a cost for some children with autism

Finally, one last distinctive feature of the social world of Kyle and his group was the strength and quality of Kyle's imagination. Children and adults alike described this as something that stood out culturally within this setting, though they framed it mostly in positive terms, as enriching and driving much of the children's play. The development of play and imagination is seen as one of the goals of intervention with children with autism, development in these areas seen as key to the development of other areas of functioning in language, cognition and sociability. However, the experience of play for Kyle suggests that imagining may be at a cost for some children with autism.

> Kyle appeared to imagine on a more continuous basis than other children. Not only did he always play imaginative games, but also most of his talk and many of his interactions were based on his knowledge of imaginary superhero characters, actions and narratives. Kyle turned almost any conversation or action into one that related to some aspect of the media culture in which he

was interested. In interactions with adults and children, his response was almost always based on this. For example, asking a child to move from his seat in the dining hall, he said, 'I'll huff and I'll puff and I'll blow your house down', and when told to listen in class he pressed an imaginary switch on his ears, made a 'Nnnn' machine noise and angled his ears like satellite dishes.

One notable behaviour was that Kyle continued to play imaginatively at the end of playtimes. When the end of play was signalled with a bell, Kyle joined his class promptly in lining up, but continued to act out the imaginary play he had just been doing, talking to himself and making pretend fighting moves. This was something that he did at the end of most playtimes, though other children seemed not to notice. Some children, mainly boys, sometimes carried out this behaviour too, though not with the same frequency or visibility as Kyle.

Kyle's class teacher felt that it was the intensity of Kyle's imaginative experience that really marked him out as different from other children. She thought that he was 'more imaginative' than other children and that the boundary between what is real and not real was much less clear for him. Kyle's support worker agreed with this. She said that staying on task was the thing Kyle found most difficult in school and that this was because 'his imagination goes off'. She described how Kyle could turn the content of most lessons into something aligned with his interests in action, adventure, fighting, superheroes, monsters and machines. She mentioned the fact that she often had to 'bring him out of' his imaginative play and prepare him for lessons, or else he would be 'Terminator till home time'.

Interestingly, though Kyle's intense imaginative engagement in his play resulted in difficulties with the curriculum, many adults and children expressed their belief that it is socially positive, equating his ability to play in inventive ways that attracted and amused peers with the peculiarly rich and ongoing nature of his imaginary experience. This aspect of Kyle's participation appeared to be experienced by his peers as essentially the same as their own and one which they could appreciate in some way. Other children were described as being enthralled by his imagination. As Kyle's class teacher pointed out, when he imagined 'he takes his group with him'. Kyle's mother thought other children had a much greater capacity than adults for appreciating Kyle's imagination. She said they valued his referencing of the media in a way adults did not and could not, having less knowledge about what was being referenced.

Other children's experience of Kyle's imagination illustrates the fact that social processes have outcomes that cannot be foreseen or assumed in advance. Though Kyle's inability to switch off his imagination was a difficulty, it was not necessarily experienced as such by other children in his group. Taking these descriptive accounts together, it is apparent that social processes can have different outcomes, only some of which result in individual difficulty and perceived differences between children which are commented upon or criticized. This chapter will conclude by highlighting the different possible outcomes of social processes that are illustrated by these descriptive accounts of children with and without autism playing and interacting together.

The differing outcomes of social processes

Corsaro's model of interpretive reproduction was used in this and the previous chapter to describe the structure and purpose of children's communication. This model highlights the fact that social processes have elements of continuity, familiarity and predictability for children, and also crucially involve creativity and change. For this reason, social processes are emergent and have different outcomes which depend on the participation of the communities involved. The fact of this has been illustrated here in relation to children's peer groups that include a child with autism, with information gathered about several possible outcomes:

Outcome 1: differential forms of social participation are not perceived

Within the information gathered about Richie, it was apparent that differential forms of his participation in interaction were not noticeable to others. Careful observation and analysis of his behaviour indicated that he sometimes jumped ahead in conversation; for example, answering a question before it had been asked. It was as if Richie was anticipating an interaction routine before it had happened and experiencing social engagement more as a learned routine rather than an unfolding event, but in a very subtle way. This slightly different way of interacting appeared to be experienced by other children and adults as a kind of 'blip' that did not occur clearly enough or often enough to disrupt the interactional flow and therefore be noticed by others. Information collected from people who participated in the research confirmed this, with no adult or child singling Richie out as 'different' in any way.

Outcome 2: differential forms of social participation are perceived only over time

It has been suggested that this might have been the case for Richie and Joey when they role played motorbikes, the play eventually – but only over time – leading to conflict. It is perhaps the case that Richie did not produce new pretend elements or enough new elements in repeated playing of the game for it to feel socially appropriate, and that this was the source of conflict with his friend Joey. In case study 2, changing perceptions of difference over time was also raised as an issue in relation to Kyle's use of an American accent. His support worker mentioned that this was something which other children had asked questions about before they really knew Kyle, but had stopped asking and seemed no longer to notice this aspect of his behaviour once he was a familiar member of their class group. It is perhaps the case that differential forms of participation, continually and regularly used, are no longer perceived by others as of special interest or note over a period of time.

Outcome 3: differential forms of social participation are perceived and incorporated into group processes

Within both these case studies, research yielded the most data in relation to this outcome with a number of illustrations provided by both case studies. An example from case study 2 would be Kyle's need to be a leader in imaginative play. This need was most probably linked to his autism and was perhaps related to a difficulty in sharing at an interpersonal level, especially of imaginative ideas. However, it appeared to be experienced by his peers as something that was 'natural', a situation of play leaders and followers that was within their social knowledge and easily accommodated within the group. From this case study too, children and adults described Kyle's use of media referencing as outside the 'norm'. However, it was much appreciated by them and linked to what many children aspired to producing in their play and interactions. Kyle's class teacher said the situation was one not where Kyle imagined and left his peers behind but where he imagined and took them along with him. From case study 1, Richie's irrational fears would also provide an example of this type of outcome. His fear was extreme and perhaps different in nature from that of other children because of his autism. However, it was not experienced as such by others, other children having their own experiences of irrational thoughts and fears and shifting in terms of their position to the perceived reality and fearfulness of something that is imagined.

Outcome 4: differential forms of social participation are perceived and give rise to comment and criticism

Interestingly, neither case study provides many examples of this type of outcome. This is surprising given that, in the literature on autism, negative attitudes and social exclusion are reported features of school experience for a child or young person with autism (Humphrey and Symes, 2011). Kyle's role of leader in his peer group's superhero play was described as the source of conflict with one peer in his group, and Kyle's best friend, Joshua, did criticize him for dominating their sharing of books, but these were the only two instances of difference being viewed critically by peers. It is perhaps significant that this research was carried out with pre-adolescent children for whom negative views of difference are less of an issue than they are for fully adolescent groups (Corsaro, 1999). It is possible to see that criticism and teasing was a possibility for Kyle, who did stand out from his peers as different. However, close analysis of what was going on within this group of children showed that this was not a feature of social relations at this point in time.

Indeed, time is an ongoing feature of social outcomes and it is important to remember that any description of a social context is a 'snapshot' only of social experience at that moment in time. Children's social experiences require monitoring and awareness that change is a constant factor to keep in mind.

Summary

This chapter has used case study material to describe the quality of social experience for two children with autism and their friends. Narrative descriptions have been provided to illustrate the differing ways in which children with and without autism participate in social processes and use culture in their interactions with each other. What has been illustrated is that a child with autism is able to appropriate and produce culture and can be viewed by those who know them as a social player. Through careful observation and reconstruction with children and with the adults who know them well, it is possible to see the ways in which the participation of a child with autism is viewed by others as appropriate and of interest, as well as inappropriate and different. The descriptive accounts illustrate four possible outcomes to social processes that involve a child with autism. These range from differential forms of social participation not being noticed by others, to only being noticed over time and repeated instances, being noticed and incorporated into ordinary group processes, and finally, being noticed and viewed negatively or criticized in some way.

Chapter 5

Researching autism in natural contexts

Time/Activity/ Location	Focus child/ Activity/Response	Partner 1	Further partners
2.00 pm Free play session Play corner	Jack tries to put a road mat on the floor. He has difficulty, the mat not lying flat and having bumps in it. Jack begins to push a car over the bumps of the mat.	Lee straightens the mat, directing Jack to do the same. Lee looks at Jack's car going over a bump and says, 'Ramp!' Lee directs Ethan and Anthony to move out of the way of the mat.	Ethan and Anthony do this, moving to the far corner of the mat.
	Jack moves his car towards Lee's.	Lee narrates where the cars are going, saying 'Town is over there'. He talks to Isaac and Anthony.	Isaac, Anthony and Mia start playing with their cars on the mat.
	Jack giggles and removes the car.	Lee says the road is now a car park and directs Jack to remove his car.	

Above is an excerpt from an observation record of the play and interaction of a few children in the setting of a mainstream school. One child, Jack, aged 5 years, has autism and the other children are part of his class group. The children's activity is recorded on a structured observation schedule that seeks to systematically note the actions of the focus child – in this instance Jack – and the actions of his play partners. Only a few minutes of play are recorded, but it is apparent that much happens in that time. It is possible to see the dynamic of the interaction, with Jack's partner, Lee, clearly in the leadership role, directing others and creating a narrative for the imaginative play with cars, which the rest of the group, including Jack, mostly follow.

The advantage of using this close-up method of gaining information is that it allows micro-details of interaction to be seen (in this instance that one child leads and that others follow) and that the child with autism is engaged, but non-verbally. However, there are disadvantages too. This interaction actually involves up to six children at different times on the play mat (even within these few minutes), moving about, looking, acting and talking, but there is little sense of this. The activity of the wider group forms part of the social experience of the child being observed and may be influencing their behaviour, but this is hard to deduce. Using this method, it is difficult to record interaction and communication as anything other than straightforward sequences of behaviour, but from watching young children engage within a play space it is apparent that much overlaps in terms of social activity, with multiple events often occurring. In addition, a schedule such as this preconceives what happens amongst children. There is a 'first partner' and additional partners, suggesting that children's social experience is primarily dyadic, but is this really the case? In fact, reading through the observation, it is not apparent who is whose primary partner, with fluidity in this respect evident at different moments. Finally, it is not clear from this account what is the precise nature of the relationship between Jack and Lee, with more questions raised than answered. There is a connection between them, interaction is sustained and some degree of shared play is occurring, but what are the two children's experience of this? Lee is directing, but is Jack comfortable with this? His giggle suggests that perhaps he is not. It is hard to know from this record whether Lee's management of Jack's involvement in the play is experienced as supportive and helpful, or as bossy and domineering.

The following is another description of the social experiences of the children in this group. This has been gained from talking to adults and children in this setting as well as from semi-participant observations of the group on different occasions written up as a narrative account.

Jack routinely interacts and plays with other children in his class and has a few particular children with whom he plays more often. His teacher elects to put Jack with these children when she can, for work tasks, in group work and for play sessions. This is as a way of enabling the maximum amount of contact and support for friendship. However, on observation, it is apparent that Jack tends to dip in and out of playing or being with the group. He plays for short periods of time with one or two children, and then tends to move off by himself, not noticing them again or seeking to reconnect in any way. His teacher reports that, though the other children are fond of Jack, there has been no evidence of a sustained friendship with any one child.

Some difficulty in peer interaction is present in the wider group in the way in which a few children perceive Jack as 'different'. A behaviour that is occurring at the moment is for some peers to ask Jack questions in order to get a 'strange' or 'funny' answer. Some peers find it funny that Jack can be made to say certain inappropriate words. They sometimes try to get him to say these out in the playground, asking him questions to which he invariably replies with an inappropriate word. The peers laugh at Jack and are told off by staff when they are witnessed doing this.

A narrative account is a description of a context which details occurrences or features that are deemed significant whilst omitting others that are thought to be less key. In this instance, significant features are those that are raised by a number of children and adults, or observed as a pattern or routine. A consideration in this is that the same information comes from different sources and so contributes to the verification of the significance of an issue. The account gives a macro-view of Jack that takes in patterns of behaviour and the wider group of which he is part. It provides a slightly different and complementary perspective of Jack's experience at school, with some information confirming that provided by the structured observation schedule. Jack is described as a follower in peer situations, though here it is more clearly within negative experiences of social interaction.

How we look at social engagement, what view we choose to take and how we record information – whether close up and focused on the dyad or wider and focused on the group – determines to some extent what we 'see'. Thinking about the two methods that are used here, it is apparent that different methods provide different types of information that can, perhaps, lead to different conclusions about individual experience and group dynamics. It is also apparent that different methods can be combined to provide a fuller and more complete picture of what is being looked at. Research into autism has been dominated by one approach – that of scientific measure – where what is being studied is seen as single variables that can be objectively quantified and compared. However, the study of complex social phenomena, such as social engagement, friendship and play, raises difficult questions, particularly around measurement and objectivity. How does one measure variables that are hidden (such as mental states), that are hard to quantify (such as children's collaboration) and that are highly subjective (such as the experience of satisfaction or enjoyment in play)? How can one begin to think about and describe children's social experience in ways that are recognizable and meaningful to those being described?

We have already seen how children with autism are partly socially engaged and this chapter will look at issues that exist within approaches to researching the social engagement of children with autism in natural contexts. A critical consideration in any research is finding the right match between the method of study and the nature of the subject matter being studied. A central argument here is that the social activity of children within a natural setting is not suited to scientific measure alone. The chapter will describe a sociocultural approach to research that is more typically used in studies of children's ordinary social worlds. This describes individual experience in the light of the wider and unfolding culture of which it is part, seeking to engage with complexity and providing contextualized accounts of individual behaviours. Issues that are particularly relevant to carrying out research with children will be discussed and the chapter will conclude with an outline of essential conditions for research with children with autism in natural contexts.

Approaches to researching autism in natural contexts

Research into autism typically aspires to a knowable 'truth' about how behaviour relates to the cognitive capacity of the individual with autism and this truth, once uncovered, is seen as applicable across populations. The ontological position – the understanding of what it is that is being studied – is that there is one reality of 'having autism' and that it can be apprehended through close and objective study. The purpose of study is to verify hypotheses as a way of establishing the facts about autism and so build up an 'edifice of knowledge' (Guba and Lincoln, 2005). Cause and effect linkages that operate in the same way across a large number of cases are seen as key aspects of knowledge as is generalization to a much wider population. Such an approach to research comes fully within the positivist paradigm or 'logical empiricism' that originates in the traditions of the nineteenth century. Within this paradigm, the image of the researcher is one of the 'disinterested scientist' who, through focused observation and careful use of research instruments, is able to objectively study the world and see what is 'real'. The researcher, who stands outside what is being studied, reduces the subject to knowable parts that are observed, measured and tested. Initial thoughts about the subject are compared with what is quantified and the truth about the subject generated.

In autism research, conventional benchmarks of scientific 'rigour' are typically used. These are based on experimental research designs and are concerned with 'validity'. Mertens and McLaughlin (2004) define validity as a combination of both internal coherence (for example, the quality of instrumentation and discreteness of the time-scale) and external coherence or how replicable the experiment is. Further criteria include the systematic application of method, the objectivity of the researcher and the reliability or consistency of findings. Details of how the research is carried out, including details of any tests used and the scoring of tasks, are made explicit so that the research can be carried out by a different researcher and produce the same results. Researchers take steps to reduce any 'novelty effects' and pay attention to how any instrumentation is used, trying to devise clear systems for calibrating and grading. They systematically analyse the data, often using standardized statistical procedures, and try to come up with clear indications of significance.

The positivist position of autism research fits well with the medical model of disability that is used to view the condition, both having the same historical roots. However, in the last decade there has been recognition of the need to conduct research into the social engagement of children with autism in a slightly different way, focusing more on research into behaviour within naturalistic-type environments rather than under laboratory-type conditions. This need has been highlighted by research findings that show children with autism having differential behaviour in everyday situations compared to controlled situations. Like all children, children with autism demonstrate that they interact differently with different people (El-Ghoroury and Romanczyk, 1999) and that the presence of ordinary feeling is important to their levels of socialization, their ability to carry out pretend play, for example, enhanced where play is invested with emotion (Sherratt, 2002). High-functioning children with autism demonstrate a gap between what they understand about social situations in controlled settings and what they actually do in practice (Bauminger et al., 2003). It is also the case that the best results for the development of social play (Jordan, 2003) and of peer interaction skills (Rogers, 2000) occur in everyday situations.

Research into children's ordinary understanding of other people's mental states has also served to influence our understanding of research approaches to autism. Theory of mind research has largely generated quantitative data obtained from controlled scientific trials that provide insight into how children perform in set tasks, but takes little or no account of social, emotional and cultural influences. However, research into children's understanding of mental states in everyday situations shows that they have different theory of mind abilities depending on whom they are with (Astington, 1994). There is now a well-established understanding that less focus is needed on laboratory-based performance and more on actual functioning in natural settings, the capacity of children for social understanding viewed not 'as an undifferentiated whole', but in relation to their 'growing sophistication in different realms' (Dunn and Brown, 1994: 135).

Taken together, such findings have led some theorists to argue for more to be known about the social–emotional understanding of children with autism in ordinary contexts, with the case made for greater use of qualitative measures and a field of research that encompasses ecological variation and spontaneous interactions in natural settings (Bruner and Feldman, 1993; McConnell, 2002; Rogers, 2000; White et al., 2007). The issue is often framed as one of finding real-life correspondence within naturally occurring behaviour to children's performance in laboratory-based tasks. Research design increasingly reflects this with more focus on natural settings and the quality of children's engagement and more use made of a range of methods and measures. The appeal is to 'bring the social world, with its emotional content and vividness, into the laboratory' (Peskin and Ardino, 2003: 509) with the purpose of addressing the shortcomings of knowledge gained in test situations.

However, the emphasis in approaches to researching the social engagement of children with autism in natural settings has remained resolutely on scientific measure. Quantitative data are increasingly being presented alongside more qualitative descriptions of individual social responses and emotional reactions, but the way in which both quantitative and qualitative data are handled has remained largely within the positivist paradigm. Investigations into children with autism playing ordinary childhood games, such as hide-and-seek or pretend play, or engaged in playful, emotionally charged situations, such as having a friend, are often carried out as a quantification of 'correct' or unambiguous performance. Yet, the notion of 'successful play', 'errors in play' and 'failure in friendship' comes across as an unorthodox application of methodology to subject matter. Play, interaction and friendship are much more than cognitively correct behaviour and are strongly linked to the child's experience and understanding of the relational, cultural and historical contexts in which they unfold. Playful social engagement, participating in children's games and being friends are all particularly exciting aspects of children's cultural worlds, with emotion constituting a key part of the social-cognitive experience. The child's playful attitude and satisfaction with friendship – as well as their interpretations of the research context itself – are critically important pieces of information, but provide complex data that cannot easily be quantified or judged as success or failure.

Boaz and Ashby (2003) have pointed out that quality in research is partly determined by the suitability of the methodology to the subject matter and whether the methods used are 'fit for purpose' in terms of the aims of the study. The process of research is partly concerned with finding the right match between methodological approach and subject matter, a 'search for form' that contributes to the validity of the whole project (Clough and Nutbrown, 2007). In studies of ordinary childhood, quantification of children's social engagement, friendship and play is not privileged as the approach most suited to the nature of the subject being studied, with qualitative methodologies, such as ethnography, being seen as of particular relevance here (Christensen, 2004; Eder and Corsaro, 1999). Quantitative and qualitative methodologies are based on different understandings of the nature of reality, what can be known about it and how that knowledge can be obtained. Whilst the criteria for analysing quantitative research involve consideration of how far data collection and analysis can be said to be valid, objective and reliable, that for qualitative research involves more the appropriateness of the methods to the topic, the degree to which research participants would verify the findings, and the amount of self-monitoring and reflexive thought the researcher invests in the research process.

Guba and Lincoln (1994) provide criteria for analysing qualitative data which focuses on the 'extrinsic' and 'intrinsic' value of research. They relate extrinsic value to the degree to which the research is generalizable and argue that this should be judged on its credibility or degree of correspondence between the researcher's constructs and that of the participants, its progressive subjectivity or degree to which the researcher monitors their own constructs, and on how far the researcher verifies data analyses with research participants. Intrinsic value refers to the transferability of the research, in particular the extent to which the researcher provides sufficient information for readers to draw their own conclusions. The criterion of validity can also be applied to qualitative research but, as Punch (2005) cautions, it is a term that needs to be used carefully since it has different meanings specific to different paradigms. For qualitative data, validity should be judged in terms of social relevance, that is, what can be seen to be real by readers of the research, what is useful and what holds meaning.

It is seldom the case that approaches used to investigate the social engagement of children with autism in natural settings meet this kind of criteria. Researchers in the autism field typically do not reflect on constructions and subjectivities within the research or verify findings outside their own data analysis. There is seldom an attempt to present participants' views, to describe their personal responses or to give them a 'voice'. Where the views of participants are sought, they are seen as having less power as data than that gained from quantitative enquiry. In situations of conflict between data sources, participants' views may be seen simply as 'wrong'. Participants' views are not seen as the source of important insight into how the social context being investigated is experienced by those involved and therefore a reflection of what the context actually is. Seldom is the ecological make-up of the sample taken into consideration in autism research, with sample size seen as a much more critical part of research design – the 'bigger the better' making for the most reliable results. Little account is typically taken of the influence of gender, race or class to a study or of individual differences between children, such as family background, individual experience or differing emotional responses to the research situation. The aim is usually to apply experimental means to natural settings, identifying measurable variables to gain a better understanding of a bigger picture whilst seeking to maximize coherence, reliability and replicability through careful use of roles and measures. Researchers almost never reflect on their own participation, their values and influence not taken into account and their role fully one of outside observer.

Social-based research, by contrast, seeks to identify the aspects of cultural knowledge available to a community and describe the ways in which individuals within it are interpreting that culture. It emphasizes the two-way aspects of social participation, the responses of others seen as integral to and partly constitutive of the actions and reactions of the individual. Sociocultural research distinctively defines social contexts as culture and seeks to locate social interaction in the light of the cultural exchange of which it is part, the experiences of the individual being examined in relation to a wider and historically unfolding scene around them. Individual personality and behaviour traits are of less significance than cultural knowledge and comparative facility in producing culture. Social interaction is viewed as 'becoming patterned' with the individual's patterns of participation constructing the expectations that others have of them (Kantor et al., 1998). For example, a child who makes a number of unsuccessful attempts to enter group play will become viewed as less desirable as a social partner. Importantly, however, that same child in another group of children might experience different cultural relations, have more success at social entry and subsequently be viewed in a different light.

Gathering detailed information about social contexts is a key aspect of social research as is the presentation of research accounts in detailed, descriptive forms. Qualitative accounts of experience are preferentially used to investigate research contexts. Descriptive detail gained from close observation is viewed as having a research purpose that is much more than 'anecdotal' since it is the vehicle best suited to presenting data that are complex, multilayered and concerns subjective experience (Gubrium and Holstein, 2008). The purpose of descriptive accounts to research is not well understood in the literature on autism and more will be said in the next section on their role within social and educational research.

The purpose of descriptive accounts in social and educational research

Whilst the underlying assumption of the positivist paradigm is that the social world can be studied 'from the outside' in a value-free way, research paradigms that have followed emphasize researchers understanding the world of lived experience from the point of view of those who live it. From the mid-twentieth century onwards, questions about what is reality, how it is known and in what ways it is represented have been highly contested. In particular, traditionalist approaches to research are challenged by a 'crisis of representation'. This refers to the fact that research must always represent subjective reality in text and questions the nature of the link between reality and representations of reality. The ethnographic work of Clifford Geertz (1988) has been influential in this since he was amongst the first to point out that the lack of a direct link between lived experience and research text must always be overcome by the interpretations of the researcher. He pointed out that social research is not scientific investigation to establish laws, but an interpretive engagement with people's construction of meaning.

The interpretive paradigm in social research emphasizes the fact that knowledge of social phenomena must be viewed as an 'emergent construction' that needs to be created together with those who are engaged within the social world being studied (Denzin and Lincoln, 1994). Within this paradigm, social reality is not seen to exist as an entity that can be straightforwardly observed by the researcher. What is socially real must be generated from the complex understandings and experiences of all those involved in a situation, with the researcher paying careful attention to the process of their own constructions and interpretations. In his famous essay on Balinese cockfighting, Geertz (1973) argued that the researcher must use as much descriptive detail as possible in explaining human behaviour. He said that it is not enough to say a man winked, since this behaviour could have the social origins of irony or flirtation, and also the physical origin of having something in his eye. He coined the term 'thick description' to express the idea that information about social behaviour and relationships must be *contextualized* and make reference to the wider socioculture of which it is part. Thick description is 'description plus interpretation', where the validity of the interpretation is grounded in a full account of the specificities of everyday life that are being described and participants' acknowledgement of them as true.

Theorizing about the purpose of qualitative methodologies in social research has emphasized the importance of detailed descriptive accounts to the investigation of social contexts. Different forms of enquiry exist, such as the case study, ethnography, focus groups and phenomenological analysis, but all have the purpose of providing information that is in-depth, contextual and seen to be 'consensually real'. Key terms are 'complexity', 'exploration' and 'inductive logic', where the researcher does not apply their own pre-existing expectations but allows understandings to emerge from the data themselves. Rather than trying to present conclusive accounts of social phenomena, qualitative accounts provide a more 'pieced-together' description of ongoing human experience in all its variation. The image of the researcher is one of a 'bricoleur' – a maker of quilts – who produces a set of representations that are fitted to the specifics of a situation and verified through the use of multiple methods (Denzin and Lincoln, 2000). No single method is seen as capable of capturing the diversity and complexity of ongoing human experience, with triangulation of information from different sources an important tool of validation. Careful data handling and the presence of descriptive accounts within the write up of the research together ensure a continuing connection between the raw data and conceptualizations based on that data, so that theories generated do not stray far from actual contexts.

In social research, descriptive accounts are an important feature of 'local enquiry', providing a focus on 'local elements' and helping to represent 'local knowledge'. Local knowledge is knowledge that exists within the context being investigated and its presence within research accounts is seen to be a factor in judgements of the overall reliability of the research (Silverman, 2011). Local enquiry is not overtly concerned with 'grand theorizing' and generalizations deemed scientifically reliable, though generalization of research findings may come from patterns identified across a large enough number of case studies (Rogoff, 2003). However, attention to the minute details of social study remains key and serves to keep people at the centre of the research. Local enquiry thus produces *practical* knowledge that is eminently useable because it relates directly to people's lives.

Local enquiry is seen as having an important role to play in educational research, particularly research into inclusive education and children with special educational needs and disability. Within inclusive education, knowledge of individual factors is seen as key to quality in educational research and practice: children experiencing learning difficulties and disability in diverse ways and barriers to learning taking different forms in different settings (Ainscow, 1998). Where the focus of research is on the process of implementation of a programme of support, or where it is on individualized outcomes and in-depth information is needed, or where it is research that concerns diversity and the unique qualities of individuals, local enquiry to produce descriptive accounts will have a more important role than large-scale randomized control trials (Mertens, 2010). Standardized practices and programmes that are developed through science-based research are often not widely adopted by schools, any such programmes that are used are often adapted and 'watered down' through local use (Thomas and Loxley, 2007). Education research indicates that practitioners naturally form views and make decisions based on their knowledge of actual cases, specific contexts and real-life events. Research into what works in special education invariably pinpoints the importance of knowledge about the particular rather than the general, and local forms of practice are particularly important (Pollard, 2008).

As in social research, educational research often concerns the investigation of contexts that are individual and multidimensional. This makes the gaining of context-dependent knowledge of equal or greater importance than the development of general concepts about effective practice with children. It is this kind of context-rich, concrete and nuanced knowledge that is necessary to address real-life learning contexts in all their complexity. In defining what makes good educational research, Yates concludes:

> Among the reasons for the widespread shift in the late 1970s and beyond to qualitative and case-study based work was that this seemed to address better the complexity of the real-life classroom situation, and that it is 'methodolatory' to insist on laboratory-based or artificially simplified experimental programmes that may well generalize and build on themselves in other similar laboratory or other artificially simplified contexts, but that are not 'generalizable' in real world settings.
>
> (Yates, 2004: 26)

Before considering the significance of such understandings in social and educational research to autism, one further aspect of research will be explored:

that of research with children. This is an area that has developed considerably in the last two decades and is one where clear ideas have emerged about effective research design and methodology in relation to children as research participants, including children with a disability.

Research with children

Social-based research with children views them as competent 'social actors' who actively make sense of their social worlds. The researcher's role is not one of an 'expert' on children and children are not the 'objects' of research (Woodhead and Faulkner, 2008). Instead, they are considered to be capable of reflexive thinking and comparable to adults in their ability to respond to the research process, though methods may need adapting to match their differing competencies (Christensen and Prout, 2002). The notion is that research should be *with* children not *on* them, an idea which is heavily influenced by the agenda of 'listening to children' put forward in Article 12 of the UN Convention on the Rights of the Child (UN General Assembly, 1989) and in government guidance, such as *Every Child Matters* in the UK (DfES, 2004). This agenda strongly makes the point that children's viewpoints must be taken seriously. Even the most vulnerable children are seen as capable of forming their own views about matters that affect them and as having unique knowledge of their own circumstances. Listening to children posits the idea that all children are embarked on a course of making meaning in the world and puts the responsibility on adults to ensure they are able to access their communication.

Research methods advocated for use in the study of how children make sense of their worlds generally involve in-depth descriptive accounts of children's sociocultural activity. Ethnography is frequently cited as the method best suited to the study of children's cultures of communication since it ensures an engagement with the details of social knowledge and lived experiences (Corsaro and Molinari, 2008; James, 2001). Ethnography allows the researcher time to 'tune in' to the child and place their perspective centrally within the research. Fieldwork is a practical engagement with children's cultural routines and provides the researcher with an opportunity to enter into a dialogue *in situ* about their practices and experiences. For young children, being questioned about their play and interaction in the space where it occurs allows them to respond through actions rather than verbally and offers them an alternative and possibly more effective form of communication (Clark and Moss, 2005).

Interviewing children is also recommended as a method. Traditionally, children have been seen as unreliable respondents in interview situations, telling the interviewer what they think he or she wants to hear and trying to give the 'right answer' to a question (Westcott and Littleton, 2005). A preferred approach has been to talk to the adults who are involved with children. However, it has become common practice to include children within the consultation process of a research enquiry, to invite them 'to pull up another chair' alongside parents, practitioners and policymakers (Lancaster, 2006). Rather than theorizing children as unreliable research participants, the agenda is one of finding the right tools to enable children to understand the nature of the research relationship and be able to contribute more fully (Christensen and James, 2008). Examples of interview tools to use with children would include visual cue cards or sentence beginnings as a basis for discussion and to provide structure (Veale, 2005). During an interview, attention is paid to the terminology used, using children's own language wherever possible. It is important to ask open-ended questions, to repeat questions and give children enough time to respond (Lewis, 2003). As with adults, interviewing children is seen as a process through which meanings are created and where the child's possible interpretations of the situation are taken into account.

Some questions are considered more sensitive than others. In autism research, investigations into friendship networks sometimes enquire whether children have a best friend as if that question has the same emotionally low impact as being asked what is their name. Social-based research into children's social worlds indicates that friendship is particularly sensitive for children and an area of social identity – that they are someone who has friends – that is especially important for children to assert. The descriptions provided in the previous chapter of children with autism engaged with other children, illustrates how a child with autism can have awareness of this too. Investigation into areas such as friendship would be treated sensitively by a social researcher, who frames questions carefully and takes time to build trust by asking less sensitive questions first.

Research with children with a disability is seen as taking a similar approach to that used with all children, though with some adjustment made in terms of focus and methods. Observation and other methods that have a reduced demand on verbal ability may be especially important (Pellegrini, 2001). Extended contact with research participants may also be necessary, the researcher needing more time to be able to 'see' the child in different settings (Beresford, 1997). Participatory research techniques are viewed as important since these provide another way for the researcher to verify their interpretations of children's experience and not second-guess it. Disability studies are more concerned with children's rights and their life experiences and less with clinical cases, and participatory approaches to research are seen as a way of ensuring children's ongoing involvement in investigation that concerns them (Dickins, 2008). Finally, the participation of adults who know the child may be more critical for a child with a disability than it is for other children (Kellett and Nind, 2001).

Research with children with autism

The key challenge in social research with children with autism is to find a method that ensures as much 'ethical symmetry' of participation (Morrow and Richards, 1996) as possible, in line with social-based research methods used with all children, but that is also of value in terms of describing the child with autism's differential experience of the world. Careful consideration must be given to balancing 'listening to children' with credibility and authenticity in the research account. For children with autism, the social-cognitive difficulties of the condition must be considered alongside sociocultural factors present in the environment. However, given that children with autism are partly socially engaged, issues in social research with children must be considered in research with children with autism too. Though powerful biographies do exist of the experience of children and young people with autism, the 'voice' of the child with autism has been absent in much of the research into autism and this must constitute a concern.

A framework for research should minimize the challenges posed by research with children with autism – without necessarily being able to eliminate them completely – whilst giving a voice to the child and to those who know the child well. Like other children with a disability, research into autism would require extra consideration of issues such as the language content of methods, the involvement of adults who know the child and extended engagement by the researcher to allow them to 'see' the child. The following six research conditions are identified as key conditions of research with children with autism:

- naturalistic enquiry;
- a strength-based model;
- mixed methods design;
- participation;
- reflexivity and shared interpretation;
- orientation to practice.

Naturalistic enquiry

Autism research has been dominated by propositional enquiry and an experimental approach, but increasingly the need is seen for more understanding of actual behaviour in natural settings. Social-based research into children's participation in culture is concerned with naturalistic enquiry, that is, the natural ways in which children produce culture. Though children's participation may be seen as patterned, it is not the case that it exists independently of place and context or that it can be abstracted for the purpose of predicting the behaviour of others in comparable circumstances. It is not possible, for example, to make formal generalizations and propose that two children who are in a similar social situation will act in a certain way. They may act in the same way, but there will always exist a richness of possibility in terms of action. Sociocultural research accounts depend for their meaning on retaining a connection with the concrete circumstances from which they arise. Naturalistic enquiry also helps to align research with the social model of disability which puts forward the idea that disability is at least partly socially derived, impairment not necessarily leading to disability and society contributing to disablement by failing to see and accommodate individual differences.

A strength-based model

Typically in autism research, the focus of enquiry is on within-person capacity using a deficit model that measures behaviour against pre-given categories. By contrast, social-based research is concerned with 'seeing things as they are' (Clark, 2005). In research with children, the emphasis is on children's actual lived experience, what they are doing rather than on what they cannot do. Activity rather than deficit is the key term. Focusing on competencies provides insight into cultures of childhood, particularly how children make sense of things and use that understanding in interactions with others. This opens up the possibility of seeing how a child's autism manifests itself within a group as well as the differences that exist between all children. Looking at what children are doing, at their knowledge, understanding, participation and competency within a group, allows for the possibility of seeing the details of what is different as well as what is the same about a child with autism compared to their peers.

Mixed methods design

The argument being put forward here is that an essential condition for research into the social engagement of children with autism is the use of mixed methods research design. The use of mixed methods is seen as a way of overcoming the limitations of using one method only to investigate complex data, such as social data. At the beginning of this chapter, we saw that close observation by itself may be problematic, but that observation combined with interviews and other kinds of conversations provides a fuller and clearer picture of the nature of a child's social functioning.

Natural settings are essentially a much more complex field than experimental situations and would require an impossible number of measures of behaviour to replicate a quasi-experimental approach. However, it is possible to combine approaches that yield 'micro-level' information about individual behaviour with ones that allow a 'macro-level' view of peer and adult perceptions of children's participation and the appropriateness of participation within the group. This latter kind of knowledge is primarily knowledge of group processes and is more practical and valuable educationally than extremely detailed knowledge about one individual child within the group. However, what are being studied are similar processes of participation as those available to a micro-analytical approach, that is, one focused at the individual, intrapersonal or even neural level. In the UK, the Medical Research Council recommends that more rigorous methods, such as randomized control trials, should come later on in the process of research, with time spent first using exploratory, macro-level, socioculturally focused methods to define the parameters of research (Daniels, 2010).

Outside autism research, the value of mixed methods design is well understood. Siraj-Blatchford (2010b) notes that the established and widespread use of mixed methods as an approach to social and educational research marks the end of the 'paradigm wars' or false duality of positivist and interpretive approaches. In particular, it is understood that the combination of approaches allows 'progressive focusing' on a subject and a more effective collection of data (Siraj-Blatchford, 2010a). Information gathered from different sources and in different ways can be used to inform further data collection; for example, background information about the wider culture giving rise to a priori categories that are then used in more focused investigations of parts of the same community of children, or of an individual child. In the case of researching social engagement in children with autism, social-based research can provide a wide perspective of the sociocultural world of which the child is part, ensuring that research takes a view of the particular nature of social relations and cultural practices in a setting. Given the specific social-cognitive difficulties of autism, psychology-based research can provide a more focused view of the individual child's abilities, which interact with sociocultural factors. This background plus foreground information is crucially important in providing rigour *plus* social relevance in autism research accounts.

Participation

The voice of the child is a central concern in research with children, although the voice of the child with autism is something that is mostly missing from research into autism. Cognitive explanations of autism question whether it is possible for an individual with autism to have insight into their own experience (Frith and Happé, 1999), but in line with sociocultural concepts being used here, accounts by children with autism are 'real' since they reflect their experience and should be viewed as of value. Children with autism participate less in culture and will have less social knowledge than their peers, including knowledge of themselves and their social performance. However, rich and varied accounts of the experience of school for children and young people with autism do exist (Humphrey and Lewis, 2008; Ochs *et al.*, 2001). The descriptions provided in Chapter 4 (of children with autism engaged with others) illustrate that they can have their own constructions of what is going on socially, some of which are aligned with other children's understandings in the same setting.

Participatory research originates in methods used with non-literate adults in developing countries to enable their decision-making on local issues (Freire, 1970), and have since been applied to research with children as a way of gaining insight into their point of view and giving them a stakehold in research that concerns them. Tools used in participatory research with children typically involve ones that allow them to express their views in a variety of ways; for example, through drawing, mapping and children using cameras to take photographs. Different amounts of participation are possible, from 'shallow participation' that is designed by adults but positions children's views centrally, to 'deep participation' where research is designed and carried out by children (Hagey, 1997; Miller, 2003). What is essential is the foregrounding of children's subjective experience with methods used to open up the research context for participants, allowing them to describe their experience and feelings and benefit from the research process (Mauthner, 1997).

Methods used with children with autism would require close attention to the design of research tools, including the language content and the use of visual information. Researchers cannot assume that information produced by children with autism is open to the same kind of interpretive analysis as that produced by children without autism. Interpretive methods are contingent on the researcher being able to access meaning at some level, but this may not always be possible in the case of autism. It is better to think in terms of ordinary research tools that are used in simple, pared down ways, with language used clearly and unambiguously, questions about interaction possibly asked in the setting where it occurs, and the verification of information gathered from children through triangulation with other data sources (Conn, 2013a).

In research with children with a disability, the participation of familiar adults is thought to be especially important to serve as a 'network of advocates' commenting on and helping to clarify the nature of the child's participation in the research process (Kellett and Nind, 2001). The use of multiple informants contributes to verification in the process of research and to validity in the research account. It is important that this kind of information is seen as 'local knowledge' and not merely 'perspective'. Research indicates that parents of children with autism hold reliable knowledge about their child's functioning and specific social difficulties (Stone and Lemanek, 1990; Wimpory et al., 2000) and the contribution of adults should be seen as an important reflection of the life experiences being investigated.

Reflexivity and shared interpretation

An autism research framework should include reflexivity, but crucially this should involve children, parents, teachers and the researcher thinking together about the research agenda. Reflexivity refers to an awareness of what we bring to the understanding and construction of a subject, requiring reflection on our own knowledge, understanding, ideas, attitude, experiences and behaviour. Investigations of autism are usually outside the researcher's own experience of the world (unless of course the researcher has autism) and reflexivity together with participation can make an invaluable contribution to the process of data review and analysis in research, with an emphasis on the shared nature of interpretation. When the researcher and research participants reflect together on data, differences of opinion and different interpretations are not a weakness in the process but add to the richness of the data collected, giving further insight into the nature of social experiences being studied. A collaborative and active role for participants within the research process should be seen as a positive aspect of research rather than a possible 'contamination' of findings (Christensen and James, 2008). In addition, the process of shared interpretation is seen as a way of minimizing the possibility of mistaken assumptions made by the researcher acting alone.

Orientation to practice

An important aspect of research with children is that the process should be well understood by participants and seen to have local in addition to academic benefits. The research process should be practically oriented with the gathering of information part of a wider discussion about quality and good practice. Interestingly, social-based methods for use in research with children, some of which have been outlined here, are influenced by ideas in early childhood education about the importance of the child's experience of the world and their ways of making meaning as starting points for teaching and learning. These ideas should be particularly relevant to research with children with autism since early childhood education is particularly focused on the social and emotional development of the child, as is autism theory and practice. It seems odd, therefore, that a gap exists between autism research and practice, though this has been well documented in the literature on autism (Humphrey and Parkinson, 2006; Kasari and Smith, 2013). It could be argued that the importance of the issue of 'seeing' autism in both education and research means that there is actually a significant overlap between the role of teacher and that of researcher, perhaps more than is the case for other areas of special educational needs and disability. An approach to research that is oriented to educational practice makes sense particularly in the case of autism and a research process that seeks to gather information about the experiences and views of children, teachers and parents follows well-established ideas around good practice in teaching and learning. This is an area that will be explored further in Chapter 7 where the importance of a reflective approach to autism education is discussed, one which prioritizes the teacher taking time to tune in to and investigate the child's experiences of learning contexts.

Summary

This chapter has questioned the privileging of scientific measure as the method best suited to researching the social activity of children with autism in natural settings. It has been argued that the micro-focus on the individual child and single instances of interaction provides a narrow view only of social engagement. The benefits of qualitative research design to investigate the behaviour of the individual within their sociocultural context and of descriptive information to provide a fuller account of complex data such as children's social and play activity have been outlined. Developments within social research with children are described, including the agenda of enabling children to contribute to the research process. A framework of conditions for research with children with autism has been provided which recommends the use of mixed methods design and progressive focusing within a participatory and reflexive approach.

Part II

Educational practice in inclusive school settings

Part II focuses on practical issues within autism education. In supporting children's learning and social development, the emphasis has been on devising special interventions and strategies, but a case is made for greater use of ordinary teaching methods within a reflective approach. Chapter 6 sets out the inclusion agenda in schools describing the issues that are particularly relevant to the inclusive education of students with autism and describing established ways of working. Chapter 7 argues that a key issue for school practitioners working with children with autism is to know about their competencies, the quality of engagements and the dimensional nature of difficulty, identifying how a child participates in actual peer processes and the appropriateness of their participation as viewed by their peers and adults who know them. Guidance is provided on evidence-informed educational practice that focuses on real-life learning contexts and uses a protocol of observing, listening to children and documenting their social activity to identify clear learning targets. The problems associated with a structured approach to teaching play with children with autism are discussed in Chapter 8 in relation to sociocultural theory. Methods for supporting the development of play in children with autism in educational settings are described in relation to the different contexts of children's play. From a sociocultural perspective, the emphasis is on finding ways of supporting ordinary play processes and the ability of all children to engage with these, but other forms of support are also discussed, including individualized support for children and support for the adults who monitor children's play.

Chapter 6

Inclusive education for children with autism

Individual Education Plan

Child's name: Charlie Williams   Class: 1M

Today's date: January 7   Review date: End of half-term

SMART target	Contexts for learning	Success criteria
To follow class routines for transition times.	Clear communication about what is happening now and next using visual timetable and verbal countdown. Lining up routine (front of line). Personal book taken into assemblies.	Is able to go into assembly without distress.
To have an awareness of another child's social needs.	Ryan's needs explained to Charlie, supported by visual information. Clear routine provided for how to interact with Ryan. Staff to reinforce routine in situ as social opportunities arise.	Incidence of conflict with Ryan decreases by agreed percentage.
To be able to make basic shapes in relation to handwriting.	Gross and fine motor skill programme three times weekly in a small group. Make large-scale circle, square, line, diagonal shapes with streamer and overwriting in chalk. Look for opportunities in class, particularly in outside learning area.	Can make all four shapes large scale following a visual cue.

Charlie, aged 5, who has a diagnosis of autism, is educated in an ordinary mainstream class along with twenty-five other children, some of whom also have additional learning needs. He has been making good progress in school. When he first entered the nursery he had poor speech, spoke only a few words, many of which were echoed from phrases he had heard, and preferred to sit apart from the group. He did have one friend, a girl named Helen, who was herself quite isolated from the general peer group and with whom Charlie interacted in mostly non-verbal ways. During his time in school, Charlie's speech has become clearer and he is able to produce language more reciprocally and appropriately in ordinary conversations. He is now in Year 1 and has become more sociable too, working with and talking to a wider number of peers.

Charlie's class teacher, his support worker who works with him in the mornings, the special educational needs co-coordinator and his parents meet every half term to review his learning progress. New learning objectives are agreed or existing ones adjusted within this meeting, which is also sometimes attended by other professionals who support Charlie and the school, including the speech and language therapist, a specialist teacher for autism and the occupational therapy service. Different areas of learning are targeted within Charlie's individual education plan (IEP), including his social communication, social understanding and peer integration as well as the development of motor skills, which is an area of weakness for him. The idea is to set SMART targets, that is, ones that are specific, measurable, attainable, time-limited and relevant to Charlie's actual social-emotional experiences. A key consideration in this is the social contexts with which he must engage, including other people's communication, understandings, needs and responses. Targets thus refer to the behaviour of others within relevant contexts, setting aims that incorporate aspects of their communication and social awareness. Targets also concern specific settings and events; for example, making the transition from the classroom to the school hall for assembly each morning, something that Charlie is finding difficult at present. All targets are short term and inform the weekly planning of the teacher who thinks about how to organize the learning environment and structure pedagogical opportunities.

On this occasion, the discussion about Charlie's progress centres on the fact that he has recently shown aggressive behaviour towards another child, Ryan. Charlie, who is a gentle child, has been observed on several occasions trying to prevent Ryan physically from joining or leaving a game, becoming upset, shouting at him and hitting out. School practitioners remark on the fact that Ryan is a forceful, antagonistic and unpredictable child who other children complain about and tend to avoid. They say that they have concerns about his learning and progress. The meeting agrees that Charlie becomes frustrated in his interactions with Ryan, like some other children in the group, but is not as good at dealing with this frustration. They decide to provide Charlie with a range of support strategies, including explaining Ryan's needs in social interaction and providing Charlie with ideas about what to say and do when he is around Ryan. They also plan separate targets for Ryan's individual learning plan.

Within this process of target setting, the school practitioners and Charlie's parents use their knowledge and understanding about the specific social contexts and group processes with which Charlie ordinarily engages. Practitioners regularly carry out observations and assessments of children's activity within their early years classroom, trying to make sense of their learning experiences in order to understand what children know and can do. Charlie's parents too attend closely to his experiences of the world and try to understand them. The fact that Charlie has autism means that adults must work harder to do this, and indeed may never fully know exactly how he experiences the world. Nevertheless, careful thinking and sharing of their ideas and interpretations with other adults will help them gain a better understanding of Charlie's experiences and how they can support his learning.

This chapter and the two chapters that follow concern the inclusion of children within ordinary mainstream school settings, describing similar educational practices to those used to support Charlie's learning. This chapter will introduce the agenda of inclusive education, describing features of educational practice that are particularly relevant to the inclusion of children with autism in mainstream settings. It will be noted that key amongst these is the issue of practitioners finding out about the learning experiences of the children with autism with whom they work, though it will also be noted that the process by which they do this is not a straightforward one. The chapter will go on to outline the range of approaches that are available within autism education in school settings, discussing these in relation to sociocultural theory.

Barriers and benefits of inclusive education for children with autism

Inclusion is a term that that has in recent years replaced the idea of integration for children with special educational needs and disability. Inclusion presents a more radical proposal than integration since it implies the accommodation rather than assimilation of all children irrespective of need or disability and puts the burden of change upon the school rather than the individual child (Slee, 2001). It introduces the language of human rights to education with the aim of eliminating exclusionary practices that originate in people's attitudes and responses to diversity and difference (Ainscow, 2007). Inclusion promotes the social model over the deficit model of disability by framing the difficulties that are experienced by individual children as partly the product of a disabling environment. The emphasis is less on essential differences between children, less on the idea of a 'norm' that is desirable for all, and less on the need for specialized treatment packages. In place of this, inclusion highlights capacity over deficit, entitlement over need, and similarities and differences over difference alone (Norwich and Lewis, 2005).

Research into the inclusion of children with autism in mainstream school settings presents a mixed picture. In the UK, the majority of children with autism are educated in the mainstream sector (DfE, 2010), with a sharp increase in numbers occurring in response to the introduction of the inclusion agenda (DfEE, 1997). Despite this, considerable challenges exist for students with autism in mainstream schools, who are much more likely than other students to be excluded and who report higher levels of social rejection and bullying (Humphrey and Symes, 2010; Symes and Humphrey, 2011). Even compared to other children with special educational needs and disability, they appear to encounter more barriers to inclusion in ordinary settings, with school experienced by children and young people with autism as increasingly difficult as they become older and move on to secondary school education (Humphrey and Lewis, 2008; Ochs et al., 2001).

However, it is clearly the case that inclusive schools provide important opportunities for learning and social inclusion for students with autism. Research indicates that where school leadership strongly supports inclusion and where there is a culture of collaboration, positive attitude and respect, inclusion can result in positive outcomes and experiences (Ainscow, 2007; Symes and Humphrey, 2011). Like all children, children and young people with autism often express the same desire to be socially included and have friends (Beresford et al., 2007), and inclusive schools are seen as the setting best suited to realizing these goals. We know what are the common features of an effective approach to achieving important learning aims for students with autism, though which aspects of various strategies and techniques are significant and what works for whom remains unclear (Parsons et al., 2009). Supporting the social development of a child with autism is key amongst these and the lively and engaging presence of other children that exists within a mainstream setting is, of course, an important factor in this.

A critical context for successful inclusion of students with special educational needs and disability is other people's understandings, attitudes, beliefs and responses, that is, the adults and children who engage with them. Change and development within this context is viewed as the basis for positive experiences of inclusion and progress in a child's learning and is discussed more fully below.

The importance of attitudes and knowledge to inclusive practice

In much of the literature on inclusion, the realization of inclusive practice is thought to depend largely on changing attitudes and a re-conceptualization of the role of school practitioners. The school resource pack, *Index for Inclusion*, reframes 'special educational needs' as 'barriers to learning and participation' and advises that a way of minimizing these is through reflection by practitioners and the school community on their values and understandings (Booth et al., 2000). Inclusion requires teachers to be more critically aware, more reflective practitioners who are capable of greater depth of thought on inclusion issues and of making changes in their day-to-day actions and interactions (Giangreco, 2003). Rose (2001) argues that inclusive practice should include a more collaborative framework with clear roles, effective use of support staff and closer family involvement. Teachers are seen as centrally placed to bring this about since it is they who have the immediate information about a child's engagement with their learning and who can see what really goes on.

Perhaps not surprisingly, the inclusion agenda has given rise to an interest in teachers' attitudes and investigations of their values and understandings. In an extensive review of teachers' attitudes towards integration and inclusion, Avramidis and Norwich (2002) found that teachers hold differing opinions about inclusion and that attitudes correlate strongly to the nature and severity of a student's disability. Positive attitudes are contingent upon how well the inclusive placement has been organized, the presence of supporting factors such as specialist equipment and specialist advice, and on whether the teacher has had previous positive experience of inclusion. Croll and Moses (2000) found an 'I am committed to inclusion *but...*' attitude where school practitioners qualify their support depending on the special educational need in question, children designated as having 'emotional and behavioural difficulty' being seen as the least likely to be included successfully. They make a distinction in practitioners' attitudes between what is felt to be morally right – full inclusion – and what is thought to be realistic, that is, partial inclusion based on the severity of a child's behaviour and needs. Practitioners identify a number of prerequisites for successful inclusion which include appropriate professional development (Nutbrown and Clough, 2006), additional staffing in classrooms and time for pre-planning and liaison (Rose, 2001), and advice on effective ways of working provided by outside agencies such as school psychologists (Farrell, 2004).

It is notable that in the literature on general attitudes towards inclusion, autism is not singled out as especially difficult to include, unlike children with emotional and behavioural difficulty. McGregor and Campbell (2001) found that, at 86 per cent, the majority of mainstream teachers agree with inclusion of children with autism, though only where sufficient support, resources and training is available. Reflecting findings about teacher attitudes to inclusion in general, Helps *et al.* (1999) found from their survey of teachers' views that support for inclusion of children with autism was partly contingent on the severity of their needs and whether behavioural difficulties were present. This was also the finding of Robertson *et al.* (2003), who reported that teachers generally experienced positive relationships with their students with autism, but that the presence of challenging behaviour had a negative impact on this and on the level of the child with autism's social inclusion within the class group.

Research into inclusive education for students with autism raises the possibility that it is not only teachers' attitudes that are relevant to successful inclusion, but that the attitudes and understandings of support workers and peers involved with a student with autism are also key contexts for inclusion. Emam and Farrell (2009), for example, found that where teachers experience difficulty in understanding the social-emotional needs of a student with autism, they rely heavily on the support worker who is working with the child and who knows that child well. In a similar vein, Ochs *et al.* (2001) found that the pressure on teachers to deliver academic progress and manage discipline meant that the inclusion of students with autism often becomes the responsibility of the peers within their group, who experience greater and more continuous amounts of social contact. Both these studies suggest that change needs to be thought of in terms of teacher attitudes and roles as well as in relation to the knowledge, understandings and attitudes of all those involved with a child or young person with autism.

Importantly, research into attitudes towards the inclusion of students with autism has highlighted the issue of knowledge – the knowledge that children and adults have about autism as a condition and knowledge about the specific needs of the student with autism – as one that is at the heart of autism education. Ochs *et al.* (2001) found that inclusion was positively experienced where people had knowledge of the student's diagnosis of autism, whilst Emam and Farrell (2009) found that lack of knowledge about autism as a condition leads to an experience of tension and anxiety in teachers. Indeed, investigation into what works in practice indicates that knowledge is *the* issue of autism education since teachers must first be able to understand the particular experience of learning for the individual student with autism in order to be effective in their practice (Jones *et al.*, 2009). Writing about whether special pedagogies are necessary for children with autism, Jordan (2005) points out that gaining this knowledge is not, however, a straightforward process. She challenges the 'curriculum for all' argument by pointing out that autism education is not simply about adapting the curriculum but concerns specific knowledge about the condition and how it 'transforms meaning' of the world for the individual. She argues that the normal intuition of teachers is not helpful where autism is concerned and can be misleading (see also Powell and Jordan, 1993). Research indicates, moreover, that school practitioners can have significant misconceptions about autism compared to specialists in autism, some teachers believing that autism has an emotional basis and is not a developmental disorder or associated with learning difficulties (Helps *et al.*, 1999; Stone and Rosenbaum, 1988).

Knowledge about the individual and their behaviour is a social process that may involve the feeling we definitely know something, but can also involve the feeling that we know something only in part or that we do not know. Knowing – particularly about something as complex as social phenomena – often involves a continual alignment of existing knowledge to new information, experiences and understandings. Adjusting knowledge can have a strong emotional impact on the individual that gives rise to mental states of ambivalence, worry, concern and resistance to change. In the general literature on inclusion, this is often conceptualized as a major barrier to the realization of inclusion. Practitioners knowing about students with special educational needs and disability and trying to work out if they are different from or the same as other students, can give rise to tension and 'internally contradictory' views even within one professional (Croll and Moses, 2000). With autism education, the issue of knowledge must be seen as particularly problematic. Children with autism often do develop, but their needs are highly individual and it is unclear what works for whom. Sometimes support strategies work, but sometimes they do not. Some children have needs that are intractable to any kind of intervention and the advice of autism specialists is not always reliable. There is little clarity at the level of policy or research, the latter often reporting complex, confusing and sometimes contradictory results. Again as Jordan (2005) points out, there is knowledge, but there is no *established* knowledge base within autism education.

Advocates of inclusion argue that the difficult issue of knowledge means effective inclusionary practice can only be achieved where there is sufficient depth of thought and the continual questioning of strategies. Practitioners must be reflective and develop 'an enhanced capacity to think' about the experience and subjectivity of the included student. As Giangreco comments:

> You don't gain the ability to deal with the complexity of people just by acquiring an abundance of strategies. You gain the ability to deal with the complexity of people from depth of thought.
>
> (2003: 40)

Hart (2000) recommends the use of 'interactive viewing' by teachers where, in supporting the child, they explore the connections between the child and their environment and re-examine their own assumptions, trying to see things more from the child's point of view. Thus, they may choose to value diversity, appreciate difference, focus on ability, reflect on their own attitudes, beliefs and expectations, and view the environment as more or less enabling. The process by which school practitioners are able to do this in relation to included students with autism is looked at in much more depth in the chapter that follows. This concerns the professional practice of teachers and the nature of teaching and learning contexts, and outlines how reflective practice can enable practitioners to develop their knowledge about the learning experiences of children with autism and so plan and deliver teaching more effectively. Before that, this chapter will go on to outline methods that are used to educate students with autism in inclusive settings and discuss the key rationale underpinning these methods taking a sociocultural perspective.

Approaches to autism education in mainstream schools

Though no one approach to the education of children with autism is seen as able to address the range of needs that exist for students with autism, there is a generally agreed consensus about the key principles of effective teaching and learning. Children with autism have a wide range of learning needs in cognition, language and communication, social development, emotional understanding and perceptual-sensorimotor development. They may have specific difficulties with the achievement of skills in literacy and numeracy, and difficulty understanding concepts within the topic content of curriculum areas. Their sensory processing needs may additionally mean that their capacity to access aspects of ordinary learning environments is reduced. The principles of autism education, therefore, involve provision for different learning needs using a range of strategies and techniques.

First and foremost amongst these is the use of unambiguous and simply phrased instruction that is sometimes repeated, written down or visually supported as an aid to understanding and memory. The social communication difficulties of autism mean that children may need to be individually addressed and provided with extra explanation and instruction of teaching content with higher levels of adult support and guidance (Sherratt, 2005). A system of structured teaching is often used to address difficulties in receptive and expressive language, attention, working memory and personal organization. Structured teaching aims to maximize students' independence in thinking and learning by breaking down learning tasks into single steps, clearly setting out expectations within a task using larger amounts of visual information and instruction than is usually the case (Mesibov and Howley, 2003). Individualized learning tasks may be more appropriate for students with autism compared to other students, with a closer link made between the student's personal experience of the world and the content of teaching material. This is by way of overcoming the difficulties that people with autism have in acquiring knowledge and understanding of the world and generalizing their own learning. It is also the case that areas of social-emotional learning may have to be specifically addressed educationally with students with autism using special curriculum materials designed for this purpose (Iovannone et al., 2003).

The shared nature of difficulty in autism, where difficulty in social communication and understanding is experienced not only by the person with autism but also by those with whom they interact, means that a key principle of autism education involves the development of other people's awareness and understanding. As with inclusive education generally, effective practice in relation to students with autism is seen as involving a whole-school approach where all staff demonstrate an awareness, understanding and acceptance of the child's needs (Symes and Humphrey, 2011). Clear policy and guidance, strong leadership and a positive attitude towards difference and diversity are further features of successful inclusion for children and young people with autism in school settings, though the attitudes and understanding of peers is also seen as important. Disability awareness training, adult mediation of friendships and closer than usual monitoring of peer relations to ensure that teasing and bullying does not occur are all seen as crucial areas of support. Effective partnerships with parents are also seen as critical to effective practice since this contributes to the development of understanding of a child with autism and makes support for families possible.

For children and young people with autism in educational settings, social and learning experiences, the busyness of the school day and the whole environment of the school can give rise to considerably raised levels of stress and anxiety. Inclusive education for children with autism thus makes provision for consistent routines in addition to clear communication, and prior warning about transitions and changes to routine. The behaviour of children and young people is often considered in the light of challenges that exist within the social and sensory environment, the processing of social, sensory and perceptual information seen as more tiring and stressful for students with autism who may need regular breaks from their learning with minimal social contact and permission to pursue special interests (Fletcher-Campbell, 2003).

The challenges posed by the actual environment of the school may additionally require environmental audits and adaptations. Consideration may need to be given to the amount of sensory stimulation they contain for a student with autism; for example, the quality and amount of noise, lighting and movement. Sensory-integration difficulties may raise issues about where a student sits, what is in their sightlines and how often they are allowed breaks from learning. Additionally, students with autism may be provided with a non-social 'safe haven' or 'grey haven', a low arousal environment where they can go when feeling stressed and overwhelmed by sensory and social experiences.

The rationale that underpins these principles of autism education is that having the condition means an essential difference in the individual child with autism, one that gives rise to a different kind of learning profile. Educational practice is seen as needing to suit the particular ways in which students with autism understand and learn with special attention given to the communication processes that are used. However, the inclusion of children and young people with autism in mainstream settings is also driven by the understanding that it is possible for students with autism to acquire social learning within ordinary contexts, through social participation and cooperation with other children and adults. Thus, support for the development of children with autism in schools is seen as needing to maintain a balance between providing ordinary experiences of relationships and shared communication within natural contexts and the strategic application of support and teaching of specific skills and social understandings. As Jordan points out (2005), the challenge is to provide a common pedagogy that is suitable for all children as well as aspects of a therapeutic model of learning that addresses what is unique in the learning of the child with autism.

Autism education is sometimes described as having pedagogical features that are 'social' and 'non-social', where social learning involves teaching that is delivered in ordinary ways; for example, through teacher instruction and social interaction within the classroom, and non-social learning involves a student being instructed 'asocially'; for example, through access to visual instruction or a computer-based programme (Powell, 2000). This perceived dichotomy, however, highlights a misunderstanding in the literature on autism about what 'social' means. The idea that social experience is encountered only within social interaction is in fact too narrow a view since the social world can take a multitude of forms: in written texts, images, cultural practices, ideas, routines and so on. Thus, visual instruction has a social basis and refers to people's ideas, communications and practices. Similarly, using a computer programme is accessing culture that has been socially produced and participating in a cultural routine that is increasingly present within some social communities, albeit ones that are more active outside schools.

What is different about the social participation of the individual with autism is the reduced richness of their social sharing and difficulty in producing culture flexibly and appropriately to suit particular contexts. Taking a sociocultural perspective on the principles of autism education and the teaching strategies that are typically used allows one to see a common factor. This is the adjustment of social contexts and support for social experiences in order to facilitate access by a child with autism, with a possible added element of reducing sensory processing interference. There are many methods used in autism education that, in essence, serve to slow down, simplify and delineate sociocultural experiences, thereby reducing very rich, continuous and multilayered social processes to more manageable amounts. The communication forms that are used in the TEACCH method and in other visual communication systems could be seen in this light: as language or social information that is 'slowed down' and 'fixed on paper' as opposed to produced very fast and 'disappearing into the air'. These approaches may take away the physical presence of another person or dictate that the communicative partner acts in highly socially predictable ways – such as in the Picture Exchange Communication System (PECS) – but this does not make the experience 'non-social'. Rather, it ensures that social experience is less rich, less complex, less dynamic and therefore more comprehensible to the child with autism.

The strategic teaching of aspects of social knowledge, skill and understanding could also be viewed in this way. There is some theoretical disagreement about whether the individual with autism has fewer 'scripts' than other people and so needs to learn more (Bauminger, 2004), or whether they are too scripted and artificial in terms of their social responses (Kasari *et al.*, 2001), but the answer probably lies somewhere in between. Children who do not have autism are socialized and participate in cultural routines, but they do so in a way that is so dynamic and fast-paced that it is a barely conscious process. Sociocultural practices do contain ideas, understandings and routines that are learned and shared, but the rich and constantly changing nature of socioculture means that socialization processes are not fixed and cannot be taught reliably across different communities, cultures or periods of time. Children with autism may be supported to gain a better understanding of what is 'going on socially between people' in their setting, though it is the case that they may never be fully fluent in appropriating and using culture, or even see this as a proper personal goal.

However, social communities are varied and culture is incredibly diverse. Not all children are socialized in the same way and social processes have unexpected outcomes. There are also cultural forms of sharing that are more available than others to the individual with autism; for example, ones that involve less person-to-person contact or that are more about physical presence rather than verbal communication or that focus on certain practices and cultural preferences. It is important, therefore, to think about development as taking different forms for different individuals and of children finding their 'social niche', where social sharing and inclusion *for them* can maximally occur. The next two chapters will discuss this further, looking at how education for children with autism must take account of difference and diversity in terms of social learning and the differing features of social contexts in which all children engage.

Summary

This chapter has described the inclusive education agenda as one that is concerned with the accommodation of difference and diversity within schools and focuses on the elimination of exclusionary practices. The attitudes and understandings of school practitioners and peers are key indicators of effective inclusion, including in relation to students with autism. However, knowledge about the particular subjective experience of autism is seen as a particularly important, unique and difficult challenge within autism education. Key principles of approaches to autism education have been described and discussed in relation to sociocultural processes. It has been suggested that an important rationale underpinning these principles is the reduction of social information and simplifying of social experience as a way of enabling the social participation of children with autism.

Chapter 7

From intervention to reflective teaching in autism education

School field note, Monday 10.30 am

Emily approached different groups of children at playtime today, all groups of girls. She sat near to where they were playing and watched them intently, but none of the girls noticed her, probably because she always sat out of their view. At one point, Emily pulled the rope of the swing seat on the adventure trail where some girls sat as if to indicate her presence and interest in them, but she was standing to one side of the trail and the girls did not notice her.

Emily did engage with a small group that included Nathan and Sara, who themselves are often on the edge of the children's play. They played a game of walking along a low wall, jumping down and laughing when they reached the end but mostly not talking to each other. Emily laughed and looked at the others, appearing to enjoy the play. At one point, however, the other two reached the end of wall before Emily and suddenly ran off. Emily did not to notice them going (she was concentrating on moving her feet along the wall) and when she reached the end was surprised to find them gone. She looked around but could not spot them. By the end of playtime, she was on her own again.

This field note that has been written by a support worker following a playtime observation of the child with autism with whom she works, Emily, aged 6. The school is pleased with Emily's progress, especially in terms of her learning in class, but is concerned by her lack of inclusion with her peers. The decision is made to carry out systematic observations at playtimes to see what is happening within her interactions with her peers: how interactions begin, what happens in interactions and why they break down. The observation provided here, one of a series of observations that are carried out over the course of three weeks, records a similar pattern of behaviours. Emily shows an interest in her peers, often sitting near them and watching them, but tending not to talk to them and not signalling her interest in them in ways they notice. She does not track the social movement of other children well, with the result that she often loses contact with a child with whom she is playing.

The support worker discusses the findings of her observations with Emily's class teacher and the school coordinator for children with special educational needs, both of whom have made observations of their own. It is decided that Emily's interest in and willingness to go up to others are positive behaviours and that her interest in girls of her age is socially appropriate and should be encouraged. They also note that Emily has a small group of children with whom she plays in a more sustained way, which includes Nathan and Sara. The practitioners feel that a non-intrusive approach is needed, one that does not encroach too much on what is happening socially for Emily and that can support interaction as it happens. A plan of support is agreed which involves the support worker monitoring Emily at playtimes from a distance and intervening on occasion. Monitoring is for the purpose of knowing when to intervene in peer interactions and support is to take the form of encouraging peers to notice Emily's presence and notify Emily of peer intentions in play; for example, to move to another area of the playground. Finally, it is decided that the class teacher will pair Emily with Nathan and Sara for classroom activities as a way of encouraging these friendships.

It is notable that this way of supporting the social development of children with autism in schools involves a considerable amount of time watching children and thinking about what they do. Planning support and the delivery of teaching on the basis of information that is gathered about children's actual experiences can be a powerful way of facilitating their learning and development. Paying attention to what is going on within the group also allows support to be provided to other children and influences their patterns of behaviour. This form of teaching, where practitioners spend time watching and learning about what children naturally do then apply support strategically, is known as reflective teaching and is considered to be the most effective way of supporting children's learning. It reflects understandings in the psychology of education about how children are active as learners and engage with experience in different ways, constructing their own knowledge and understandings. Reflective teaching involves the understanding that teachers must find out about children as learners in order to be able to guide further learning.

This chapter concerns the education of children with autism in ordinary school settings and how it can best be aligned with what we know about quality in educational practice. Best practice in education involves the teacher accurately knowing the needs of the learner. It is closely linked with making educational assessments of learning contexts and with reflective teaching where teachers and students think together about learning processes. This chapter outlines how autism education can produce value in children's learning by focusing on real-life learning contexts and children's engagement with these. It will describe the teacher as a professional working closely together with other professionals and with parents in a team approach to support the needs of children with autism and their peers. The focus of this support is on careful analysis of social contexts, since this is where learning occurs, and the application of tailor-made strategies of support. It will be argued that it is in this way that autism education is most likely to identify effective learning targets and create an impact on children's learning.

Children as learners

In the literature on educational approaches to supporting the social development of children with autism, the concept of 'intervention' is often used to convey the idea that educational practice in autism is about using teaching to target a 'deficit skill' in the individual – much like a drug might target symptoms of a disease – and so support development, though interventions are not in themselves seen as a cure. It is a view of education that is influenced by the dominant medical discourse of autism theory and practice and is different from that found in current educational theory. This conceptualizes education as a process that involves both teaching and learning. Education is conceived of as the instruction of educational material but also, crucially, the learner's experience of learning contexts (Kyriacou, 2009). Learning is a rich process that encompasses natural stages in the development of the child together with the provision of educational experiences. The teacher sets up the learning environment and provides learning experiences, but it is the child as learner who engages in and makes sense of these. Highly influential to contemporary understandings of children as learners is the work of psychologists such as Margaret Donaldson (1978) in the 1970s and Barbara Tizard and Martin Hughes (1984) a decade later. Their investigations into young children at home and at school showed that children's learning is responsive to the social and language contexts in which it occurs, children having greater intellectual ability where learning situations are meaningful to them. Learning is an interactive process that involves a number of pedagogical features including the needs of the learner, relationships and the learning environment, as well as the selection of appropriate teaching strategies. The process of education is one of teaching plus the way in which learning is experienced, itself dependent on the attention, motivation and well-being of the learner (Skinner, 2010).

The concept of teaching and learning that exists in schools today moves education on from behavioural approaches to learning, that conceive of it as a situation of stimulus and response, as well as Piagetian constructivist ideas about education, which view the child as individualistically accommodating learning experience. It is influenced by sociocultural theory which highlights the fact that children as learners are active in engaging with learning and constructing their own meanings about experience and that the teacher is active too, in engaging children, making sense of what they know and moving them on.

Teachers must engage with children's existing conceptual and cultural understandings in order to 'scaffold' and extend children's knowledge.

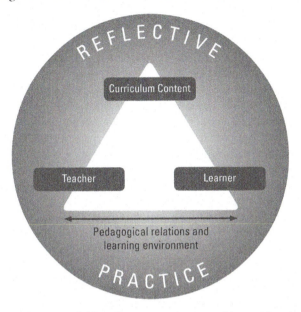

Figure 7.1 The pedagogy model for effective practice in teaching and learning (adapted from Hudson, 2000)

The model for pedagogy showing the components of effective educational practice is depicted in Figure 7.1. Learning is a social process that is dynamic and dependent on the nature of pedagogical relationships. The teacher makes teaching decisions and uses teaching strategies about what is being instructed, but based on the experience of learning for the learner. Teachers are encouraged to be reflective and think about the learner, adjusting contents, strategies, relationships and expectations depending on need. Even aspects of learning that can be thought of in terms of teaching fixed skills may require some consideration of how learning is experienced. Learning multiplication tables, for example, may be a straightforward teaching exercise for a student who is numerically able and a confident learner. For a student who has some learning difficulty or lacks self-confidence, however, there may need to be more consideration of their experience of learning and attention to the quality of pedagogical relations.

Teaching and learning is a dynamic process that is best described in terms of individual variation, creativity and resourcefulness. This is the case for both teachers and learners. Teachers are professionals who continuously plan, adjust and develop their practice as they assess learner needs. There is much evidence to show that original ideas behind teaching strategies are changed and adapted with use and over time (Meyer *et al.*, 1998; Thomas and Loxley, 2007). Autism education emphasizes programmes and practices that have been developed through research with the expectation that these will be strictly and identically applied by practitioners, but critically this does not factor in the processes that operate in teaching and learning. The fact that procedures are not used in their original form is part of the folklore of autism, but there is little consideration of whether the expectation of strictly standardized practice in terms of social-emotional teaching and learning is a reasonable one.

Effective teaching practice is based on knowing about students' progress and difficulties and this makes educational assessment an essential process within teaching and learning. Practitioners must first assess where the learner is at in terms of their learning before decisions can be made about how to instruct. They have varied means by which they do this, but all would be described as assessment for learning. Assessment and teacher reflection are the key to effective practice in education because they provide the link between the two components of education: teaching and learning. They are so central to educational practice, yet so overlooked in autism education, that it is worthwhile giving some consideration to the form and purpose of assessment and the nature of reflective teaching as a way of thinking more clearly about the education of students with autism.

Form and purpose of educational assessment

Assessing children's learning and development cannot be separated from delivery of the curriculum and takes two basic forms. Summative assessment refers to assessment that is carried out periodically and measures students' attainment. Examples of summative assessment would be end of year profiles, end of unit tests and state examinations. In summative assessment, the focus is on student learning relative to a set of standards and the information gathered is used for the purpose of grading and reporting. Generally speaking, its use in classroom management, the delivery of the curriculum and everyday teaching decisions is minimal.

Summative assessment is viewed as separate from the assessment that practitioners carry out in an ongoing, everyday way to inform their teaching. The distinction is made between assessment *of* learning, which would be described as summative assessment, and assessment *for* learning. This second type of assessment is known as formative assessment and is seen as integral to the education process. Formative assessment – assessment for learning – provides information about the way in which the learner is experiencing learning and the nature of their understanding and helps the teacher to know how to proceed in their teaching and whether any adjustments are necessary. It is part of practice and as such is not about holding children accountable for what they know, as it is in summative assessment. Assessment for learning allows for the fact that students are in the process of learning a skill or concept and as such may not have full understanding or capacity. It is more about the teacher gaining knowledge about how the student is learning and where they are in terms of their learning.

In the UK, the Assessment Reform Group (2002) has provided ten principles of assessment for learning to help guide classroom practice. These set out the essential features of assessment and focus on the fact that it can be used to inform the planning of teaching and learning. Much of what teachers and learners do in a classroom could be described as assessment, with learners prompted to show their knowledge and understanding and teachers taking time to observe, analyse and interpret learners' contributions. Assessment for learning is sensitive to the emotional impact of learning and constructive in viewing strengths as well as difficulties. An important principle of assessment for learning is that teachers share what is happening within the teaching and learning context with the student. Students can be helped by knowing what it is they are learning as well as by being given feedback on what they have achieved. They can also be informed about next steps in their learning, with information about these also informed by the assessment process. Providing students with feedback is seen as important since it makes the link for the student between what is being taught and what is being learned. Research indicates that talking to students about their learning and providing feedback on their experience of learning are the most effective instructional tools to use to move them on in their development (Airasian and Russell, 2008).

Assessment for learning is increasingly seen as the approach to education that is most likely to deliver quality and the raising of standards (Wiliam and Leahy, 2007). It is an approach that encourages a thoughtful and reflective style in practitioners and ensures that teaching is aligned with learning. Perhaps more importantly, it ensures teaching and learning reflect understandings in the psychology of education about learning motivation and how human beings develop. It focuses on social contexts and incorporates the social and emotional aspects of learning, seeing these as the foundational experiences out of which all learning emerges (Wood, 1998).

Unsurprisingly, ideas about assessment for learning are strongly present in early years education, the area of education most concerned with the early capacities that underpin our development as human beings. Assessment is a critical part of curriculum delivery in the early years and seeks to gain an understanding of how young children's actions are related to thought, making extensive use of observation, talking to children and parents, and careful analysis and interpretation of pupil profiles (Nutbrown and Carter, 2010). Early years assessment usually takes an ecological and sociocultural perspective, focusing on naturally occurring learning situations, looking at the whole child within social contexts – perhaps at home and at school – and taking an interest in what the child is able to do and does know (Williamson et al., 2006). Influenced by developments in early childhood education, particularly the Reggio Emilia schools system in northern Italy and the New Zealand early years curriculum, Te Whāriki (Ministry of Education, 1996), the emphasis is on a child-centred approach that does not impose a predetermined framework of educational expectations and norms, but starts with the child's experience, interest and knowledge of the world. It uses understandings about the social basis of learning and the different processes involved that are taken from sociocultural theory. Thus, what the child is doing is highlighted, as is the experience of relationship within the learning context, the existence of mutual understanding and reciprocity and the degree of collaboration involved (Dunphy, 2008). Early years assessment acknowledges that there are many naturally occurring factors that impact on children's learning, not all of which are planned by the teacher, but some of which may be the key to a child moving on in terms of their understanding.

Early years education theory has most fully conceptualized children's learning as the acquiring of new understandings within social contexts, children's attainment of knowledge seen to come out of social relations in the classroom. Defining the learning process within the early years, Rinaldi (2006) describes it as a process of construction rather than one of transmission. She rejects the idea of learning as a tree pattern, with pre-determined and overarching branches of concepts-to-be-learned, and uses the analogy of a rhizome that has no hierarchy but does have a multiplicity of connections. Children move themselves forward in terms of their learning, with the support and encouragement of the adults around them and building on what they already know.

It could be said that early years practice has most overlap with autism education since both are strongly interested in children's social-emotional engagement, interactions and experiences of relationships, communication and social sharing. Autism education is also concerned with the early capacities that support human development, but guidelines for autism practice seldom reflect what is considered good practice – including in assessment – in early years education. Autism education does not tend to take an interest in social contexts, the holistic development of the child and their experiences of relationships. The emphasis is invariably on the individual child with assessment methods often reflecting diagnostic measures, involving tick lists to record single capacities. Indeed, actual diagnostic screening tools are sometimes recommended for use in schools with no recognition that the purpose of educational assessment is different from that of assessment for diagnosis, being much more interested in learning contexts. The use of individual screening tools can result in large amounts of information being collected about one child with autism, with no insight provided into the nature of social relations within a setting and therefore no practical information about how adjustments can be made or learning support provided. Screening-type measures also focus on deficits and do not highlight what the child can do and what exists within the environment to support their learning and development.

European guidelines on special educational needs highlight the fact that children with special educational needs can benefit from an approach to teaching and learning that includes the use of individualized profiles, created from observations, talking to children and parents, and other methods in assessment for learning (EADSNE, 2009). In a report on educational assessment and autism in the UK, Wilkinson and Twist (2010) point out that assessment for learning is viewed as having an important role in inclusive education, but note that there is no guidance and little research into the use of assessment for learning strategies with students with autism. It was noted in Chapter 6 that research into inclusive practices in autism education indicates that autism remains poorly understood in mainstream schools, teachers feeling that they lack the appropriate knowledge and resources to deliver quality in their practice (Emam and Farrell, 2009; Jones et al., 2009). It is the case that the application of assessment for learning principles to the inclusive education of students with autism could go a long way in addressing this identified need in practitioners. It is also the case that assessment for learning could make a valuable contribution to individualized education plans and the personalized learning agenda that is seen to be critical within autism education (Humphrey and Parkinson, 2006; Parsons et al., 2009).

Reflective teaching

Assessment for learning is closely tied up with the concept of reflective teaching. This encompasses the idea that adults do not know everything about children's experiences and must take steps to understand them. The child's lived experience is crucial to their learning, but an adult cannot necessarily immediately apprehend it. As we saw in the descriptions of children playing in Chapter 4, neither do adults have full access to children's experiences of group processes and may need to reconstruct these with children to gain a proper understanding. Reflective teaching thus involves investigation into and a process of thinking about the nature of children's experiences. The child is envisaged as an 'expert' on themselves and the teacher's role is more one of 'follower'. The reflective teacher accepts a less powerful role than, say, the didactic teacher, but ultimately is more effective in terms of their impact on children's learning.

Reflective teaching has blurred the boundaries between teaching and research, with the teacher and the process of teaching both described using the language of social research (Clark and Moss, 2005). The image is of the 'rich child' who is embarked on a course of constructing knowledge about the world around and of the 'teacher interpreter' who does not impose themselves but tries to explore, make sense of and reflect on this, and so move the child on (Rinaldi, 2006). Engagement with the learning process means, above all, the practitioner engaging with complexity, taking an interactive view that suspends judgement, tries to understand the child's point of view and takes time to explore connections between a child's actions and influences within the environment (Hart and Travers, 2003).

Reflective teaching is concerned with the professional expertise of the teacher and views teaching as a highly skilled activity which requires teachers to reflect on their own practice. Pollard (2008) describes this as 'evidence-informed professionalism' and sets out the range of methods of enquiry that can be used to provide an adequate analysis of the complex factors involved in the process of learning. Observation is seen as key amongst these, but questioning children and finding ways to record and share information with children and adults are further features. Different methods of observation are possible, but the emphasis is on trying to see and understand what the child can do without imposing pre-given, adult-driven expectations and norms. Observation can take a systematic form, with the teacher intentionally focusing on certain aspects of behaviour, skill, groups or times of the day, but decisions about what to observe are informed by their knowledge of the learning context gained from preliminary and exploratory investigations. Thus, the emphasis is much less on categories of 'normal development' taken from developmental psychology and more on the social constructions that are in place within a particular setting.

Observation is combined with questioning children about their activity. Again, questioning can take different forms and can be part of classroom talk, an interruption of group activity or within individual sessions between teacher and child, but it is always sensitive to children's cultures and concerns. The teacher is required to pay attention to their use of language in questioning, adopting the child's own language and level of language where possible and trying to understand the child's construction of meaning. 'Active listening' is a concept used in connection with reflective practice. This concerns the idea of 'tuning in' to the child by paying attention to all aspects of their communication – not just the spoken word – and giving children time to communicate without jumping to hasty conclusions. Building trust within relationships is seen as important and both questioning and observing should be within positive and constructive experiences of relationships. Constructive enquiry focuses on strengths, considers feelings and tries to see things from the child's point of view.

Recording and sharing information about children's learning are further features of reflective practice. This is sometimes described as 'documentation' and also involves a range of possible methods. Choosing which method to use is contingent on the nature of what is being investigated and can include producing descriptive accounts based on information gathered from observation and talking to children, recording information in diaries which are kept by the teacher or student, taking photographs and video, and using children's output from classroom tasks. The purpose of documentation is to profile students' learning and make the learning process visible and shareable. Sharing information with students enables them to 'see' their learning and this can aid the process of consolidation of knowledge and produce further learning. In Chapter 8, we will see how documentation of children's play using observation, recording and subsequent sharing of information gathered in this way can support the inclusion of a child with autism in imaginative playground games. However, the process of sharing can also be for the purpose of allowing teachers to reflect on their own knowledge and understanding and can be used to inform planning. Information that is documented can be discussed with other adults, including parents and outside support agencies, and can contribute to the development of an appropriately individualized curriculum.

The process of enquiry is itself a powerful method that can produce development in the child without recourse to further teaching strategies. It can bring about change in teaching practice too as well as change in other aspects of the learning environment. As outlined in the previous chapter, inclusive education requires teachers to be critical and reflective practitioners who are able to consider and adjust their own practice. Attitudes, values, understandings, resources and systems within a setting contribute to the creation of barriers to learning, and attention to these is seen as the basis of a properly inclusive environment (Booth et al., 2000).

Teachers as professionals reflecting on learning in discussions with students and developing their own practice is removed from the view of the teacher that exists in autism education. This largely conceives of education as a fairly rigid practice and teaching strategies developed by researchers rather than teachers. The emphasis is on evidence-based practice with the view taken that evidence of what works educationally for students with autism must be gained from large-scale randomized controlled trials written up as educational manuals (Smith et al., 2007). In an interesting discussion of what constitutes evidence-based practice, Mesibov and Shea (2011) point out that differing ideas exist about what evidence is. They note that, in the United States, different guidelines for best practice in psychology use different sets of criteria, some of which strictly promote practice that has been tested within experimental designs and others which also recognise 'the best available research and clinical expertise within the context of patient characteristics, culture, values and preferences'. They also note that, where best practice in education has been described in strictly science-based terms, this has led to protest within the educational community to 'a myopic view of science in general and a misunderstanding of educational research in particular' (quoted in Mesibov and Shea, 2011: 116–18).

The argument here is that reflective teaching has much to offer autism education. A reflective approach to autism education makes sense when one considers the issues that exist in both the teaching and the learning of students with autism. Autism education is focused on social learning, but often uses the idea of hypothetical social contexts in social skills training. Students learning about what they might do in imagined situations is at odds with the idea of learning emerging from experiences of actual social contexts. Reflective teaching focuses on actual contexts and the fact that children with autism tend to be partly engaged with these means that some degree of reflection is possible. In Chapter 4, the descriptive accounts of children with and without autism interacting and playing together illustrates that enquiry into actual contexts is of value in highlighting what a child with autism knows and can do, as well as the nature of difficulty. The idea that reflective teaching facilitates planning for further steps is just as relevant to autism education, the engagement with children's actual social experiences allowing the specifics of any difficulty to be seen. It is the specificities of a social context that often suggest the way forward in terms of learning, without reference to performance indicators or developmental pathways. A child and their friend who do not talk to each other may need prompting and reminding of possible scripts *in situ* – the situation itself suggesting the content of talk – rather than a more abstract learning of 'conversation skills' within separate social skills groups.

In fact, the idea of students with autism reflecting on social experience is already present within autism education. Approaches such as social skills training, Social Stories[TM] and discussing video footage of social engagement are predicated on the idea that children with autism need to pay special attention to aspects of social experience that are not fully understood. Sociocultural theory adds the idea that learning must always be based on actual social contexts and real-life relationships, and that learning can occur for all those involved. There is a debate within the literature on autism about whether it is possible for individuals with autism to follow the same developmental pathway as typically developing individuals, with the idea put forward that it is better to think of children with autism having to consciously, rather than naturally, learn social strategies and understandings (Kasari *et al.*, 2001). Reflective teaching provides just this kind of approach, where real-life experience is highlighted, visualized in some way and the meaning made more explicit so that students can learn.

Reflective teaching has an important contribution to make to the learning process, but it has value in terms of teaching practice too. In Chapter 1, it was noted that a key aspect of autism education is working with an 'autism lens' to see and understand the behaviour of the child with autism. It is by virtue of the teacher being able to see and understand behaviour that effectiveness in communication and other aspects of teaching practice is often achieved. Being able to see and understand autism is not the exclusive preserve of autism specialists and is something that can be learned (Theodorou and Nind, 2010). Clearly, reflective evidence-informed practice has an important role to play here since it encourages thinking through teaching and is concerned with the development of professional practice. Ordinary classroom teachers and support workers may need initial support in doing this, but many do go on to develop a good understanding and awareness of the nature of behaviours seen in children with autism.

Evidence-informed practice in autism education

Evidence-informed practice in autism education recognizes social-emotional learning as a key goal of pedagogy and emphasizes the need for close attention to children's experiences in real-life here and now contexts. Real-life social experiences within actual group processes are viewed as foundational to the child with autism's social development and learning. Evidence-informed practice recognizes that learning contexts are diverse, rich and complex, even for a child with autism, and require careful analysis of the individual features of specific contexts. There is the understanding that support for development of a child with autism does not necessarily involve the delivery of direct teaching, but does necessitate taking time to consider children's lived experience and the strengths and weaknesses of the child, the social context and the learning environment. Recognition is thus given to the fact that autism education concerns both the development of the individual child with autism within a particular setting and the development of the setting, including other people, children and adults. Autism is a lifelong condition and a disability and the expectation of change cannot be on the child with autism only.

Recent prevalence studies of children and young people in the UK suggest that 1 per cent of the population is affected (Baron-Cohen *et al.*, 2009), with two-thirds of these educated in mainstream settings (DfE, 2010). All teachers, therefore, can expect to be a teacher of children with autism. Evidence-informed practice recognizes that teachers are professionals who plan and adjust their practice based on their assessments of students' learning needs. Autism education should concern the facilitation of teachers to more effectively do this. However, what constitutes evidence should be viewed in local as well as general terms. Evidence exists in information about what works in practice gained from research findings and written up in professional publications. But methods of local enquiry should also be employed by teachers and other professionals involved in supporting a child with autism to gather evidence of learning strengths and needs.

To support the social development of children with autism in schools, practitioners should be less concerned with individual behaviour and more with group processes and individual participation in these. These processes are public, performative and open to being observed and involve patterns of participation that exist over time. What is of interest is sociocultural activity within the particular setting, including children's use of cultural resources and the comparative facility of all children in producing these. Questions to be explored might be: 'What social competencies do children demonstrate in this setting?', 'What roles exist in children's play?', 'Is "best friends" a norm?' and 'What do children talk about?' Investigation of the wider peer group would be carried out to gain information about the pattern of social mixing within the general group, dominant play themes and patterns of cultural interests and concerns. More focused investigation of the child with autism and members of their peer group, if one exists, would be used to gather information about social activities, interests and roles. Areas to assess would include the similarities and differences in sociocultural activity between the focus child and their peer group, and between that peer group and the wider group. In this way, the appropriateness of activity as it is experienced by the child, the peer group and the wider group could be assessed alongside, crucially, the nature of peer responses.

Box 7.1 Questions for formative assessment of children's experiences of social processes within everyday contexts

Play activity

- What are the dominant play themes in the wider group, focus group and for the individual child with autism (for example, superhero play, physical play such as running and jumping, ball play, chatting)?
- What cultural resources are typically used in the wider group, focus group and by the child with autism (for example, television programmes, make-believe characters, sporting figures)?
- How is the larger play space used by different groups and for different play activities?
- Where does the focus group/individual child play and how do they use their play space?
- What play equipment is available and who uses it?
- What forms of communication are typically used in play?
- What social roles are typically being taken in play and who is taking what role?
- How do games begin?
- How much enjoyment do children derive from their play?

Children's talk

- What are children's preferred communicative modes (for example, verbal, non-verbal, movement, sound effects)?
- What is the proportion of verbal to non-verbal language used in the wider group, focus group and by the individual child?
- What do children talk about?
- What is the 'flow' and quality of talk (for example, conversational, single words or short phrases only)?
- How do children describe themselves and each other?

Friendship

- What patterns of friendship exist in the wider group and focus group (for example, large loose groups of friends, small tight groups of friends, strongly gender specific friendship groups)?
- Is having a best friend a norm or are there few best friend dyads?
- How much is conflict an issue in friendships?
- How do friends talk about their friendship and describe each other?
- What friendship activity goes on outside of school?

Box 7.1 outlines questions to ask when carrying out assessment for learning, though, given the diverse and rich nature of culture, these should not be seen as universally appropriate or as a finite list. What is being assessed is *comparative facility* and questions such as these should be addressed for the small group that includes a child with autism as well as for the individual child with autism, but always in relation to what is going on within the wider context.

Methods for gathering information about children's social learning

In autism education, methods of enquiry and processes of assessment for learning are determined by the fact that enquiry concerns a child with autism whose participation in socioculture will be individualistic and only partly socially based. Investigation of sociocultural activity often involves analysis of language use, but the use of language cannot be viewed as straightforward in the case of autism. Methods of enquiry would not therefore rely on language-based methods alone or, as with research into autism outlined in Chapter 5, be left open to individual interpretation. Observation will be the most powerful method of enquiry for educational practitioners and outside support agencies investigating social processes that include a child with autism, and should be an ongoing feature of practice, but other methods of enquiry also exist. Assessment, moreover, is of the whole sociocultural environment, including adult awareness and the whole social environment, though not the sensory environment which would constitute an important but separate area of investigation in autism education. What follows is an outline of possible methods of enquiry to investigate children's social learning which include the following:

- observing and recording
- listening
- systematic observation
- taking photographs
- child conferencing.

Observing and recording

Observation as a method of enquiry takes different forms, which range from a systematic look at a specific issue or behaviour to taking a more open-ended and less prescribed view. However, observing should be seen as a key aspect of professional practice and includes watching children, listening to them, and taking time to note down observations and think about what has been seen and heard. Educational practitioners often feel the pressure to *do*, that is, deliver teaching, but observing children should be viewed as part of teaching practice. This is something that early years practitioners understand well, but, given the particular social needs of children with autism that require focused support for social development well after the early years, it is something that practitioners working with older children must learn too.

Participant observation is a non-intrusive form of observation that occurs as the practitioner is involved with children and will probably be the starting point for enquiry into children's learning. Participant observation is an effective way of gaining information about the quality of children's experiences and interactions and so is particularly relevant to autism education. Observations can be carried out in different places, at different times of the day and on different days of the week so that comparisons can be made of responses to different conditions and where different people and activities are involved. Regular observation is important because it allows patterns within social activity to be seen. Of interest are questions such as: 'What patterns of activity exist for individual children and particular groups?', 'How do patterns change depending on who or what is involved?' and 'How do established patterns change over time?' Making observations allows us to see new skills and abilities in children emerge and keeping a record of observations means having evidence of progress.

A limitation of participant observation is that it relies on the ability of the observer to remember the small details of what they see. Knowing what to observe and improving one's memory for detail are skills that can be improved, but keeping quickly jotted notes during an observation is a useful practice. These can be compiled into a record of observation or written up as field notes or a diary shortly after an observation. Notes can be made of the routines, experiences and activities that children enjoy, move towards, seek out and have skills in. Notes can also be made of what children find difficult, move away from and what makes them feel anxious. Recording children's emotional responses to experience – and changes in these – is a central feature of making observations and something that should be carefully analysed by practitioners in reviewing observational information.

Keeping an open mind and trying to be objective is an important aspect of practice. Being open to what children's experience is and paying attention to one's own preconceptions and judgements is part of professional practice. In doing this, it is helpful if observations are carried out by more than one practitioner, with school staff and the multiprofessional team taking time to discuss and analyse observations and compare findings. This in itself is a key process in reflective practice and is discussed more fully below.

Observation as a method of enquiry can be combined with other methods to provide a fuller and richer picture of social processes and a child's social participation in these. Methods can be used interactively so that they help to inform and extend each other. What methods are used will be determined partly by whose perspective is being considered. Addressing this question as well as the question of how and when best to capture this perspective will narrow down what methods of enquiry to employ. Figure 7.2 shows the process of assessment for learning that begins with the child and actual social

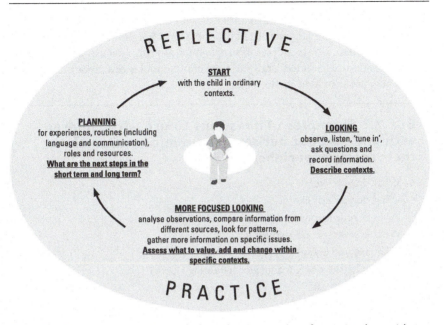

Figure 7.2 The process of gathering evidence for the purpose of assessing the social strengths and difficulties of a child with autism within specific contexts (adapted from DCSF, 2008)

contexts and uses observation and a system of progressive focusing to assess strengths and difficulties, and the similarities and differences of the child within the particular setting. This process very specifically identifies learning needs and leads to the setting of highly informed and precise targets. Further methods for gathering information are outlined below.

Listening

Informal questioning of children during an observation is an effective way of providing more detailed information about what is being observed. Children can be asked what they just said to each other (if that cannot be overheard by the adult), what game they are playing, what they are doing in this particular bit of the game, whose idea it was first and what they are planning to do next. If observing and questioning children is done on a regular enough basis, children get used to this kind of interruption so that it does not overly intrude on their interactional flow.

Questioning children is a language-based method and so needs to be used with caution with children with autism. Keeping language simple, phrasing questions straightforwardly and questioning children *in situ*, so that objects or parts of the play space can be visually referred to, are all effective methods for listening to children, including children with autism. Research indicates that children with autism typically make friends with children who also have special educational needs and language used in simple and straightforward ways will be of benefit to them too. Examples of simple question forms to use with children, ones that are open-ended and do not draw conclusions about children's experience, are provided in Box 7.2.

Box 7.2 Examples of questions to use with children with and without autism to gain information about their social experiences

- What do you like?
- What do you not like?
- What is your favourite...?
- What is your second favourite?
- What are you doing?
- What is he/she doing (naming or indicating a peer)?
- Who did this first?
- What happens next?

Listening to staff and parents would also be a method of enquiry. Different adults hold different kinds of knowledge about children, some having more access to children's social experience. Observing and listening to children might give rise to a more formal set of questions to address to parents or to practitioners who work in specific areas; for example, who supervise in the playground. Listening to adults is for the purpose of gathering further information about children's social functioning and adds to the creation of an overall picture of a child or a group.

Systematic observation

Observation can be carried out in more planned and formal ways. Preliminary investigation into children's social experience might give rise to particular issues that require more focused investigation and a preconceived set of behaviours about which observational information is sought. Equally, there may be a focus on particular cultural routines, times of the day or a group of children. Practitioners might systematically carry out an observation or allocate a time of day. They may use a structured schedule to record particular aspects of behaviour that have been identified by other means as significant. Methods of quantifying behaviour may be appropriate at this stage. A timed interval method may be used to determine the frequency of a behaviour, event sampling may be used to track the use of an identified routine, and mapping procedure may be used to systematically record a child's use of the play space if this is seen as a key issue in their learning.

Taking photographs

Taking photographs and obtaining video footage is often recommended within evidence-informed practice as a way of gathering visual evidence of children's social experience. This is valuable when it comes to sharing and reviewing information with children and adults and as evidence of learning and progress. Methods in reflective practice often recommend giving cameras to children to take photographs, but images produced by children with autism will not be open to the same level of cultural sharing and interpretation as those taken by their peers and it is probably better to think in terms of adults taking photographs. If this is done regularly enough and carried out in a sufficiently discreet way, children will become accustomed to having their photograph taken. An effective way of obtaining this type of evidence is to identify places or routines about which visual evidence is required through non-intrusive participant observation and then, at a later date, ask children to pose in that routine, game, interaction or behaviour. Except in cases where children believe a behaviour or routine may prompt some kind of adult control or reprimand, they are usually happy and eager to do this.

Attention to the sounds and borrowed phrases children use in their play and interactions may also be an important source of information. These are the aspects of play that children often say they particularly enjoy and appreciate in each other. Making sound recordings of these and playing them back for children to comment on can provide valuable information about how all children are experiencing play and interaction, including that of a child with autism.

Child conferencing

Children can be invited to talk about their peers and review social experiences in structured ways. Child conferencing is a short interview with a child or small group of children that can be used to review information that has been gathered about them or explore further a theme or issue that has been raised by other methods of enquiry (Clark and Moss, 2001). For children with autism, basing the conference on visual information can be an effective way of working. Children can be asked to draw a peer and say what they like about them and their favourite things to do together. Or they can be shown photographs of children in their peer group or of activities in the playground and asked to describe them. Child conferencing is not a strictly formal question and answer session but more a conversation with a purpose where children are engaged in talk about their social experiences, supported by review material and visual evidence wherever possible.

Consideration should be given to whether conferencing is carried out with individuals or in groups. The presence of a peer or peers will probably influence a child's responses and individual sessions may be preferred for this reason.

However, group interviews allow the social structures that are naturally in place within a group to be seen and can be helpful.

Organizing and reviewing information for the purpose of identifying learning targets

The process of gathering and documenting information about children's social experiences is for the purpose of providing concrete examples upon which to reflect. It provides the means by which practitioners are able to engage in conversations with children and adults about children's learning processes. In educational theory, it is conceptualized as a process of 'visualization' that allows the sharing of the child's experience, with the child as well as with others in their world (Dahlberg et al., 2006). It is the teacher who enables children to revisit their actions which in turn becomes integral to their process of understanding and knowledge-building (Rinaldi, 2005).

Organizing information can take a number of different forms, including creating pictorial displays, social profile booklets and Learning Stories (Carr and Lee, 2012). Information can be organized according to dominant themes within interaction and play or the key skills that children demonstrate, but it is important to remember that it should centrally address group processes within a setting and the child's engagement with these. Children's concerns and areas of difficulty can also be addressed, although these will need to be handled constructively when setting out information, since all children can be sensitive on matters relating to difficult aspects of social experience.

Reviewing information can also take different forms and involve conversations between practitioners, between practitioners and children, and between practitioners and parents (Clark, 2005). The role of outside agencies is important in this respect since professionals who specialize in autism can help school practitioners to make sense of the information they have gained about the child and the group. They can also assist in the assessment of what needs to be valued within learning contexts and what needs to be added or changed. It is at this point that the need for further information about a specific issue may be highlighted as important.

For children and adults who are reflecting on this kind of rich information about children's experiences and the ways in which they are making sense of things, the experience of review can provide a powerful form of learning, as well as further information about what children know and understand. Reviewing information can also support planning for next steps in learning.

In the literature on autism, the setting of learning targets is often conceptualized as the addressing of single aspects of individual behaviour in the child with autism. Measurement of single skill areas is frequently recommended as clear evidence of progress, but this is problematic when one considers the complex and interactive nature of social learning. In their survey of the quality of individual education plans (IEPs) for young children with autism, Ruble et al.

(2010) found IEPs to be generally poor according to their criteria of having specific goals for the individual child and measuring these in unambiguous ways. However, what these authors did not question is whether the uniformity of failure in the IEPs they surveyed to meet these criteria reflects the unsuitability of using standards that conceptualize social-emotional learning as involving single skills and individual behaviour alone. Social-emotional learning and the details of what is happening within dyadic and group processes do not lend themselves to the setting of learning targets that concern the individual child with autism only. Moreover, measurement of the social-emotional experiences that are crucial to learning and development – that is, quality in social engagement, emotional experience and group dynamic – require much more in the way of detailed and contextualized information.

Children with autism are partly engaged in social learning and, as with other children, the process of setting targets needs to be one where evidence is used to devise a plan of support that takes a holistic, ecological and sociocultural approach to development. Sociocultural theory emphasizes the need to think in terms of group processes and social contexts when thinking about the development of the individual. The social model of disability adds the idea that the individual's experience of disability rests partly in the social constructions of others. This makes the consideration of group targets or individual targets – but for a peer other than the child with autism – an important one (Conn, 2013b). Research shows that children with autism often make friends with children who also have some kind of learning or developmental need and it is wholly sensible that target setting should seek to support the development of all the children concerned. As well as other people's behaviour, target setting might concern aspects of the environment, including sensory features, social routines and general levels of knowledge and understanding.

From the examples that have been provided throughout this chapter, it is possible to see that reflective teaching and assessment for learning strategies give information about specific issues in relation to children's social learning. These approaches are engaged with the specificities of learning and so give rise to clear indications of learning competency and areas of learning need. It is possible to see too that measurement of progress and identification of learning targets need to be based more on the judgements of professionals and parents, making reference to socialization goals that exist within curricula for social-emotional education but also taking into account local, individualistic and one-off factors.

Summary

This chapter has outlined our understanding of children's learning as being closely linked to the social contexts in which it occurs, contingent upon how children engage with and make sense of learning experiences and how adults support them in this. Educational theory views children's learning as involving processes in both the delivery of curricula and the learner's engagement with their learning and prioritizes the teacher taking time to consider the needs of the learner. Methods in educational assessment and reflective teaching which allow teachers to explore children's experiences of real-life learning contexts are seen as key to attaining quality in education. Methods for gathering information about the social learning of children with autism and their peers have been outlined. It has been argued that information gathered using these methods provides a firm foundation for the identification of clear learning targets and planning of teaching.

Chapter 8

Supporting the development of play

Laurie plays Families

Laurie sometimes plays a game called Families with Ella and Aesha. She plays Families in the playground at breaktime, on the bench by the classroom door. Ella is the leader and tells the story. She pretends that the area around the bench is home and that she is Mum. Laurie and Aesha are the children and the bench is where they go to sleep. They pretend that the kitchen is by the windowsill and that there is a table on the ramp. Laurie, Ella and Aesha pretend to cook in the kitchen, make cakes out of leaves and eat them at the table.

Sometimes Ella tells Laurie and Aesha to go to bed. They pretend to brush their teeth, lie on their bed and sometimes listen to a bedtime story. Laurie pretends to go to sleep and then get woken up in the morning.

Laurie really enjoys playing Families with her friends. When she plays, she smiles and looks at what her friends are doing. She lies on the bench with the others and pretends to cook in the kitchen. She listens to Ella tell the story and imagines that she is in bed or eating her dinner.

When Laurie plays with her friends she can try to talk to them and say, 'Night-night Mum' and 'Dinner's ready!'

Laurie, aged 7, a young girl with autism, attends her local mainstream school and is included in an ordinary mainstream class. She has some language and is interested in other children, interacting with them regularly, though often in non-verbal ways. In recent months, she has begun to join in with the imaginative play of her classmates, particularly a small group of girls who often play together. These girls play a variety of games including one they call Families. Laurie's support worker, who helps her in the mornings, and her teacher have taken time to observe the girls. The children have been playing the same game over and over again, repeating many aspects of the story, and this makes it possible for the adults to identify patterns in their play. Laurie's support worker and her teacher have noticed that Laurie really enjoys Families and is particularly good at joining in with her peers when they are playing this game. Laurie's support worker writes a Learning Story about Laurie playing the game, making sure she uses simple language in her description. She asks the children to pose for photographs in different parts of the game and also takes photographs of the bench, the windowsill and the ramp outside the classroom door, all of which feature in the story. She asks Laurie to help her decorate the story with pictures of homes and families using storybooks from the classroom and children's drawings.

Laurie reads the Learning Story with her support worker. It documents her increasing ability to attend to and follow what her peers are doing in play, to copy their actions and to think of pretend actions of her own. The story gives Laurie an overview of what is going on in the game, including the different uses of the play space and the roles that she and her friends adopt. It points out what skills she is using as a way of highlighting for her what is important in her social behaviour. In this way, the Learning Story supports Laurie's participation in the play, deepening her understanding of what she and her friends are doing. When Laurie is playing Families and other imaginative games, it is apparent to the adults who support her that she does not always fully share the imagined pretence. It may also be the case that Laurie's imaginary experience within these games is different, her imagining taking a more sensory-based form; for example, more focused on the lighting in her imagined bedroom, the feel of being in bed or the taste of the food. Nevertheless, reading the Learning Story with her support worker helps to transmit more explicitly to Laurie the culture that is being naturally and collectively produced by her and her friends and encourages her to use more social routines in her play.

This chapter explores what we do when we support the development of play in children with autism and describes a number of ways in which children can be facilitated to join in more effectively with others. Support for the development of play is viewed as needing to be based on the actual games that children create and on their real-life play experiences, such as Laurie's experience of Families. The focus of support, moreover, needs to be on the essential ingredients of play, that is, the child's attitude in play – their playfulness, personal investment in the play and experience of positive affect – as much as if not more than on the play actions they carry out. The perspective on children's play is a sociocultural one that views play as a complex phenomenon. Children's play is varied and includes not only imaginative play but also motor play, language play, sensory play, rough and tumble play, and risk-taking play amongst many other forms (Burghardt, 2011). Play serves different purposes too, supporting the child's development in different domains including intellectual development, the development of a capacity for social-emotional participation and the development of the child's integration of movement. Development itself is seen as occurring as the result of the interrelation of different areas of cognitive, social-emotional and motor-perceptual operation; for example, the child's development of motor function having an important impact on their social inclusion and capacity to join in with the games of other children.

Play is viewed as occurring within different contexts where differing goals, influences and understandings are present. Support for the development of play requires consideration of the particular features of a context and the range of influences on play that are specifically present. What are the personal resources, interests and play preferences that this particular group of children bring at this time? What are their cultural understandings as well as the understandings of the adults who encourage and support the play? What are the social, physical and intellectual demands of this particular play form or game and how are children interpreting and resolving these? The play space itself is a further consideration since this also provides play opportunities and constraints. How do children collectively understand the uses of the play space for this play activity and how does this understanding change over time?

Children with autism are described in this chapter as having particular preferences in play, carrying out play with stronger than usual sensory, perceptual and motor features that are, nevertheless, within the knowledge and understanding of other children who do not have autism. Children without autism also have their own preferences, skills and interests in play and the differing ways of supporting groups of children to participate together more effectively in ordinary, naturally occurring play processes are discussed in relation to different social contexts.

Sociocultural perspectives on play differences in autism

Play is a defining feature of autism, children with autism typically producing less play, showing less sophistication in play and playing at a slower rate than other children. In Chapter 1 it was noted that research findings show children with autism can play and do develop in terms of their play, but tend to generate fewer ideas, produce more repeated acts and spend more time looking away. In episodes of shared play, they are less likely to engage the playful interest of others. It was also noted that the difficulties children with autism experience in relation to play are not only in relation to the creation of pretence – their experience of other forms of play also showing differential participation and areas of challenge. Children with autism appear to have certain play preferences that include play with a sensorimotor component, physical forms of play such as rough and tumble play, and play that is socially organized in unambiguous ways. Many writers with autism emphasize these aspects of play, describing intense sensory play experiences and other experiences, such as collecting and categorizing objects, that stand apart from what is typically thought of as children's play.

Sociocultural explanations for the differences that exist in the play of children with autism would focus on the social basis of play itself. Almost all forms of ordinary play have a social component where children use objects in culturally informed ways or play out narratives that are based on real-life social experiences. Children bring social knowledge, understandings and practices even to solitary play, and engage with objects and other children in playful ways that are strongly influenced by their experiences of their families and the wider world around them (Howes, 2011). They coordinate their play to that of others and produce shared ideas through collectively produced actions. The well-documented difficulties children with autism have in producing pretend play would also be seen as a result of the strong social basis of this area of development. Research into the creation of pretend play no longer sees it as individual cognitive behaviour but something that is social in origin (Lillard, 2011). Children initially perform symbolic acts in the ways they have first seen adults do, developing their use of objects as symbols in the same way that they develop language (Striano et al., 2001). Using the research method of slowed-down video footage of mother and baby interactions, Lillard (2006) vividly describes how children's first pretend acts emerge out of social engagement with their primary carer. She found that verbal cues are insignificant in carrying out early pretence, mothers not saying to the infant that they are pretending and the word 'pretend' seldom used. In early pretence, the mother's language is simpler and more repetitive and the voice louder and more sing-song. However, what is most marked in the behaviour of both mothers and infants in pretend play is their social behaviours. Mothers use a range of non-linguistic markers to cue for the infant that 'this is pretend', including using actions in a faster way that involves an exaggerated use of space and more repetition. They also look at the infant much more, smiling more and for longer periods of time. When mothers perform real acts they look more at the object, but when they are pretending they look more at the child. Children of all ages bring their own social skills to pretend situations too. They do more back and forth looking – between the mother and the object used in pretence – than would normally be the case in real-life situations and also interpret the mother's smiling when carrying out a pretend action as a form of social referencing, that this is pretence.

Children with autism are less socially engaged than typically developing children and participate in fewer social experiences and cultural routines. They have less awareness of the world around them and will be engaged with family members, teachers and friends in ways that are only partly social. Gunilla Gerland (1997) is one of many writers with autism who has described how her experience of relatedness to others was derived more from their sensory impact on her than any socially formed sense of personality, relationship or interaction. In autism, knowledge of others and what they do is much less known as back and forth experiences of shared social meaning. Gerland describes how her feelings about people were based on an accumulation of rich sensory data – the sensory quality of their voice, the sensory quality of the situation in which the person was first perceived – and that this constituted her 'thinking' about the person and the situation. From a sociocultural perspective, the development of play in children with autism is affected by this kind of reduced capacity for social participation. Autism has a genetic basis and is not caused by social factors, but the effect of having the condition impacts on development that is largely socially based. Reduced levels of social motivation, differential forms of social orientation, reduced experiences of joint attention and cumulatively less knowledge of people, culture and the world around would all impact on the capacity of the child with autism to join in with socially based forms of play, that is, most forms of ordinary play. Equally, the differences in the play of children with autism (for example, their preference for sensory and physical forms of play) would be a result of the reduced social content that is present in these types of play. Again from a sociocultural perspective, children with autism are viewed as moving away from play that is strongly socially based, such as pretend play, and towards play that is less socially arduous and demanding of high levels of social participation.

However, it must not be forgotten that socioculture is characterized by diversity and play difference in autism should be viewed in relation to this too. Children's ordinary play worlds are varied, not all children playing in the same way and children without autism also having their own play preferences. All children play at different levels of sophistication and have differing play interests. Some children without autism, for example, show very little interest in imaginative play whilst others play only in imaginative ways (Sutton-Smith, 1997). Different forms of play exist too, ones involving differing amounts of cultural activity and social engagement. Some forms of play, such as motor play, mastery play, risk-taking and rough and tumble play, may emphasize physical exertion over social orientation. Other aspects of ordinary children's play, such as dizzy play, involve children momentarily experiencing play as purely physical and sensory pleasure that is independent of culture and thought (Caillois, 1958). The play preferences of children with autism could be seen, therefore, as further variation within cultural diversity and affirmed as a natural outcome of the differential subjective experience of individuals with autism.

Importantly from children's perspectives, the play of a child with autism will not necessarily be judged as outside the experience of other children and as something with which they cannot engage. Play involves processes of communication and children may try to play with each other, with varying degrees of success and varying experiences of pleasure in this. A key consideration is the issue of the outward appearance of play. When we look at the play activity of children with autism, we cannot know just by looking that it does or does not take the same social-based form as that of ordinary play. We do not know, for example, whether a child with autism we see performing karate chops in the playground next to their peers is acting according to a culturally shareable schema – of martial arts, say, or masculinity, bravery and strength – or whether they are simply responding at a motor-perceptual level to the actual or remembered physical actions of others. To put it another way, we cannot know whether a child with autism who is performing karate chops alongside his peers is interpreting an episode of imaginary role play as one that, for them, involves physical play. It is possible that the outer features of children's play and interactions have some degree of stand-alone quality in children's play worlds that makes them open to simple perceptual appreciation, by a child with autism say, as well as a more sophisticated, interpersonal and mentalistic experience of shared cultural meaning. It stands to reason that what we as adults cannot fully discern, cannot be discerned by children, though it is the nature of their participation in sociocultural processes to try anyway to interpret what is going on and act according to those interpretations. The experience of playing with a child with autism who is performing karate chops in the playground, therefore, would depend on who is doing the perceiving. If the child without autism is also interested in physical play, the situation of play might continue to be enjoyed by both players but within a context of physical relatedness. The essential ingredients of play (that is, the experience of positive affect, a playful attitude and intrinsic motivation to engage) would continue to exist, but the play itself would take a slightly different form. The child without autism who has a strong investment in the imaginary aspects of the play, however, may become frustrated at this point and seek ways of controlling, changing or ending the play.

Hobson's (1993b) discussion of the differing forms of self-experience in relation to perceptions of the environment provides some helpful insight on this point. He notes that differing forms of self co-exist within human consciousness, with a fundamental distinction existing between the self that perceives and operates within the non-personal world of objects and actions, and the self that relates interpersonally with other people. He makes reference to the work of Martin Buber (1958) who distinguished between 'I–It' and 'I–Thou' forms of relatedness. I–Thou relatedness concerns an interpersonal self that has the capacity for reflective self-awareness and an emotionally based consciousness of other people's mental states. By contrast, I–It relatedness involves a more primitive awareness of an 'I' in relation to a non-personal world that does not have a sense of being an object to itself or within the perspective of others. Hobson also cites Neisser (1988) who characterized I–It relations as belonging to an impersonal 'ecological self' which perceives the self as separate from the environment and from 'things'. This stands in contrast to the interpersonal self, I–Thou, that perceives the self as separate from other people who are experienced by the individual as mentally as well as physically present. Crucially, however, Hobson notes that I–It relatedness does involve some cognitive, conative and affective states, having a sense of physical location, bodily coherence, personal agency and understanding of simple goal-oriented actions. There can thus be a relation to other people, but not people conceptualized as 'persons', but rather people experienced as objects within the environment.

Along with other theorists, Hobson makes the connection between the experience of impersonal I–It relatedness and autism (see also Zahavi, 2005). He cautions against too simplified a distinction between interpersonal and impersonal relatedness given that autism involves difficulty in relating to the world of things as well as to the world of people. Nevertheless, he points out that there exists an overlap between relating to people as objects in the environment and people as subjects since both are located in the same place – the body of the person – and are engaged in the same activity. As Hobson (1990) writes, 'I–Thou and I–It relations converge on the bodies of others'.

Conceptualizing the self as ecological as well as interpersonal may help us to understand how children with and without autism are able to have a sense of a shared experience in play despite social-cognitive differences. Play could be described as concerned with levels of meaning that are culturally and intersubjectively shared, but also with ecological aspects of relatedness, perhaps especially for a child with autism. Some forms of play will be more relevant in this respect than others. Shared meaning in play that is less contingently based on social understandings or involves simpler forms of social sharing (for example, physical play) may be more readily experienced interpersonally as shared ideas but also impersonally as straightforwardly discernible features or 'objects' within the environment. The performative, physical, often non-linguistic communicative modes favoured by some children in play may be more suitable to this kind of sharing too, that is, one that is available as interpersonal experience as well as and alongside one that is impersonally and objectively striking and open to appreciation by children who are not, or not as, interpersonally engaged.

A programme to support the development of play in children with autism needs to take account of the fact that children with autism probably have different experiences of play. Supporting play in autism is not simply about facilitating children with autism to play 'more like typically developing children', who in actuality do not all play in the same ways. Supporting play in actual real-life contexts should be focused on developing the richness and mutuality of enjoyment in play experiences for children with and without autism whilst valuing the existence of differences. It is about finding children who can be supported to play with each other in ways that are sufficiently enjoyable to motivate them to carry on playing and being together. Supporting play should concern supporting playmates who share some common features in their play, personal resources and interests, and who are more likely to want to engage with each other in ordinary, natural social contexts. Organizing the play environment, planning for play activities, observing and analysing children's play, and playing alongside children are all useful forms of support that adults can provide. However, children's rights in relation to play is an issue that is relevant here. As Mastrangelo (2009) points out, an important definition of play is that it should be enjoyable, voluntary and intrinsically motivating. It would be a paradox, for example, to think of play as something that adults direct children to do. Behavioural interventions that involve an adult imparting play skills to a child and setting play goals could not be seen as proper play. The right of children to play is part of the agenda of children's rights set out in the UN Convention on the Rights of the Child (UN General Assembly, 1989), and the right of children with autism to play in ways that are differential but nevertheless described by those with the condition as playful and enjoyable, must be taken seriously.

Taking all this together and in a similar vein to other areas of autism theory and practice that have already been discussed, the development of play in children with autism needs to take account of different factors, some of which may be hard to reconcile but which nevertheless encompass features within the play of children with autism and ordinary play contexts. To summarize, these are:

- children with autism can play to some extent and do tend to develop in terms of their play;
- there is no indication that their experience of play takes the same form as typically developing children with the possibility that, as a child with autism develops, play continues to be a more sensorily- and perceptually based experience than it is for other children;
- children with autism have certain preferences in terms of play, which include sensorimotor play and physical play;
- all children have their own play preferences and play at different levels of sophistication;
- children's play in ordinary contexts is characterized by variation and diversity, some forms of play, such as pretend play, having a stronger social component than others;
- children's play in ordinary contexts is emergent, being a process of communication between players with outcomes that cannot be assumed in advance.

The next section will look more closely at the underlying concepts that are involved in thinking about how to support the development of play of children with autism and their friends in ordinary school settings. A framework for conceptualizing the development of play of children with autism, one that takes account of the differences in children's play, will be outlined. It will be argued that, from a sociocultural perspective, it is important to identify the appropriate form of play for the individual, dyad or group, acknowledging children's diverse experiences of play, valuing their differences and seeing personal enjoyment as a key feature of play.

Conceptualizing the nature of development of play in autism

Different frameworks are used to conceptualize the development of play in children with autism. Most frequently used is one based on Piaget's (1954) developmental stages of intellectual growth. This focuses on the development of the capacity for pretence and fits well with what was considered a key feature of autism. Piaget envisaged children as moving from an early stage of sensorimotor experience of objects to later and more sophisticated stages in which objects are related to other objects in ways that involve their properties (relational play) and the everyday uses of an object (functional play). The final stage of pretend play initially involves almost identical actions to real-life actions, what Piaget referred to as 'deferred imitation', but is later 'decoupled' from here and now experience to exist as mental schema that is available for symbolic use.

The important concept underlining this framework is Piaget's notion of the child's developing capacity to move from egocentric thinking, where experience is processed in concrete ways only, to sociocentric thinking, where children are able to process experience from the point of view of others. Piaget conceptualized young children's exploration of objects as a process of assimilation to their own mental schema that also involves an adjustment of these mental conceptions to accommodate influences within the environment. Piaget argued that intellectual growth comes about through the child reconstructing ideas that were formed at an earlier stage, higher-order thinking taking a more abstract and less concrete-based form.

Though Piagetian theory has been hugely influential on ideas about child development, subsequent theorizing has questioned aspects of his developmental model. Most importantly, it does not take account of the cultural support provided by the environment, in particular the child's primary carers, to the development of mind. Children do not develop in isolation but through interactions with their carers. It is the child's internalization of co-constructions of meaning about these shared experiences and increasingly complex use of language, symbols and social participation that provides the foundation for the development of cognition (Dehart et al., 2003). Piaget's model disregards the fact that children at different ages have some flexibility about how they engage with objects depending on the nature of the play activity itself (Hughes, 2009). It is also the case that other forms of play exist in children's worlds that do not clearly fit this model and so are overlooked (Sutton-Smith, 1997). These include forms of play with which children with autism more readily engage, such as physical play, and that, from some children's perspectives, are equal to pretend play in their enjoyment and legitimacy as play activities.

Another framework that is used in the literature on autism to conceptualize the development of play concerns the idea of stages of children's participation in play (Parten, 1932). This was developed from watching young children's activity in free play sessions and involves six stages of children's social involvement with others: the child moving from unoccupied to solitary, onlooker, parallel, associative and finally cooperative forms of participation in play. According to this model, the child becomes increasingly able to associate with others, communicate ideas, cooperate and share intentions. As with Piaget's stages of play, this model is useful in thinking about autism since it focuses on a key aspect of difficulty: social participation in play with others. However, like Piaget's model, it too overlooks the fact that age is not the only determinant of children's participation in play with others, the form of play children engage in also being an influencing factor.

Whilst individualistic stages of development, increasing capacity to symbolize and more sophistication in terms of relatedness all remain relevant to our thinking about the development of play, there needs to be consideration of other issues in relation to autism and play. The idea of stages of play and cooperation in play provides part of the picture, so to speak, without addressing the whole complexity of play. They focus on some types of play and aspects of relatedness in play, but do not acknowledge other features of play that are critical to a consideration of autism and play. There is no possibility of conceptualizing a differential form of development of play in autism, for example, or of children playing flexibly with each other, depending on the type of play they are engaging in and who they are playing with.

A framework for the development of play in autism that accounts for a differential experience of play in autism and tries to encompass a wider developmental and sociocultural perspective on play is provided in Figure 8.1. This framework has the advantage of highlighting the continuing existence of a differential experience of play in autism, one that remains more sensorily and ecologically based throughout development. It starts with the natural form engagement with the environment takes for children with autism – sensory engagement – and does not focus on the development of one type of play only. It makes the distinction between sharing social meaning in play – what is often first achieved in play encounters with adults – and playing with other children. Sharing social meaning is the focus of many developmental approaches used in autism education to develop two-way communication and usually involves an

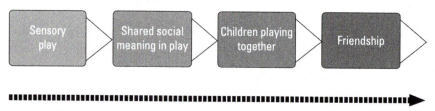

Sensory, perceptual and motor features remain strong features of play

Figure 8.1 A framework for conceptualizing the development of play in children with autism within specific contexts

Table 8.1 The contexts of play for a child with autism at different stages of play development

Stage of development	Social context	Examples of group processes	Complexity of experience	Quality of emotion
Sensory play	No social context.	No group process.	May involve sensory, perceptual and motor complexity, but no social complexity.	Probably rich.
Shared social meaning in play	Intense experiences of one-to-one relationship, usually child–adult. Adult tries to 'tune in' to child and follow their lead. Play context is carefully organized, e.g. play materials matched to child's interests and tolerances.	Circles or cycles of communication characterized by repeated gaining, sharing and withdrawing of attention. Shared attention to single objects or experiences, exaggerated affect on part of adult. Sensory-perceptual experience given gloss of social meaning by adult, e.g. by adding rhythm, social gesture and language.	Simple, pared down social experiences with reduced use of language, body posture, movement, etc on the part of the adult, though may be amplified use of face and vocalization.	Mixed – the adult must work towards maximizing pleasure in social contact and reducing anxiety caused by social and environmental features.

Table 8.1 The contexts of play for a child with autism at different stages of play development (continued)

Stage of development	Social context	Examples of group processes	Complexity of experience	Quality of emotion
Children playing together	Spontaneous play and playful interaction in natural settings. Age, gender and race influences may operate differently from children without autism. Adults structure and monitor play environments and support children to find suitable playmates. They encourage and give positive feedback.	Processes of communication between play partners are emergent and have socially positive as well as negative outcomes. Children use a range of communicative modes. Adoption of different social roles in play, e.g. one child leads, the other follows. Play partners may share some preferences in terms of play, e.g. both enjoying physical aspects of play or play that involves minimal communication.	Naturally occurring play and playful activity has social complexity, though child with autism's experience may have stronger sensory, perceptual and motor features.	Mixed for all children – play and interaction may feel appropriate and enjoyable, or socially disjointed, frustrating and unsatisfying. Differing emotional experience leads to different social outcomes: continued play and interaction, or communication breakdown, discord and criticism.
Friendship	Children seek each other out to be with. Adult (parents/teachers) mediation of friendship to arrange meetings, suggest activities, negotiate interactions – more than for children without autism and until an older age.	Shared enjoyment of play preferences and cultural interests. Children enjoy the social roles they have adopted within the friendship. Modes and levels of communication are shared, but there may be little verbal communication or virtual presence only via media sources.	Socially complex, but possibly less so than in friendships where neither partner has autism, e.g. experience is of physical presence rather than mental companionship.	Mostly positive and rich for child with autism and their friend – feelings of satisfaction and enjoyment, affection, safety and trust. Some conflict may exist, but is managed by children or adults.

adult play partner following the lead of the child with autism, rather than a more reciprocal experience of relationship. Playing with children would also include sharing social meaning, but this would be a stage of greater mutual enjoyment and satisfaction in play encounters, and sense of reciprocity in social engagement. The framework also expresses the fact that play, interaction and friendship are closely interrelated within children's social worlds. Children's friendships are based on their experiences of play, affection and trust, and partly grow out of the coordination of play.

Features of these different contexts of play for children with autism are outlined in Table 8.1. This describes each context and provides examples of group processes that operate at each stage of development for a child with autism as well as the level of social complexity involved and the possible quality of emotion.

Using this framework, methods that can be employed to support the development of play at each of these stages are explored below. As with the discussion of support for children with autism in mainstream schools, a combination of methods is required for supporting play too, focusing on the differing contexts of children's play. Children can be individually supported to join in with play, but a more important area of support is for dyadic and group processes, with groups of children being supported to more effectively engage with each other. Other influences on children's play also exist, such as adult understanding of children's play and the environment of the play space, and ways of supporting these contexts of play will be discussed too.

Engaging with sensory play

Sensory play is the natural starting point for thinking about the development of play in children with autism. The experience of living and working with children with autism tells us that a primary form of engagement in autism is a sensory one that is strongly visually based and may also include motor elements. This is what many writers with autism say is their primary experience of the world, often describing an intense, passionate and highly emotional engagement with the sensory properties of people, objects and features within the environment.

Sensory play involves playing with the physical properties of an object and the environment in ways that do not involve the application of social meanings or construction of a social self. Playing with a mirror, for example, would be less about 'me in the mirror' or 'my bedroom in the mirror' and more about playing with the quality of light produced by the mirror or with 'myself as a sensory object' in the mirror. Children with autism sometimes use mirrors to explore the visual movement of their eyes, mouth and tongue without any consideration of the social context, 'this is me'. Sensory play involves engaging with the shape of things and the look of things, with movement and with light, and can achieve considerable levels of sophistication. Situations that are not often thought of as 'sensory', such as distance, perspective or objects that are 'here and gone' (for example, the opening and closing drawer of a DVD player) can nevertheless be experienced in sensory-perceptual ways that are intensely exciting (Janert, 2000).

There are many books and resources that focus on the sensory play of children with autism and explore different aspects of it. Moor (2008) reassesses ordinary toys and play activities for the purpose of finding new uses that are sensorily compelling for a child with autism, Sher (2009) focuses on play activities that have sensorimotor appeal, and Shields (1999) explains how non-toy objects, such as flap-books, can be used for enjoyable sensory play. Keay-Bright (2009) has produced software to support experiences of sensory and physical play which coordinates movement of the child with beautifully produced visual and musical digital outputs. What these resources have in common is a recognition of the importance of sensory experience for children with autism and many see this as the place where the development of social communication needs to begin.

From a sociocultural perspective, one important aspect of sensory play is that it is a feature of all children's play experience. The sensory play of children with autism is often characterized as something strange that stands apart from the activity of other children, but all children can become fascinated with the sensory properties of ordinary objects, their shape, movement and function evoking powerfully emotional reactions. Typically developing children can become fascinated with objects that disappear and suddenly reappear, with objects that have gaps through which things can be posted or buttons that can be pressed. They can become intensely engaged with the movement of objects, with objects that flow, plop or move erratically, this last type of movement often provoking real fear in very young children. Children with autism are described as being preoccupied with objects that are not considered as play items (for example, washing machines, hoovers and other household items), but this is well within the experience of children who do not have autism too.

Early education pioneers such as Friedrich Froebel (1897), Rudolph Steiner (1968) and Maria Montessori (1965) took a great interest in children's sensory-perceptual and motor experiences, seeing these as the foundation blocks for children's construction of meaning. Their methods often sought to harness sensory-perceptual resources within ordinary educational pedagogy for the purpose of maximizing children's motivation and progress in learning. In contemporary early years educational theory, there has been a renewed interest in the young child's experience of temporal, spatial and material motor-perceptual experiences, seeing these as the basis for intrinsic forms of thought that occur early on in development. Young children have patterns of experiences – of going back and forth, over and under, round, in and through – and it has been argued that these give rise to mental 'schema' that reflect the child's first constructions of reality (Nutbrown, 2006). Within cognitive science, indeed, there is the idea that human cognition is partly derived from meanings based in the embodiment of patterns of these kinds of affectively arresting, sensory-perceptual experiences (Varela *et al.*, 1993). It is probable, of course, that the experience of children without autism differs from that of children with autism, their sense of themselves in relation to these experiences being different. Unlike children with autism, the schema of children without autism will have a stronger social component. They will have a sense of themselves in relation to these experiences, 'my hand moving this back and forth', but also a sense of others who are also engaged or engaged as a virtual presence, 'here I am watching Mummy's dress going round and round (in the washing machine)'.

Sharing social meaning in play

Sensory-perceptual play is frequently used as the starting point in developmental relationship-based approaches for the development of communication in children with autism. Developmental approaches seek to provide experiences of relatedness and shared communication and use play-based intervention, often in the form of sensorimotor play, as a platform for engaging hard to reach children with autism (Gallo-Lopez and Rubin, 2012). Approaches such as Intensive Interaction (Nind and Hewett, 2005), the Developmental, Individual-Difference, Relationship-Based (DIR) model (Greenspan and Wieder, 1998) and the smile programme (Seach, 2007) see support for the development of children's communication as needing to reflect a natural model of relationship. Methods of support are based on forms of communication that exist in ordinary parent–infant interactions and these are characterized by rhythmic, repeated and emotionally rich experiences of togetherness. Establishing child–adult 'circles of communication' is prioritized so that shared attention, language and exaggerated affect can be added to experiences that may originate as sensory, motor, perceptual and child-based only. A key aim is to share instances of social meaning within real-life spontaneous interactions that mainly follow the child's lead. The child's behaviour is treated by the adult as socially purposeful even when it is not, as a way of developing self and other awareness and an experience of two-way communication. The idea is to put a gloss of social meaning onto activity that is largely sensory-based and to bring the child into social engagement through the provision of enjoyable experiences of being together.

Inevitably, this kind of approach is used with children with autism who have very reduced capacities in social communication and who are processing information in mostly sensory ways. It involves intense experiences of togetherness and high levels of social attunement on the part of the adult and is a natural mode of communication in the sense of early experiences of human interaction only. Developmental approaches are predicated on the idea that it is not possible to directly teach sociability and play as a separate set of skills and see experiences of relatedness as the basis for development of language and cognition in children with autism as they are for all children.

Sharing social meaning as a form of support for children with autism is established within autism theory and practice and is somewhat outside the focus of this book, which concerns children with and without autism being together, playing and being friends. Children playing together is a stage beyond the intense interactive exchanges that exist in relationship-based developmental approaches. Within child–child interactions it is not possible to achieve the level of support for communication that is required in child–adult interaction approaches, nor can it be guaranteed that a child without autism will carefully follow the lead of a child with autism, though some children are adept in this. As we have seen in Chapter 3, children also communicate with each other in ways that differ somewhat from adult communication. Children use more non-verbal and multimodal communication within group processes that also involve peer-produced culture. Working with groups of children that include a child with autism thus requires a consideration of the sociocultural contexts in which all children operate. There needs to be a sense of the play and interactional flow that exists within a dyad or group and all children's experience of this. Support needs to be for naturally occurring contexts rather than the created interaction spaces of child–adult relationship-based approaches. Supporting children's natural play contexts necessitates having an understanding of the cultures of communication that exist for all children within a group and to be able to view the experience of play and interaction from their perspectives.

Children playing together and becoming friends

The facilitation of children playing together, interacting and being friends can take a variety of forms to reflect the different contexts of naturally occurring play. Individual support can be provided for a child with autism but, more importantly, support can be given too to the dyad or group of which they are part. Further contexts for the development of play is support for the play space, provision of suitable play materials and support for the adults who oversee the play. Adults have an important role in supporting children's play since it is they who often structure the play space and supply play materials, monitor and assess children as they play and sometimes engage as play partners. However, play is an area of children's experience that is often difficult for adults to understand fully and know how to support, and this is especially the case in autism. Ideas for facilitating children playing together across all these contexts are provided below, addressing each context in turn and suggesting possible strategies for support. The contexts of play are:

- support for group processes;
- individual support for the child with autism or for a peer;
- support for adults;
- support for the play space.

Support for group processes

Within a sociocultural perspective, the key area of support for the social development of the individual child is support for the group processes with which they engage, or are likely to engage. Support for group processes in connection to play would include such things as helping children find each other as playmates, providing suitable play materials, helping children to generate play ideas, and providing them with positive feedback for staying together and being friends. Support for group processes focuses on the shared nature of play, friendship and interaction and prioritizes ways of developing all children's participation. Children's play worlds are characterized by diversity of roles, resources and interpersonal relations and require consideration of the particularity of play contexts and of the group processes that occur within them.

Helping children to find playmates is usually the starting point for supporting children playing together since children with autism often lack the social knowledge and skill to enter play or interaction situations, though they may indicate a desire for greater involvement in relationships with others (Bauminger and Kasari, 2000). There is skill involved in a child identifying another child who might be a good playmate and companion. Even quite young children can demonstrate this skill however, but a child with autism may lack it, sometimes seeking out children who are very different from themselves, who have different levels of social skills and different interests and who are unlikely to make good friends. Satisfying experiences of play emerge from contexts where children have a similarity of skill in play, communication and interaction and this means it is better to think in terms of children who have similar skills and interests becoming friends (Dunn, 2004; Howes et al., 1994). Research into the social networks of children with autism in ordinary settings find that the beginnings and maintenance of friendships require more in the way of adult mediation than is usually the case (Bauminger and Shulman, 2003; Chamberlain et al., 2007), but it is problematic to think in terms of pairing up a child with autism for the purpose of play and friendship with a child who is socially adept and provides a good role model.

Adults who know a group of children are often good at identifying who might be a *potential* friend for a child with autism, someone who might share their interests and levels of skill, whose personality or personal resources may differ but who would make a good match anyway, or who might need a friend themselves. Children take on differing roles in play and this needs to be a consideration. If a child with autism is playing imaginative games which require a situation of leader and followers, a non-equality of participation – where the child without autism leads the child with autism or vice versa – can be socially successful. What type of leader a child is needs further consideration; for example, whether they are bossy and exclusive or inclusive and encouraging of other children and their ideas. Gender, race and age may also need special consideration and an alternative perspective since these structures can operate differently in play situations that include a child with autism. A child with autism may naturally gravitate towards children who are younger and sometimes form cross-gender friendships, boys with autism, for example, not viewing gender as an exclusion to close friendships with girls. There are no hard and fast rules about this however, some children with autism viewing gender difference as highly prohibitive of friendship or even social interaction.

Once playmates and potential playmates have been identified, it is possible to provide support for children's play activity. Teachers are able to organize classroom groupings on the basis of friendship and put children together for learning activities as a way of providing experiences of being together. Adults, whether parent or teacher, can give children an activity to do, offer play materials or suggest a game. It is also possible for school practitioners, once they have identified a possible dyad, to put parents in touch with each other as way of encouraging play dates outside school. Research indicates that this is a key factor in encouraging children's friendships (Frankel and Myatt, 2003). Children can be praised for staying together, playing and 'being a good friend', children without autism probably benefitting more from this type of approach.

In some settings, friendship groups are offered as a way of supporting children playing together and of 'kick-starting' friendships. Friendship groups differ from social skills groups in that the focus is more one of supporting actual social relations. The aim is not to develop the sociability of the child with autism only and is more concerned with the whole group participating in social processes more effectively and with maximum enjoyment. The idea is to try to bond children who already exist as a group of friends or who show some interest in being together. Positive experiences of being together and responding to others would also be a suitable group aim since all children interact more effectively the more they enjoy the experience. For a child with autism who is unsure and wary of other people, an important piece of learning is that it is possible to take pleasure in the company of others, though the quality of emotion that is present in relationships will be a socially motivating experience for all group members.

When thinking about supporting children's play through friendship groups, an important consideration is children's cultural interests and concerns as they already exist. What are these children like as individuals and as a group? What play preferences exist and how do they naturally communicate with each other? Children create their own peer cultures based on their personalities, interests and resources and are influenced in part by the dominant adult culture. For children who like to play in physical, mostly non-verbal ways, or for children who like superhero play and acting out stories, or for children who like to sit and chat, these forms of play and communication should be reflected in the activities and resources used in the friendship group. Gender is a further cultural consideration that might be relevant when thinking about a group of children. Boys tend to favour large groups and physical play, whilst girls participate more in smaller groups with strong emotional attachments. It is important to consider whether a peer group is, for example, a 'boyish group', that is, one partly defined by the distinct ways in which boys organize themselves socially and construct their identities. Peer cultures can also be seen in terms of group values; for example, whether there is a high level of conflict between children or whether children are particularly accepting of each other and any differences. Using children's own cultures of communication, play preferences and cultural concerns means that a closer link is made between what happens in the friendship group and what children go on to achieve in real-life contexts.

Individual support for the child with autism or for a peer

Sociocultural support can also be provided for the individual child with autism or for a peer with whom they interact. As with support for group processes, individualized support would be for actual play contexts and real-life relationships, experiences and understandings. Rather than an abstract learning of 'what is a friend' or 'how do I play', the focus is on developing a child's awareness and social understanding of features within known play experiences, play relationships and the play space itself. In schools, methods in reflective teaching can be employed for this purpose: to identify what a child's experience of play is and to know what areas require support. Chapter 7 described how methods in educational assessment and reflective teaching help practitioners uncover processes in children's learning that are often hard to see but nevertheless critical to their development. Information gathered about children's experiences of play can be used as the basis for describing and reflecting on what is happening within these learning contexts as a way of encouraging deeper understanding and richer participation by a child with autism or a peer. The use of visual information is part of reflective practice and has the added benefit of highlighting and 'fixing' play experiences, social interactions and aspects of relationships that are fleeting and not easily apprehended, particularly by a child with autism.

A method of reflective teaching that is especially useful in supporting the development of children's play is that of Learning Stories, which is essentially a descriptive narrative of children's activity (Carr *et al.*, 2005). It has been discussed elsewhere in this book how descriptive narratives are particularly good at capturing complex human experiences, including the inter-relationships of, for example, cognitive, social, emotional and motor features (see Chapter 5). Narrative, descriptive accounts of children's social activity focus on contexts and seek to describe the range of influences that are operating at any one time, including ones that are not visible such as mental processes. They involve making interpretations of behaviour, but all descriptions of behaviour that involve hidden processes in cognition and emotion use some degree of interpretation. Learning Stories is a descriptive form of educational assessment that is typically used as a method of describing young children's learning experiences. Learning Stories focus on 'critical moments' in children's activity when they are in the process of actually learning something. Critical moments are those where a child is taking an interest, being involved, persisting with a difficulty or uncertainty, expressing an idea or feeling, or taking another person's point of view (Carr, 2001). The story of this process of learning can be written as a descriptive account which is accompanied by relevant visual information, such as photographs and children's drawings. For a child with autism, a Learning Story needs to take a simple form, using straightforward language that is supported or structured visually. The Learning Story at the beginning of this chapter is simply worded and well within the understanding of Laurie, the girl with autism for whom it is written. This Learning Story concerns imaginative play, but stories can be produced about any form of play and learning activity. Stories can be produced about the learning of motor skills; for example, a story in picture sequence of a child learning to hop, balance and bend in the game of hopscotch, or they can be produced about physical play; for example, a story about a child with autism who enjoys the game of chase and who is in the process of learning to look back and keep track of the child who is chasing them.

Learning Stories help children to understand more fully what is going on in play, what roles are being taken by the players and what are the important skills being used. This is as a way of developing a child's ability to participate in richer ways in the play contexts with which they are already engaged. Learning Stories should ask questions about the next steps in learning and so contribute to the setting of short-term learning targets. It is a method of support that reflects the process of children's learning better than performance indicators since it focuses on motivating aspects of the child's actual learning experience and accounts for the unpredictability of key moments of learning.

Learning Stories can be shared with adults as well as children as a way of deepening *their* understanding of what is happening within group processes and the individual child's participation in these. It has been discussed elsewhere in this book how adults do not know everything about children's experiences and must take steps to reconstruct them together with children to gain a proper understanding. The process of adults reflecting on and knowing more about children as learners contributes to the development of the learning environment and can be a powerful influencing factor on children's development. The complexity and hidden aspects of children's play requires adults to make significant efforts to understand children's experiences in this realm. Support for adults to know and understand more about children's play can therefore be a significant influencing factor on their development.

Support for adults

It has already been noted that a particular feature of autism education is working with an 'autism lens' to see and understand the behaviour of a child with autism. This is something adults must learn to do, gradually developing their capacity to see how autism affects the child's perception of ordinary experience and understand why children make the responses they do. The inclusive agenda and accommodation of increased numbers of children with autism in mainstream school settings means that there is a greater number of adults who need to develop these kinds of skills in careful thinking and analysis of children's activity.

Nowhere is the idea of being able to 'see' and understand what the child with autism is doing more relevant than it is to play. Children's play even in ordinary contexts can be something that adults feel they do not fully comprehend and do not have full access to. The particular forms play takes for children with autism means adults may feel that it is overwhelmingly incomprehensible and strange. However, they can be given support to be able to see more clearly what is going on for a child in play, why they are acting or responding in the way they do, what their communication means and how they provide support within a particular context. A useful technique for doing this would be a method such as the 'thinking aloud' procedure. Thinking aloud involves someone speaking out loud their thoughts as they carry out an activity. It is a method that is used in research to gather data from research participants, but is also used in education as a form of instruction, particularly in relation to the teaching of reading and problem-solving (Kucan and Beck, 1997). As a form of instruction, it involves a more experienced partner speaking aloud as they perform a learning task, saying what they are looking at, thinking and feeling. This is for a less experienced partner to understand their thought processes at first-hand. The second partner should simply listen and take in what is being said, not making any comments or interpretations of their own about the task.

Inclusive education invariably involves specialists supporting the work of teachers and support staff in ordinary educational settings. For specialists in autism, a helpful way of doing this, particularly in relation to children's play and interactions with other children, is to use thinking aloud procedure to convey what it is they are focusing on in looking at children and what it is they are seeing in children's behaviour. They can impart their knowledge and understanding to another adult by saying out loud as they watch children interact and play, though non-intrusively of course and to one side so that children cannot hear what is being said. What is communicated is the more experienced adult's thinking about the experience of the play context for the child with autism as well as their understanding of all children's communication, behaviour and responses within the group. This second-hand experience of situated learning can have a powerful impact on the understanding of the adult who has less experience of autism. In this way, they can be supported to have a better understanding of what children are able to do, the nature of any difficulty, and what they as educators need to focus on. They can be helped to be more effective as practitioners, more able to plan for further steps in learning, to support other children in negotiating play interactions and to make any necessary adjustments to the learning environment.

It is perhaps worth pointing out here that the issue of adults with autism being involved in the education of children with autism could be just as relevant to this area of special educational needs and disability as it is to other areas. In some areas of special education, an adult who has the same disability as the child in need of support is seen as having advanced skills that can deliver quality in terms of provision; for example, in deaf education, a deaf educational practitioner who has fluent signing skills providing richer language than the acquired skills of a hearing worker. In autism education, the difficult though central concern of practitioners being able to see and understand the behaviour of a child with autism means that perhaps more thought should be given to adults with autism sometimes supporting children with autism as a feature of best practice within an educational approach.

Support for the play space

The play space is the final context in which children with autism can be supported in the development of their play. The play space is the area in which children play a game, defined in terms of its size, boundaries and strategic use of parts of the space. The game of chase, for example, will be in a large play space, imaginative games will use features within the play space in symbolic ways, and competitive games may functionally use an area as a target. The same physical space can differ as a play space depending on the game being played, and this itself can change over time. However, the play space is largely an invisible concept that is held in children's minds as they play a game. Children cease to apply their concept of the play space once a game is finished and re-apply it when the game recommences. Children without autism are able to be flexible in this, but children with autism may struggle with many aspects of the play space. They may not know the boundaries of a game or understand the symbolic and strategic uses of the space, and they may not know that the space is being used flexibly. Helping children with autism to understand the play space can thus be an effective way of supporting their ability to participate in ordinary play contexts (Conn, 2010). Play spaces can be described according to specific games, they can be mapped out on a piece of paper, a child can be taken on a tour of the play space and a book made with photographs explaining the different uses of space. Visual cues, such as small flags as boundary markers, can be added to the space itself to point out to a child what is happening in a game as they are playing. As with other aspects of sociocultural support, what is important to remember is that this support for children's learning in play needs to be specific to a particular game and focused on actual play contexts and the child's experience of these.

Social-emotional learning can be a rich process even for a child with autism and, as for other areas of support in autism education, supporting the development of play may take different forms. Only one or two examples have been provided here for each context of play, but the richness and variation that exists within socioculture means that many methods of support will be possible. Any special attention to a social context will introduce new influences and change the nature of experience within that context and the learning that takes place as a result. Always of consideration is that having autism means a different way of being but does not necessarily preclude children's social engagement and play that is intrinsically motivated, meaningful at some level and, most importantly, mutually experienced as fun.

Summary

This chapter has described a sociocultural perspective on the play differences that are seen in children with autism. Children with autism have been described as able to play and participate in some aspects of play contexts, but with difference existing in their preferences in play, the amount of their participation in the social contexts of play and possible difference in their subjective experience of play. The differential experience of play in relation to autism has, however, been set against the complexity of play itself and the different experiences of play that exist within children's ordinary play worlds. Support for the development of play in children with autism needs to take account of the differences that exist for them in relation to play and provide support for their real-life play experiences. Methods of support for the differing contexts of play have been outlined including support for peer group processes and individualized support for the social understandings of children and adults.

References

Abrahams, B.S. and Geschwind, D.H. (2008) 'Advances in autism genetics: On the threshold of a new neurobiology', *Nature Reviews Genetics*, 9: 341–55.

Ainscow, M. (1998) 'Would it work in theory? Arguments for practitioner research and theorising in the special needs field', in C. Clark, A. Dyson and A. Millward (eds) *Theorising Special Education*, London and New York: Routledge.

Ainscow, M. (2007) 'From special education to effective schools for all: A review of progress so far', in L. Florian (ed.) *The Sage Handbook of Special Education*, London, Thousand Oaks, New Delhi: Sage Publications.

Airasian, P. and Russell, M. (2008) *Classroom Assessment: Concepts and Applications*, London: McGraw-Hill.

American Psychiatric Association (2013) *Diagnostic and Statistical Manual of Mental Disorder*, 5th edn, Washington DC: American Psychiatric Publishing Inc.

Anderson, A., Moore, D.W., Godfrey, R. and Fletcher-Flinn, C.M. (2004) 'Social skills assessment of children with autism in free-play situations', *Autism*, 8: 369–85.

Asher, S.R., Parker, J.G. and Walker, D.L. (1998) 'Distinguishing friendship from acceptance: Implications for intervention and assessment', in W.M. Bukowski, A.F. Newcomb and W.W. Hartup (eds) *The Company They Keep: Friendship in Childhood and Adolescence*, New York: Cambridge University Press.

Assessment Reform Group (2002) *Assessment for Learning: 10 Principles. Research-based Principles to Guide Classroom Practice*. Online: www.aaia.org.uk/content/uploads/2010/06/Assessment-for-Learning-10-principles.pdf (accessed 2 January 2013).

Astington, J.W. (1994) *The Child's Discovery of the Mind*, London: Fontana.

Avramidis, E. and Norwich, B. (2002) 'Teachers' attitudes towards integration/inclusion: A review of the literature', *European Journal of Special Needs Education*, 17: 129–47.

Barnes, C. (2004) 'Disability, disability studies and the academy', in J. Swain, S. French, C. Barnes and C. Thomas (eds) *Disabling Barriers, Enabling Environments*, 2nd edn, London, Thousand Oaks, New Delhi: Sage Publications.

Barnes, P. (2003) 'Children's friendships', in M.J. Kehily and J. Swann (eds) *Children's Cultural Worlds*, Chichester and Milton Keynes: John Wiley/Open University.

Baron-Cohen, S., Scott, F.J., Allison, C., Williams, J., Bolton, P., Matthews, F.E. and Brayne, C. (2009) 'Prevalence of autism-spectrum conditions: UK school-based population study', *British Journal of Psychiatry*, 194: 500–9.

Barton, E.E. and Wolery, M. (2008) 'Teaching pretend play to children with disabilities: A review of the literature', *Topics in Early Childhood Special Education*, 28: 109–25.

Bateson, G.A. (1972) 'A theory of play and fantasy', in G.A. Bateson *Steps to an Ecology of Mind*, San Francisco: Chandler.

Bauminger, N. (2004) 'The expression and understanding of jealousy in children with autism', *Development and Psychopathology*, 16: 157–77.

Bauminger, N. and Kasari, C. (2000) 'Loneliness and friendship in high-functioning children with autism', *Child Development*, 71: 447–56.

Bauminger, N. and Shulman, C. (2003) 'The development and maintenance of friendship in high-functioning children with autism: Maternal perceptions', *Autism*, 7: 81–97.

Bauminger, N., Shulman, C. and Agam, G. (2003) 'Peer interaction and loneliness in high-functioning children with autism', *Journal of Autism and Developmental Disorders*, 33: 489–507.

Bauminger, N., Solomon, M., Aviezer, A., Heung, K., Brown, J. and Rogers, S. (2008) 'Friendship in high-functioning children with autism spectrum disorder: Mixed and non-mixed dyads', *Journal of Autism and Developmental Disorders*, 38: 1211–29.

Beresford, B. (1997) *Personal Accounts: Involving Disabled Children in Research*, London: The Stationery Office/Social Policy Research Unit.

Beresford, B., Tozer, R., Rabiee, P. and Sloper, P. (2007) 'Desired outcomes for children and adolescents with autistic spectrum disorders', *Children and Society*, 21: 4–16.

Bernard-Opitz, V., Ing, S. and Kong, T.Y. (2004) 'Comparison of behavioural and natural play interventions for young children with autism', *Autism*, 8: 319–33.

Bishop, J.C. (2011) 'The visual playground: Children's use of communicative resources in schoolyard play and games', paper presented at International Play Association Triennial Conference, UK, 4 July.

Blatchford, P., Pellegrini, A., Baines, E. and Kentaro, K. (2002) *Playground Games: Their Social Context in Elementary/Junior School*. Final Report to the Spencer Foundation. Online: www.breaktime.org.uk/SpencerFinalReport02.pdf (accessed 28 July 2010).

Boaz, A. and Ashby, D. (2003) 'Fit for purpose? Assessing research quality for evidence based policy and practice', Working Paper 11, ESRC UK Centre for Evidence Based Policy and Practice, University of London.

Bock, M.A. (2007) 'The impact of social-behavioural learning strategy training on the social interaction skills of four students with Asperger Syndrome', *Focus on Autism and Other Developmental Disabilities*, 22: 88–95.

Booth, T., Ainscow, M., Black-Hawkins, K., Vaughan, M. and Shaw, L. (2000) *Index for Inclusion: Developing Learning and Participation in Schools*, Bristol: Centre for Studies in Inclusive Education.

Boucher, J. (1999) 'Interventions with children with autism: Methods based on play', *Child Language Teaching and Therapy,* 15: 1–5.

Boucher, J. and Wolfberg, P. (2003) 'Editorial', *Autism*, 7: 339–46.

Boyd, B.A., Conroy, M.A., Asmus, J.M., McKenney, E.L.W. and Mancil, G.R. (2008) 'Descriptive analysis of classroom setting events on the social behaviours of children with autism spectrum disorder', *Education and Training in Developmental Disabilities*, 43: 186–97.

Bronfenbrenner, U. (1979) *The Ecology of Human Development*, Cambridge, MA: Harvard University Press.

Brown, J. and Whiten, A. (2000) 'Imitation, theory of mind and related activities in autism', *Autism*, 4: 185–204.

Brownlow, C. and O'Dell, L. (2009) 'Challenging understandings of "theory of mind": A brief report', *Intellectual and Developmental Disabilities*, 47: 473–8.

Bruner, J. (1968) *Processes of Cognitive Growth: Infancy*, Worcester: Clark University Press.

Bruner, J. (1986) *Actual Minds, Possible Worlds*, Cambridge, MA and London: Harvard University Press.

Bruner, J. (1997) 'Celebrating divergence: Piaget and Vygotsky', *Human Development*, 40: 63–73.

Bruner, J.S. and Feldman, C. (1993) 'Theories of Mind and the problem of autism', in S. Baron-Cohen, H. Tager-Flusberg and D.J. Cohen (eds) *Understanding Other Minds: Perspectives from Autism*, Oxford: Oxford University Press.

Buber, M. (1958) *I and Thou*, trans R.G. Smith, 2nd edn, Edinburgh: T & T Clark.

Buckingham, D. and Willett, R. (eds) (2006) *Digital Generations: Children, Young People, and the New Media*, London and New York: Routledge.

Burghardt, G.M. (2011) 'Defining and recognizing play', in A. Pellegrini (ed.) *Oxford Handbook of the Development of Play*, New York and London: Oxford University Press.

Burn, A., Marsh, J., Bishop, J.C., Willett, R., Richards, C., and Sheridan, J. (2011) *Children's Playground Games and Songs in the New Media Age.* Project Report. Online: http://projects.beyondtext.ac.uk/playgroundgames/uploads/end_of_project_report.pdf (accessed 6 August 2011).

Caillois, R. (1958) *Man, Play and Games*, Urbana and Chicago: University of Illinois Press.

Carpenter, M., Pennington, B.F. and Rogers, S.J. (2002) 'Interrelations among social-cognitive skills in young children with autism', *Journal of Autism and Developmental Disorders*, 32: 91–106.

Carr, M. (2001) *Assessment in Early Childhood Settings: Learning Stories*, Los Angeles, London, New Delhi, Singapore, Washington DC: Sage Publications.

Carr, M. and Lee, W. (2012) *Learning Stories: Constructing Learner Identities in Early Education*, London, Thousand Oaks, New Delhi, Singapore: Sage Publications.

Carr, M., Jones, C. and Lee, W. (2005) 'Beyond listening: Can assessment practice play a part?' in A. Clark, A.T. Kjørholt and P. Moss (eds) *Beyond Listening: Children's Perspectives on Early Childhood Services*, Bristol: Policy Press.

Chamberlain, B., Kasari, C. and Rotheram-Fuller, E. (2007) 'Involvement or isolation? The social networks of children with autism in regular classrooms', *Journal of Autism and Developmental Disorders*, 37: 230–42.

Christensen, P.H. (2004) 'Children's participation in ethnographic research: Issues of power and representation', *Children and Society*, 18: 165–76.

Christensen, P. and James, A. (eds) (2008) *Research with Children: Perspectives and Practices*, New York and London: Routledge.

Christensen, P. and Prout, A. (2002) 'Working with ethical symmetry in social research with children', *Childhood*, 9: 477–97.

Christensen, P. and Prout, A. (2005) 'Anthropological and sociological perspectives on the study of children', in S. Greene and D. Hogan (eds) *Researching Children's Experience: Methods and Approaches*, London, Thousand Oaks, New Delhi: Sage Publications.

Clark, A. (2005) 'Ways of seeing: Using the Mosaic approach to listen to young children's perspectives', in A. Clark, A.T. Kjørholt and P. Moss (eds) *Beyond Listening: Children's Perspectives on Early Childhood Services*, Bristol: Policy Press.

Clark, A. and Moss, P. (2001) *Listening to Young Children: The Mosaic Approach*, London: National Children's Bureau.

Clark, A. and Moss, P. (2005) *Spaces to Play: More Listening to Young Children Using the Mosaic Approach*, London: National Children's Bureau.

Clough, P. and Corbett, J. (2000) *Theories of Inclusive Education: A Student's Guide*, London: Paul Chapman Publishing.

Clough, P. and Nutbrown, C. (2007) *A Student's Guide to Methodology*, 2nd edn, Los Angeles, London, New Delhi, Singapore: Sage Publications.

Cole, M. (1996) *Cultural Psychology: A Once and Future Discipline*, Cambridge, MA: Harvard University Press.

Cole, M., Cole, S.R. and Lightfoot, C. (2005) *The Development of Children*, 5th edn, New York: Worth Publishers.

Conn, C. (2010) *Play Better Games: Enabling Children with Autism to Join in with Everyday Games*, Milton Keynes: Speechmark.

Conn, C. (2013a) 'Essential conditions for research with children with autism: Issues raised by two case studies', *Children and Society*, 18 April. DOI: 10.1111/chso.12018.

Conn, C. (2013b) 'Investigating the social engagement of children with autism in mainstream schools for the purpose of identifying learning targets', *Journal of Research in Special Educational Needs*, 20 May. DOI: 10.1111/1471–3802.12010.

Connors, C. and Stalker, K. (2007) 'Children's experiences of disability: Pointers to the social model of childhood disability', *Disability & Society*, 22: 19–33.

Corsaro, W.A. (1985) *Friendship and Peer Culture in the Early Years*, Norwood, NJ: Ablex Publishing Corporation.

Corsaro, W.A. (1992) 'Interpretive reproduction in children's peer cultures', *Social Psychology Quarterly*, 55: 160–77.

Corsaro, W.A. (1999) 'Preadolescent peer culture', in M. Woodhead, D. Faulkner and K. Littleton (eds) *Making Sense of Social Development*, London and New York: Routledge.

Corsaro, W.A. (2003) *We're Friends Right? Inside Kid's Culture*, Washington DC: Joseph Henry Press.

Corsaro, W.A. (2011) *The Sociology of Childhood*, 3rd edn, Thousand Oaks, London, New Delhi: Pine Forge Press.

Corsaro, W.A. and Johannesen, B.O. (2007) 'The creation of new cultures in peer interaction', in J. Valsiner and A. Rosa (eds) *The Cambridge Handbook of Sociocultural Psychology*, New York: Cambridge University Press.

Corsaro, W.A. and Molinari, L. (2008) 'Entering and observing in children's worlds', in P. Christensen and A. James (eds) *Research with Children: Perspectives and Practices*, 2nd edn, New York and London: Routledge.

Croll, P. and Moses, D. (2000) 'Ideologies and utopias: Education professionals' views of inclusion', *European Journal of Special Needs Education*, 15: 1–12.

Cumine, V., Leach, J. and Stevenson, G. (2000) *Autism in the Early Years: A Practical Guide*, London: David Fulton Publishers.

Dahlberg, G., Moss, P. and Pence, A. (2006) *Beyond Quality in Early Childhood Education and Care: Languages of Evaluation*, 2nd edn, London and New York: Routledge.

Daniels, H. (2005) 'Vygotsky and educational psychology: Some preliminary remarks', *Educational and Child Psychology*, 22: 6–18.

Daniels, H. (2008) *Vygotsky and Research*, London and New York: Routledge.

Daniels, H. (2010) 'Learning as a sociocultural process', paper presented at Doctoral Conference, Graduate School of Education, University of Bristol, 18 June.

Dehart, G.B., Sroufe, L.A. and Cooper, R.G. (2003) *Child Development: Its Nature and Course*, 5th edn, Boston: McGraw-Hill Higher Education.

Denzin, N.K. and Lincoln, Y.S. (1994) 'Entering the field of qualitative research', in N.K. Denzin and Y.S. Lincoln (eds) *Handbook of Qualitative Research*, Thousand Oaks: Sage Publications.

Denzin, N.K. and Lincoln, Y.S. (2000) 'The discipline and practice of qualitative research', in N.K. Denzin and Y.S. Lincoln (eds) *Handbook of Qualitative Research*, 2nd edn, Thousand Oaks, London, New Delhi: Sage Publications.

Department for Children, Schools and Families (DCSF) (2008) *The Early Years Foundation Stage. Effective Practice: Observation, Assessment and Planning*. Online: www.ndna.org.uk/Resources/NDNA/Generic%20Folders%202/10/33.%20EYFS%20Observation_%20assessing%20and%20planning.pdf (accessed 16 November 2013).

Department for Education (DfE) (2010) *Special Educational Needs in England, January 2010: Statistical First Release*, London: Department for Education.

Department for Education and Employment (DfEE) (1997) *Excellence for All Children: Meeting Special Educational Needs*, London: Department for Education and Employment.

Department for Education and Skills (DfES) (2004) *Every Child Matters: Change for Children*, London: Department for Education and Skills.

Dickins, M. (2008) *Listening to Young Disabled Children*, London: National Children's Bureau.

Dolan, P., Canavan, J. and Pinkerton, J. (eds) (2006) *Family Support as Reflective Practice*, London and Philadelphia: Jessica Kingsley Publishers.

Donaldson, M. (1978) *Children's Minds*, London: Fontana.

Donnelly, J. and Bovee, J.-P. (2003) 'Reflections on play: Recollections from a mother and her son with Asperger Syndrome', *Autism*, 7: 471–76.

Dunn, J. (1991) 'Understanding others: Evidence from naturalistic studies of children', in A. Whiten (ed.) *Natural Theories of Mind*, Oxford: Blackwell.

Dunn, J. (2004) *Children's Friendships: The Beginnings of Intimacy*, Oxford: Blackwell Publishing.

Dunn, J. (2005) 'Naturalistic observations of children and their families', in S. Greene and D. Hogan (eds) *Researching Children's Experience: Methods and Approaches*, London, Thousand Oaks, New Delhi: Sage Publications.

Dunn, J. and Brown, J. (1994) 'Affect expression in the family, children's understanding of emotion, and their interactions with others', *Merrill-Palmer Quarterly*, 40: 120–37.

Dunn, J. and Hughes, C. (2001) '"I got some swords and you're dead!": Violent fantasy, antisocial behaviour, friendship and moral sensibility in young children', *Child Development*, 72: 491–505.

Dunphy, E. (2008) *Supporting Early Learning and Development Through Formative Assessment: A Research Paper*, Dublin: NCCA.

Eder, D. and Corsaro, W.A. (1999) 'Ethnographic studies of children and youth', *Journal of Contemporary Ethnography*, 28: 520–31.

El-Ghoroury, N.H. and Romanczyk, R.G. (1999) 'Play interactions of family members towards children with autism', *Journal of Autism and Developmental Disorders*, 29: 249–58.

Emam, M.M. and Farrell, P. (2009) 'Tensions experienced by teachers and their views of support for pupils with autism spectrums disorders in mainstream schools', *European Journal of Special Needs Education*, 24: 407–22.

Espanol, S. (2007) 'Time and movement in symbol formation', in J. Valsiner and A. Rosa (eds) *The Cambridge Handbook of Sociocultural Psychology*, New York: Cambridge University Press.

European Agency for Development in Special Needs Education (EADSNE) (2009) *Assessment for Learning and Pupils with Special Educational Needs*. Online: www.european-agency.org/publications/flyers/assessment-materials/assessment-for-learning/assessment_for_learning_en.pdf/view?searchterm=assessment%20for%20learning%20and%20pupils%20with%20special%20educational%20needs (accessed 18 January 2010).

Farrell, P. (2004) 'School psychologists: Making inclusion a reality for all', *School Psychology International*, 25: 5–19.

Finnigan, R. (2002) *Communicating: the Multiple Modes of Human Interconnection*, London and New York: Routledge.

Fletcher-Campbell, F. (2003) *Review of the Research Literature on Educational Interventions for Pupils with Autistic Spectrum Disorders*, Slough: National Foundation for Educational Research.

Frankel, F. and Myatt, R. (2003) *Children's Friendship Training*, New York: Brunner-Routledge.

Freire, P. (1970) *Pedagogy of the Oppressed*, New York: Herder and Herder.

Frith, U. and Happé, F. (1999) 'Theory of Mind and self-consciousness: What is it like to be autistic?', *Mind and Language*, 14: 1–22.

Froebel, F. (1897) *Pedagogics of the Kindergarten, Or, Ideas Concerning the Play and Playthings of the Child*, trans. J. Jarvis, London: Edward Arnold.

Gallagher, S. (2004) 'Understanding interpersonal problems in autism: Interaction Theory as an alternative to Theory of Mind', *Philosophy, Psychiatry and Psychology*, 11: 199–217.

Gallagher, S. (2011) 'Some qualifications on the "warmth and intimacy" of bodily self-consciousness', paper presented at Meaning and Mindedness Seminar Series: Encounters between Philosophy and Psychoanalysis, Seminar 4: The Embodied Mind, Tavistock Centre, London, 25 March.

Gallo-Lopez, L. and Rubin, L.C. (eds) (2012) *Play-Based Interventions for Children and Adolescents with Autism Spectrum Disorders*, New York and London: Routledge.

Geertz, C. (1973) *The Interpretation of Cultures: Selected Essays*, New York: Basic Books.

Geertz, C. (1988) 'I-witnessing: Malinowski's children', in C. Geertz, *Works and Lives: The Anthropologist as Author*, Stanford: Stanford University Press.

Gerland, G. (1997) *A Real Person: Life on the Outside*, trans J. Tate, London: Souvenir Press.

Giangreco, M.F. (2003) '"The stairs don't go anywhere": A self-advocate's reflections on specialised services and their impact on people with disabilities', in M. Nind, J. Rix, K. Sheehy and K. Simmons (eds) *Inclusive Education: Diverse Perspectives*, London: David Fulton Publisher.

Göncü, A. and Gaskins, S. (eds) (2006) *Play and Development: Evolutionary, Sociocultural and Functional Perspectives*, Mahwah, NJ and London: Lawrence Erlbaum.

Götz, M., Lemish, D., Aidman, A. and Moon, H. (2005) *Media and Make-Believe Worlds of Children: When Harry Potter Meets Pokémon in Disneyland*, Mahwah, NJ: Lawrence Erlbaum.

Grandin, T. and Johnson, C. (2005) *Animals in Translation*, Bloomsbury: London.

Gray, C. (2009) Personal communication.

Greenspan, S.I. and Wieder, S. (1998) *The Child with Special Needs: Encouraging Intellectual and Emotional Growth*, Reading, MA: Perseus Books.

Guba, E.G. and Lincoln, Y.S. (1994) 'Competing paradigms in qualitative research', in N.K. Denzin and Y.S. Lincoln (eds) *Handbook of Qualitative Research*, Thousand Oaks: Sage Publications.

Guba, E.G. and Lincoln, Y.S. (2005) 'Paradigmatic controversies, contradictions, and emerging confluences', in N.K. Denzin and Y.S. Lincoln (eds) *The SAGE Handbook of Qualitative Research*, 3rd edn, Thousand Oaks, London, New Delhi: Sage Publications.

Gubrium, J.F. and Holstein, J.A. (2008) 'Narrative ethnography', in S.N. Hesse-Biber and P. Leavy (eds) *Handbook of Emergent Methods*, New York: Guilford Press.

Hagey, R. (1997) 'The use and abuse of participatory action research', *Chronic Diseases in Canada*, 18: 1–4.

Harris, P. (2000) *The Work of the Imagination*, Oxford: Blackwell.

Hart, S. (2000) *Thinking Through Teaching*, London: David Fulton.

Hart, S. and Travers, P. (2003) 'Learning in context: Identifying difficulties for learners', in M. Nind, J. Rix, K. Sheehy and K. Simmons (eds) *Inclusive Education: Diverse Perspectives*, London: David Fulton Publishers.

Helps, S., Newsom-Davis, I.C. and Callais, M. (1999) 'Autism: The teacher's view', *Autism*, 3: 287–98.

Hobson, R.P. (1990) 'On the origins of self and the case of autism', *Development and Psychopathology*, 2: 163–81.

Hobson, R.P. (1993a) 'Understanding persons: The role of affect', in S. Baron-Cohen, H. Tager-Flusberg and D. Cohen (eds) *Understanding Other Minds: Perspectives from Autism*, Oxford: Oxford University Press.

Hobson, R.P. (1993b) *Autism and the Development of Mind*. Hove: Psychology Press.

Hobson, R.P. (2006) 'Developing self/other awareness: A reply', *Monographs of the Society for Research in Child Development*, 71: 180–6.

Hobson, J.A. and Hobson, R.P. (2007) 'On identification: The missing link between imitation and joint attention', *Development and Psychopathology*, 19: 411–31.

Hobson, R.P., Lee, A. and Hobson, J.A. (2009) 'Qualities of symbolic play among children with autism: A social-developmental perspective', *Journal of Autism and Developmental Disorders*, 39: 12–22.

Hogan, D. (2005) 'Researching "the child" in developmental psychology', in S. Greene and D. Hogan (eds) *Researching Children's Experience: Approaches and Methods*, London, Thousand Oaks, New Delhi: Sage Publications.

Holland, P. (2003) *We Don't Play with Guns Here*, Maidenhead and Philadelphia: Open University Press.

Howes, C. (1998) 'The earliest friendships', in W.M. Bukowski, A.F. Newcomb and W.W. Hartup (eds) *The Company They Keep: Friendship in Childhood and Adolescence*, New York: Cambridge University Press.

Howes, C. (2011) 'Social play of children with adults and peers', in A. Pellegrini (ed.) *Oxford Handbook of the Development of Play*, New York and London: Oxford University Press.

Howes, C., Droege, K. and Matheson, C.C. (1994) 'Play and communication processes within long- and short-term friendship dyads', *Journal of Social and Personal Relationships*, 11: 401–10.

Howes, C., Unger, O. and Seidner, L.B. (1989) 'Social pretend play in toddlers: Parallels with social play and with solitary pretend', *Child Development*, 60: 77–84.

Hudson, B. (2000) 'Seeking connection and searching for meaning: Teaching as reflective practice', paper presented at European Conference on Educational Research, Edinburgh, 20–3 September.

Hughes, F.P. (2009) *Children, Play and Development*, 4th edn, Los Angeles, London, New Delhi, Singapore, Washington DC: Sage Publications.

Humphrey, N. and Lewis, S. (2008) '"Make me normal": The views and experiences of pupils on the autistic spectrum in mainstream secondary schools', *Autism*, 12: 23–46.

Humphrey, N. and Parkinson, G. (2006) 'Research on interventions for children and young people on the autistic spectrum: A critical perspective', *Journal of Research in Special Educational Needs*, 6: 76–86.

Humphrey, N. and Symes, W. (2010) 'Responses to bullying and use of social support among pupils with autism spectrum disorders (ASD) in mainstream schools: A qualitative study', *Journal of Research in Special Educational Needs*, 10: 82–90.

Humphrey, N. and Symes, W. (2011) 'Peer interaction patterns among adolescents with autistic spectrum disorders (ASD) in mainstream school settings', *Autism*, 15: 397–419.

Hutchby, I. (2005) 'Children's talk and social competence', *Children and Society*, 19: 66–73.

Ingersoll, B. and Schreibman, L. (2006) 'Teaching reciprocal imitation skills to young children with autism using a naturalistic behavioural approach: Effects on language, pretend play and joint attention', *Journal of Autism and Developmental Disorders*, 36: 487–505.

Iovannone, R., Dunlap, G., Huber, H. and Kincaid, D. (2003) 'Effective educational practices for students with autism spectrum disorders', *Focus on Autism and Other Developmental Disabilities*, 18: 150–65.

Isaacs, S. (1933) *Social Development in Young Children: A Study of Beginnings*, London: Routledge and Kegan Paul.

James, A. (1993) *Childhood Identities: Self and Social Relationships in the Experience of the Child*, Edinburgh: Edinburgh University Press.

James, A. (2001) 'Ethnography in the study of children and childhood', in P. Atkinson, A. Coffey, S. Delamont, J. Lofland and L. Lofland (eds) *Handbook of Ethnography*, London, Thousand Oaks, New Delhi: Sage Publications.

James, A., Jenks, C. and Prout, A. (1998) *Theorising Childhood*, Cambridge: Polity Press.

Janert, S. (2000) *Reaching the Young Autistic Child*, London and New York: Free Association Books.

Jarrold, C. (2003) 'A review of research into pretend play in autism', *Autism*, 7: 379–90.

Jarrold, C. and Conn, C. (2011) 'The development of pretend play in autism', in A. Pellegrini (ed.) *Oxford Handbook of the Development of Play*, New York and London: Oxford University Press.

Jarrold, C., Carruthers, P., Smith, P.K. and Boucher, J. (1994) 'Pretend play: Is it metarepresentational?', *Mind and Language*, 9: 445–68.

Jewitt, C. (2006) *Technology, Literacy and Learning: A Multimodal Approach*, London and New York: Routledge.

Jones, G., English, A., Guldberg, K., Jordan, R., Richardson, P. and Waltz, M. (2009) *Educational Provision for Children and Young People on the Autism Spectrum Living in England: Review of Current Practice, Issues and Challenges*, London: Autism Education Trust.

Jones, V. (2007) '"I felt like I did something good": The impact on mainstream pupils of a peer tutoring programme for children with autism', *British Journal of Special Education*, 34: 3–9.

Jordan, R. (2003) 'Social play and autistic spectrum disorders: A perspective on theory, implications and educational approaches', *Autism*, 7: 347–60.

Jordan, R. (2005) 'Autistic spectrum disorders', in A. Lewis and B. Norwich (eds) *Special Teaching for Special Children? Pedagogies for Inclusion*, Maidenhead: Open University Press.

Kalliala, M. (2006) *Play Culture in a Changing World*, Maidenhead: Open University Press.

Kantor, R., Elgas, P.M. and Fernie, D.E. (1998) 'Cultural knowledge and social competence within a preschool peer-culture group', in M. Woodhead, D. Faulkner and K. Littleton (eds) *Cultural Worlds of Early Childhood*, London and New York: Routledge.

Kasari, C., Chamberlain, B. and Bauminger, N. (2001) 'Social emotions and social relationships in autism: Can children with autism compensate?', in J. Burack, T. Charman, N. Yirimiya and P. Zelazo (eds) *The Development of Autism: Perspectives from Theory and Research*, Mahwah, NJ: Lawrence Erlbaum.

Kasari, C. and Smith, T. (2013) 'Interventions in schools for children with autism spectrum disorder: Methods and recommendations', *Autism*, 17: 254–67.

Kasari, C., Freeman, S. and Paparella, T. (2006) 'Joint attention and symbolic play in young children with autism: A randomized controlled intervention study', *Journal of Child Psychology and Psychiatry*, 47: 611–20.

Kasari, C., Locke, J., Gulsrud, A. and Rotheram-Fuller, E. (2011) 'Social networks and friendships at school: Comparing children with and without ASD', *Journal of Autism and Developmental Disorders*, 41: 533–44.

Kasari, C., Sigman, M., Mundy, P. and Yirimiya, N. (1990) 'Affective sharing in the context of joint attention interactions of normal, autistic, and mentally retarded children', *Journal of Autism and Developmental Disorders*, 20: 87–100.

Keay-Bright, W. (2009) 'ReacTickles: playful interaction with information communication technologies', *International Journal of Art and Technology*, 2: 133–51.

Kellett, M. and Nind, M. (2001) 'Ethics in quasi-experimental research on people with severe learning difficulties: Dilemmas and compromises', *British Journal of Learning Disabilities*, 29: 51–5.

Kohler, F.W., Anthony, L.J., Steighner, S.A. and Hoyson, M. (2001) 'Teaching social interaction skills in the integrated preschool: An examination of naturalistic tactics', *Topics in Early Childhood Special Education*, 21: 93–103.

Kok, A.J., Kong, T.Y. and Bernard-Opitz, V. (2002) 'A comparison of the effects of structured play and facilitated play approaches in preschoolers with autism', *Autism*, 6: 181–96.

Kucan, L. and Beck, I.L. (1997) 'Thinking aloud and reading comprehension research: Inquiry, instruction and social interaction', *Review of Educational Research*, 67: 271–99.

Kyriacou, C. (2009) *Effective Teaching in Schools: Theory and Practice*, 3rd edn, Cheltenham: Nelson Thornes.

Lancaster, Y.P. (2006) 'Listening to young children: Respecting the voice of the child', in G. Pugh and B. Duffy (eds) *Contemporary Issues in the Early Years*, 4th edn, London, Thousand Oaks, New Delhi: Sage Publications.

Langan, M. (2011) 'Parental voices and controversies in autism', *Disability & Society*, 26: 193–205.

Laugeson, E., Frankel, F., Mogil, C. and Dillon, A.R. (2009) 'Parent-assisted social skills training to improve friendships in teens with autism spectrum disorders', *Journal of Autism and Developmental Disorders*, 39: 596–606.

Laushey, K.M. and Heflin, J.L. (2000) 'Enhancing social skills of kindergarten children with autism through the training of multiple peers as tutors', *Journal of Autism and Developmental Disorders*, 30: 183–93.

Leekam, S., Libby, S., Wing, L., Gould, J. and Gillberg, C. (2000) 'Comparison of ICD-10 and Gillberg's criteria for Asperger Syndrome', *Autism*, 4: 11–28.

Leslie, A.M. (1987) 'Pretence and representation: The origins of "theory of mind"', *Psychological Review*, 94: 412–26.

Lewis, A. (2003) 'Accessing, through research interviews, the views of children with difficulties in learning', in M. Nind, J. Rix, K. Sheehy and K. Simmons (eds) *Inclusive Education: Diverse Perspectives*, London: David Fulton Publishers.

Lewis, V. and Boucher, J. (1995) 'Generativity in the play of young people with autism', *Journal of Autism and Developmental Disorders*, 25: 105–21.

Libby, S., Powell, S., Messer, D. and Jordan, R. (1998) 'Spontaneous play in children with autism: A reappraisal', *Journal of Autism and Developmental Disorders*, 28: 487–97.

Lillard, A. (1993) 'Young children's conceptualization of pretense: Action or mental representational state?', *Child Development*, 64: 372–86.

Lillard, A. (2006) 'Guided participation: How mothers structure and children understand pretend play', in A. Göncü and S. Gaskins (eds) *Play and Development: Evolutionary, Sociocultural and Functional Perspectives*, Mahwah, NJ and London: Lawrence Erlbaum.

Lillard, A. (2011) 'Mother-child fantasy play', in A. Pellegrini (ed.) *Oxford Handbook of the Development of Play*, New York and London: Oxford University Press.

Locke, J., Ishijima, E.H., Kasari, C. and London, N. (2010) 'Loneliness, friendship quality and the social networks of adolescents with high-functioning autism in the inclusive school setting', *Journal of Special Educational Needs*, 10: 74–81.

Lord, C. and Magill-Evans, J. (1995) 'Peer interactions of autistic children and adolescents', *Development and Psychopathology*, 7: 611–26.

Luckett, T., Bundy, A. and Roberts, J. (2007) 'Do behavioural approaches teach children with autism to play or are they pretending?', *Autism*, 11: 365–88.

McConnell, S.R. (2002) 'Interventions to facilitate social interaction in young children with autism: Review of available research and recommendations for educational intervention and future research', *Journal of Autism and Developmental Disorders*, 32: 351–72.

McGee, G.G., Feldman, R.S. and Morrier, M.J. (1997) 'Benchmarks of social treatment for children with autism', *Journal of Autism and Developmental Disorders*, 27: 353–64.

McGregor, E. and Campbell, E. (2001) 'The attitudes of teachers in Scotland to the integration of children with autism into mainstream schools', *Autism*, 5: 189–207.

Malaguzzi, L. (1993) 'For an education based on relationships', *Young Children*, 49: 9–12.

Marsh, J. (2010) 'Young children's play in online virtual worlds', *Journal of Early Childhood Research*, 7: 1–17.

Mastrangelo, S. (2009) 'Play and the child with autism spectrum disorder: From possibilities to practice', *International Journal of Play Therapy*, 18: 13–30.

Mauthner, M. (1997) 'Methodological aspects of collecting data from children: lessons from three research projects', *Children and Society*, 11: 16–28.

Mertens, D. (2010) *Research and Evaluation in Education and Psychology*, 3rd edn, Thousand Oaks, New Delhi, London, Singapore: Sage Publications.

Mertens, D.M. and McLaughlin, J.A. (2004) *Research and Evaluation Methods in Special Education*, Thousand Oaks: Corwin Press.

Mesibov, G. and Howley, M. (2003) *Accessing the Curriculum for Pupils with Autistic Spectrum Disorders: Using the TEACCH Programme to Help Inclusion*, London: David Fulton Publishers.

Mesibov, G. and Shea, V. (1998) *The Culture of Autism: From Theoretical Understanding to Educational Practice*, New York: Plenum Publishing.

Mesibov, G. and Shea, V. (2011) 'Evidence-based practices and autism', *Autism*, 15: 114–33.

Meyer, L.H., Park, H.-S., Grenot-Scheyer, M., Schwartz, I.S. and Harry, B. (1998) 'Participatory research approaches for the study of social relationships of children and youth', in L.H. Meyer, H.-S. Park, M. Grenot-Scheyer, I.S. Schwartz, B. Harry (eds)

Making Friends: The Influences of Culture and Development, Baltimore, London, Toronto, Sydney: Paul H. Brookes Publishing.

Miller, J. (2003) *Never Too Young: How Young Children Can Take Responsibility and Make Decisions*, London: Save the Children.

Ministry of Education (1996) *Te Whāriki: Early Childhood Curriculum*, Wellington: Learning Media.

Montessori, M. (1965) *The Montessori Method: Scientific Pedagogy as Applied to Child Education in 'the Children's Houses'*, trans. A.E. George, Cambridge, MA: Robert Bentley. Originally published in 1912.

Moor, J. (2008) *Playing, Laughing and Learning with Children on the Autism Spectrum*, 2nd edn, London and Philadelphia: Jessica Kingsley Publishers.

Morrow, V. and Richards, M. (1996) 'The ethics of social research with children: An overview', *Children and Society*, 10: 90–105.

Mundy, P., Sigman, M., Ungerer, J. and Sherman, T. (1986) 'Defining the social deficits of autism: The contribution of non-verbal communication measures', *Journal of Child Psychology and Psychiatry*, 27: 657–69.

Neisser, U. (1988) 'Five kinds of self-knowledge', *Philosophical Psychology*, 1: 35–59.

Nind, M. and Hewett, D. (2005) *Access to Communication*, 2nd edn, London: David Fulton Publishers.

Norwich, B. (2008) *Dilemmas of Difference, Inclusion and Disability: International Perspectives and Future Directions*, London and New York: Routledge.

Norwich, B. and Lewis, A. (2005) 'How specialized is teaching pupils with disabilities and difficulties?', in A. Lewis and B. Norwich (eds) *Special Teaching for Special Children? Pedagogies for Inclusion*, Maidenhead: Open University Press.

Nutbrown, C. (2006) *Threads of Thinking: Young Children's Learning and the Role of Early Education*, 3rd edn, Los Angeles, London, New Delhi, Singapore, Washington DC: Sage Publications.

Nutbrown, C. and Carter, C. (2010) 'The tools of assessment: Watching and learning', in G. Pugh and B. Duffy (eds) *Contemporary Issues in the Early Years*, 5th edn, London, Thousand Oaks, New Delhi, Singapore: Sage Publications.

Nutbrown, C. and Clough, P. (2006) *Inclusion in the Early Years*, London, Thousand Oaks, New Delhi: Sage Publications.

Ochs, E., Kremer-Sadlik, T., Solomon, O. and Sirota, K.G. (2001) 'Inclusion as social practice: Views of children with autism', *Social Development*, 10: 399–419.

Owen-DeSchryver, J.S., Carr, E.G., Cale, S.I. and Blakeley-Smith, A. (2008) 'Promoting social interactions between students with autism spectrum disorders and their peers in inclusive school settings', *Focus on Autism and Other Developmental Disabilities*, 23: 15–28.

Paley, V.G. (1992) *You Can't Say You Can't Play*, Cambridge, MA and London: Harvard University Press.

Panksepp, J. (1998) *Affective Neuroscience: The Foundations of Human and Animal Emotions*, New York: Oxford University Press.

Parsons, S., Guldberg, K., MacLeod, A., Jones, G., Prunty, A. and Balfe, T. (2009) *International Review of the Literature of Evidence of Best Practice Provision in the Education of Persons with Autistic Spectrum Disorders*, Dublin: NCSE.

Parten, M. (1932) 'Social participation among preschool children', *Journal of Abnormal and Social Psychology*, 28: 136–47.

Paul, R. (2009) *Communication in Autism*. Yale University: Yale Autism Seminar. Online: http://autism.yale.edu (accessed 1 October 2012).

Pellegrini, A.D. (1988) 'Elementary-school children's rough-and-tumble play and social competence', *Developmental Psychology*, 24: 802–6.

Pellegrini, A.D. (2001) 'Practitioner review: The role of direct observation in the assessment of young children', *Journal of Child Psychology and Psychiatry*, 42: 861–69.

Pellegrini, A.D. (2011) 'The development and function of locomotor play', in A.D. Pellegrini (ed.) *The Oxford Handbook of the Development of Play*, Oxford and New York: Oxford University Press.

Pellegrini, A.D. and Smith, P.K. (1998) 'Physical activity play: The nature and function of a neglected aspect of play', *Child Development*, 69: 577–98.

Peskin, J. and Ardino, V. (2003) 'Representing the mental world in children's social behaviour: Playing hide-and-seek and keeping a secret', *Social Development*, 12: 496–512.

Petit, J.-L. (1999) 'Constitution by movement: Husserl in light of recent neurobiological findings', in J. Petitot, F.J. Varela, B. Pachoud and J.-M. Roy (eds) *Naturalizing Phenomenology: Issues in Contemporary Phenomenology and Cognitive Science*, Stanford, CA: Stanford University Press.

Piaget, J. (1954) *The Construction of Reality in the Child*, New York: Basic Books.

Pollard, A. (2008) *Reflective Teaching*, 3rd edn, London and New York: Continuum.

Pollard, A. and Filer, A. (1996) *The Social World of Children's Learning*, London and New York: Continuum.

Powell, S. (2000) 'Towards a pedagogy for autism', in S. Powell (ed.) *Helping Children with Autism to Learn*, London: David Fulton Publishers.

Powell, S. and Jordan, R. (1993) 'Diagnosis, intuition and autism', *British Journal of Special Education*, 20: 26–9.

Prior, M., Leekam, S., Ong, B., Eisenmajer, R., Wing, L., Gould, J. and Dowe, D. (1998) 'Are there subgroups within the autistic spectrum? A cluster analysis of a group of children with autistic spectrum disorders', *Journal of Child Psychology and Psychiatry*, 39: 893–902.

Prizant, B.M. and Rubin, E. (1999) 'Contemporary issues in interventions for autism spectrum disorders: A commentary', *Journal of the Association for Persons with Severe Handicaps*, 24: 199–208.

Prout A. (2005) *The Future of Childhood: Towards the Interdisciplinary Study of Children*, London and New York: Routledge.

Prout, A. and James, A. (1997) 'A new paradigm for the sociology of childhood? Provenance, promise and problems', in A. James and A. Prout (eds) *Constructing and Reconstructing Childhood: Contemporary Issues in the Sociological Study of Childhood*, London and Washington: Falmer Press.

Punch, K. (2005) *Introduction to Social Research*, 2nd edn, London, Thousand Oaks, New Delhi: Sage Publications.

Rakoczy, H., Tomasello, M. and Striano, T. (2005) 'On tools and toys: How children learn to act on and pretend with "virgin objects"', *Developmental Science*, 8: 57–73.

Rakoczy, R. (2008) 'Pretence as individual and collective individuality', *Mind and Language*, 23: 499–517.

Rinaldi, C. (2005) 'Documentation and assessment: What is the relationship?', in A. Clark, A.T. Kjørholt and P. Moss (eds) *Beyond Listening: Children's Perspectives on Early Childhood Services*, Bristol: Policy Press.

Rinaldi, C. (2006) *In Dialogue with Reggio Emilia: Listening, Researching and Learning*, London and New York: Routledge.

Robertson, K., Chamberlain, B. and Kasari, C. (2003) 'General education teachers' relationships with included students with autism', *Journal of Autism and Developmental Disorders*, 33: 123–30.

Roeyers, H. (1995) 'A peer-mediated proximity intervention to facilitate the social interactions of children with a pervasive developmental disorder', *British Journal of Special Education*, 22: 161–4.

Roeyers, H. (1996) 'The influence of nonhandicapped peers on the social interactions of children with a Pervasive Developmental Disorder', *Journal of Autism and Developmental Disorders*, 26: 303–20.

Rogers, S.J. (2000) 'Interventions that facilitate socialization in children with autism', *Journal of Autism and Developmental Disorders*, 30: 399–409.

Rogoff, B. (1990) *Apprenticeship in Thinking: Cognitive Development in Social Context*, New York and Oxford: Oxford University Press.

Rogoff, B. (2003) *The Cultural Nature of Human Development*, Oxford and New York: Oxford University Press.

Rogoff, B. and Angelillo, C. (2002) 'Investigating the coordinating function of multifaceted cultural practices in human development', *Human Development*, 45: 211–25.

Rose, R. (2001) 'Primary school teacher perceptions of the conditions required to include pupils with special educational needs.' *Educational Review*, 53: 147–56.

Rotheram-Fuller, E., Kasari, C., Chamberlain, B. and Locke, J. (2010) 'Social involvement of children with autism spectrum disorders in elementary school classrooms', *Journal of Child Psychology and Psychiatry*, 51: 1227–34.

Ruble, L.A., McGrew, J., Dalrymple, N. and Jung, L.A. (2010) 'Examining the quality of IEPs for young children with autism', *Journal of Autism and Developmental Disorders*, 40: 1459–70.

Rutherford, M.D., Young, G.S., Hepburn, S. and Rogers, S.J. (2007) 'A longitudinal study of pretend play in autism', *Journal of Autism and Developmental Disorders*, 37: 1024–39.

Sainsbury C. (2000) *The Martian in the Playground*, Bristol: Lucky Duck.

Schore, A.N. (1994) *Affect Regulation and the Origin of the Self: The Neurobiology of Emotional Development*, Hillsdale, NJ: Lawrence Erlbaum.

Scott-Hill, M. (2004) 'Impairment, difference and identity', in J. Swain, S. French, C. Barnes and C. Thomas (eds) *Disabling Barriers, Enabling Environments*, 2nd edn, London, Thousand Oaks, New Delhi: Sage Publications.

Scribner, S. (1985) 'Vygotsky's uses of history', in J.V. Wertsch (ed.) *Culture, Communication and Cognition: Vygotskian Perspectives*, Cambridge: Cambridge University Press.

Seach, D. (2007) *Interactive Play for Children with Autism*, London and New York: Routledge.

Sher, B. (2009) *Early Intervention Games: Fun, Joyful Ways to Develop Social and Motor Skills in Children with Autism Spectrum or Sensory Processing Disorders*, San Francisco: Jossey-Bass.

Sherratt, D. (2002) 'Developing pretend play in children with autism', *Autism*, 6: 169–79.

Sherratt, D. (2005) *How to Support and Teach Children on the Autism Spectrum*, Cambridge: LDA.

Shields, J. (1999) 'Ideas for toys and leisure' in *The Autistic Spectrum: A Handbook*, London: National Autistic Society.

Sigman, M. and Ruskin, E. (1999) 'Continuity and change in the social competence of children with autism, Down's syndrome and developmental delays', *Monographs of the Society for Research in Child Development*, 64: Serial No. 256.

Silverman, D. (2011) *Interpreting Qualitative Data*, 4th edn, London, Thousand Oaks, New Delhi, Singapore: Sage Publications.

Sinclair, J. (1993) 'Don't mourn for us', *Autism Network International*, 1.

Siraj-Blatchford, I. (2010a) 'An ethnographic approach to researching young children's learning', in G. MacNaughton, S.A. Rolfe and I. Siraj-Blatchford (eds) *Doing Early Childhood Research: International Perspectives on Theory and Practice*, 2nd edn, Buckingham and Philadelphia: Open University Press.

Siraj-Blatchford, I. (2010b) 'Mixed-method designs', in G. MacNaughton, S.A. Rolfe and I. Siraj-Blatchford (eds) *Doing Early Childhood Research: International Perspectives on Theory and Practice*, 2nd edn, Buckingham and Philadelphia: Open University Press.

Skinner, D. (2010) *Effective Teaching and Learning in Practice*, London and New York: Continuum.

Slee, R. (2001) '"Inclusion in practice": Does practice make perfect?', *Educational Review*, 53: 113–23.

Smith, T., Scahill, L., Dawson, G., Guthrie, D., Lord, C., Odom, S., Rogers, S. and Wagner, A. (2007) 'Designing research studies on psychosocial interventions in autism', *Journal of Autism and Developmental Disorders*, 37: 354–66.

Steiner, R. (1968) *The Education of the Child in the Light of Anthroposophy*, trans. G. and M. Adam, London: Rudolf Steiner Press. Originally published in 1909.

Stern, D.N. (2004) *The Present Moment: In Psychotherapy and Everyday Life*, New York and London: W.W. Norton and Company.

Stone, W.L. and Lemanek, K.L. (1990) 'Parental report of social behaviours in autistic preschoolers', *Journal of Autism and Developmental Disorders*, 20: 437–53.

Stone, W.L. and Rosenbaum, J.L. (1988) 'A comparison of teacher and parent views of autism', *Journal of Autism and Developmental Disorders*, 18: 403–14.

Striano, T., Tomasello, M. and Rochat, P. (2001) 'Social and object support for early symbolic play', *Developmental Science*, 4: 442–55.

Sutton-Smith, B. (1997) *The Ambiguity of Play*, Cambridge, MA and London: Harvard University Press.

Swain, J. and French, S. (2000) 'Towards an affirmation model of disability', *Disability & Society*, 15: 569–82.

Symes, W. and Humphrey, N. (2011) 'School factors that facilitate or hinder the ability of teaching assistants to effectively support pupils with autism spectrum disorders (ASD) in mainstream secondary schools', *Journal of Research in Special Educational Needs*, 11: 153–61.

Taylor, R. (2006) 'Actions speak as loud as words: A multimodal analysis of boys' talk in the classroom', *English in Education*, 40: 66–82.

Theodorou, F. and Nind, M. (2010) 'Inclusion in play: A case study of a child with autism in an inclusive nursery', *Journal of Research in Special Educational Needs*, 10: 99–106.

Thomas, G. and Loxley, A. (2007) *Deconstructing Special Education and Constructing Inclusion*, Maidenhead: Open University Press.

Thorp, D.M., Stahmer, A.C. and Schreibman, L. (1995) 'Effects of sociodramatic play training on children with autism', *Journal of Autism and Developmental Disorders*, 25: 265–82.

Tizard, B. and Hughes, M. (1984) *Young Children Learning: Talking and Learning at Home and School*, London: Fontana.

Tomasello, M. (1999) *The Cultural Origins of Human Cognition*, Cambridge, MA and London: Harvard University Press.

Trevarthen, C. (1979) 'Communication and cooperation in early infancy: A description of primary intersubjectivity', in M. Bullowa (ed.) *Before Speech*, New York: Cambridge University Press.

Tudge, J. and Hogan, D. (2005) 'An ecological approach to observations of children's everyday lives', in S. Greene and D. Hogan (eds) *Researching Children's Experience: Methods and Approaches*, London, Thousand Oaks, New Delhi: Sage Publications.

UN General Assembly (1989) 'Convention on the Rights of the Child', Document A/RES/44/25 (12 December), New York: United Nations.

Varela, F.J., Thompson, E. and Rosch, E. (1993) *The Embodied Mind: Cognitive Science and Human Experience*, Cambridge, MA: MIT Press.

Veale, A. (2005) 'Creative methodologies in participatory research with children', in S. Greene and D. Hogan (eds) *Researching Children's Experience: Methods and Approaches*, London, Thousand Oaks, New Delhi: Sage Publications.

Vygotsky, L.S. (1978) *Mind in Society*, Cambridge, MA: Harvard University Press.

Vygotsky, L.S. (1987) 'Thinking and speech', in R.W. Rieber and A.S. Carton (eds) *The Collected Works of L.S. Vygotsky*, trans. N. Minick, New York: Plenum.

Wang, H-T., Sandall, S.R., Davis, C.A. and Thomas, C.J. (2011) 'Social skills assessment in young children with autism: A comparison evaluation of the SSRS and PKBS', *Journal of Autism and Developmental Disorders*, 41: 1487–95.

Watson, N., Shakespeare, T., Cunningham-Burley, S., Barnes, C., Corker, M., Davis, J. and Priestley, M. (2000) *Life as a Disabled Child: A Qualitative Study of Young People's Experiences and Perspectives. Final report to the ESRC*, Edinburgh: University of Edinburgh, Department of Nursing Studies.

Westcott, H.L. and Littleton, K.S. (2005) 'Exploring meaning in interviews with children', in S. Greene and D. Hogan (eds) *Researching Children's Experience: Methods and Approaches*, London, Thousand Oaks, New Delhi: Sage Publications.

Whitaker, P. (2004) 'Fostering communication and shared play between mainstream peers and children with autism: Approaches, outcomes and experiences', *British Journal of Special Education*, 31: 215–22.

Whitaker, P., Barratt, P., Joy, H., Potter, M. and Thomas, G. (1998) 'Children with autism and peer group support: Using "circle of friends"', *British Journal of Special Education*, 25: 60–4.

White, S.W., Keonig, K. and Scahill, L. (2007) 'Social skills development in children with autism spectrum disorders: A review of the intervention research', *Journal of Autism and Developmental Disorders*, 37: 1858–68.

Wiliam, D. and Leahy, S. (2007) 'A theoretical foundation for formative assessment', in J.H. McMillan (ed.) *Formative Classroom Assessment: Theory into Practice*, New York: Teachers College Press.

Wilkinson, K. and Twist, L. (2010) *Autism and Educational Assessment: UK Policy and Practice*, Slough: National Foundation for Educational Research.

Willett, R. (2009) 'Consumption, production and online identities: Amateur spoofs on YouTube', in R. Willett, M. Robinson and J. Marsh (eds) *Play, Creativity and Digital Cultures*, New York and London: Routledge.

Willett, R. (2011) 'Friends, families, superheroes and super-sleuths: pretend play on a school playground', paper presented at International Play Association Triennial Conference, UK, 6 July.

Williams, D. (1996) *Autism: An Inside-Out Approach*, London and Philadelphia: Jessica Kingsley Publishers.

Williams, D. (2008) Conference discussion (Psychology), AWARES.org Autism2008 Conference. Online: www.awares.org/conferences/show_paper.asp?section=00010001 0001&conferenceCode=000200100012&id=194&full_paper=1 (accessed 10 December 2008).

Williams, E., Reddy, V. and Costall, A. (2001) 'Taking a closer look at functional play in children with autism', *Journal of Autism and Developmental Disorders*, 31: 67–77.

Williamson, D., Cullen, J. and Lepper, C. (2006) 'Checklists to narratives in special education', *Australian Journal of Early Childhood*, 31: 20–9.

Wimpory, D.C., Hobson, R.P., Williams, J.M.G. and Nash, S. (2000) 'Are infants with autism socially engaged? A study of recent retrospective parental reports', *Journal of Autism and Developmental Disorders*, 30: 525–36.

Wolfberg, P. (2004) *Peer Play and the Autism Spectrum: The Art of Guiding Children's Socialization and Imagination*, Shawnee Mission, KS: Autism Asperger Publishing Company.

Wolfberg, P. (2008) 'Including children with autism in the culture of play with typical peers', in C. Forlin and M.-G. John Lian (eds) *Reform, Inclusion and Teacher Education: Towards a New Era of Special and Inclusive Education in the Asia-Pacific Region*, New York: Routledge.

Wolfberg, P. and Schuler, A.L. (1999) 'Fostering peer interaction, imaginative play and spontaneous language in children with autism', *Child Language Teaching and Therapy*, 15: 41–52.

Wood, D. (1998) *How Children Think and Learn: The Social Context of Cognitive Development*, 2nd edn, Oxford: Blackwell.

Woodhead, M. and Faulkner, D. (2008) 'Subjects, objects or participants? Dilemmas of psychological research with children', in P. Christensen and A. James (eds) *Research with Children: Perspectives and Practices*, 2nd edn, New York and London: Routledge.

Yang, T.-R., Wolfberg, P., Wu, S.-C. and Hwu, P.-Y. (2003) 'Supporting children on the autism spectrum in peer play at home and school: Piloting the integrated play groups in Taiwan', *Autism*, 7: 437–53.

Yates, L. (2004) *What Does Good Education Research Look Like? Situating a Field and its Practices*, Berkshire: Open University Press.

Zahavi, D. (2005) *Subjectivity and Selfhood*, Cambridge, MA and London: MIT Press.

Zercher, C., Hunt, P., Schuler, A. and Webster, J. (2001) 'Increasing joint attention, play and language through peer supported play', *Autism*, 5: 374–98.

Index

Page numbers in **bold** refer to figures, tables and boxes.